Men Who Can't Be Faithful

OTHER BOOKS BY CAROL BOTWIN

Is There Sex After Marriage?

Love Lives

The Love Crisis

Sex and the Teenage Girl

Men Who Can't Be Faithful

How to
Pick Up the Pieces When
He's Breaking Your Heart

Carol Botwin

WARNER BOOKS

A Warner Communications Company

Warner Books, Inc., 666 Fifth Avenue, New York, NY 10103

w A Warner Communications Company

Printed in the United States of America

First printing: October 1988

Book design by Nick Mazzella

10 9 8 7 6 5 4 3 2 1

Library of Congress Cataloging-in-Publication Data

Botwin, Carol.
  Men who can't be faithful.

  Includes index.
  1. Adultery—United States—Psychological aspects.
2. Men—United States—Sexual behavior. 3. Men—
United States—Psychology. 4. Interpersonal relations.
5. Compulsive behavior. I. Title.
HQ806.B67 1988   306.7'36   88-40084
ISBN 0-446-51383-0

To Alexandra and Will
and Danielle, Gail, and Lyn

ACKNOWLEDGMENTS

My very special thanks goes to Dr. Edward L. Parsons whose suggestions and wisdom were a great help throughout the writing of this book. My gratitude also goes to Dr. Shirley Zussman who shared her insights and wise thoughts on the subject of infidelity early in this project.

There is no way to adequately thank all the men who were brave enough to be interviewed and generously bared their secrets, and the woman who shared their emotion-filled stories. Of course, as promised, I cannot name you, but you know who you are. Your contributions were enormous. My gratitude goes, as well, to the women who write to me every month, often while their hearts are full of pain, and to Pat Miller and Stephanie Von Hirschberg who make it possible for me to hear from them.

Finally, thanks to Nansey Neiman for her immediate enthusiasm for this project, and to Leslie Keenan for shepherding it through with enthusiasm, great skill and wonderful support at all times. And gratitude goes, as always, to my agent, Barbara Lowenstein, for both her professional skill and her friendship over the years.

Contents

Men Who Can't Be Faithful

ONE

Men Who Can't Be Faithful: A Growing Problem for Women

IT WAS SOON AFTER I HAD SEPARATED FROM MY FIRST HUSBAND that I met the man I will call Len. I was innocent in a way that divorcées leaving long marriages often are. My experience with men was limited to my husband—who, despite our problems, was basically a trustworthy and loyal man—to some early casual dating, and to a couple of serious suitors before marriage. I had never met anyone like Len before.

The circumstances in which I met him would have been my first clue today. He came into my life at an annual Christmas party of an organization to which I belonged. I arrived with a female friend. He was with a woman I had known over the years. I thought he was attractive and sexy. He had a strong-featured face, a full head of graying hair, a tall, slim body. We chatted. I could tell he was interested. I flirted, but also had mental reservations. After all, he had come with another woman, and I was not about to insinuate myself between them. When it was time to sit down to dinner, he departed with her, saying he would like to dance with me when the orchestra played later in the evening.

As it happened, I left before the music started. Another man, seated at my table, invited me to have an after-dinner drink at a nearby pub. I thought, why not? I was aware that by taking off like this I would probably never see Len again.

I was wrong. Two days later he telephoned. He had

found my name in the telephone book. "I've been thinking about you," he said.

"What about Lenore?" I asked, referring to the woman he had been with.

"Oh, that's nothing. We're just friends. We have been for years. Whenever Lenore needs an escort, she calls me. Whenever I need someone on my arm at a social function, I call her. It's practical, not romantic," he assured me.

I had no reason to doubt him at the time. And so we started going out. He came on strong and flattering. He loved my sense of style, he said, the fact that he could talk to me about serious matters, and that I would understand him in a way that others couldn't. On our third date he asked if I was interested in what he referred to as "a relationship." I assumed he meant something more than just sleeping together.

"I'm not capable of anything but that," I explained. "If I see a man and continue to see him, it means I am having a real relationship with him. If I couldn't, I would leave." I hesitated. It was really too early to ask, but since he had brought it up, I decided to take the plunge.

"And you?" I asked. "How about you? Are you interested in a relationship?" Len assured me he was. I thought, "How terrific!" And I assumed we were off and running. We had fun together, and a great deal in common. It turned out we had grown up in the same part of New York City. We could exchange memories—two unsophisticated kids from one of the boroughs, who had made their way into somewhat glamorous circles in Manhattan.

Our trouble was a matter of definition. Len and I meant different things by the term "relationship." I meant seeing each other exclusively and finding out from there where we would go. I knew, even though I was freshly hatched from a failed marriage, that basically I liked the institution, and I looked forward to a time when I would share my life as a wife again. Len, as I soon discovered, meant we would have a relationship, but it was to be only one of many in his life.

At first we saw each other about twice a week, and at the end of each evening he would be sure to pin down the next time we would see one another. About four weeks into the "relationship," Len stopped asking me about the next time. He would call every day on the telephone and, during one of those calls, would make a date.

Soon, although he was still calling all the time, saying wonderful things to me when we were together, but he started to see me only once a week—generally on Friday night. Naturally I wondered what he was doing with his Saturdays and, for that matter, all the other nights in the week. I may have been naïve initially, but I was no dummy. Len's conversations were sprinkled with references to his friends—all female. My suspicions were aroused. He knew an awful lot of women. I figured some were probably ex-lovers, but what about the present? Were any of them current? Were there other women he didn't even mention because he was having affairs with them too?

I was confused. In some ways Len acted as if I were his girlfriend. He still telephoned daily. He remained very flattering and attentive when we were together, but he was limiting our time together.

Anxiety took over. I wasn't used to this from men. In my limited experience I'd found that men either liked you and wanted to see you more, or the thing didn't take and they stopped calling or I stopped saying yes to dates. I wasn't quite sure what was going on now.

I decided to be brave, and over one of our romantic dinners together, I asked, "Len, are you seeing someone else besides me?"

He didn't miss a beat. "I'm seeing someone," he said, "but I'm not seeing her now."

In my desire to be reassured, I felt relieved for the moment. He had told me he wasn't seeing anyone else now. But the next day I realized that I had been handed one of the great double-talk answers of all time. What exactly did he mean by "I'm seeing someone, but I'm not seeing her now"?

I started looking forward to Len's calls to the office with more and more anxiety rather than pleasure, because he started skipping days. He may not have called me as regularly as before, but now he would occasionally send wonderful, affectionate little notes. They calmed me down and kept me hooked. I still have one in which he told me how wonderful and warm and close he had felt when we were together the night before. Anybody reading it would have thought a serious romance was in progress.

My suspicions kept bothering me, and I was feeling more and more uncomfortable in the situation, although when I saw Len we still had terrific times together.

Now he occasionally skipped asking me out for one whole week, although he continued to call frequently, if not every day. I found myself invited to have lunch or drinks with him some weeks when we didn't get together at night at all. I felt tortured and anxious, and had the growing feeling that, indeed, there were other women in his life.

One night Len took me to an off-off Broadway play in which one of his female "friends" was cast. And, although he had his hand cupped around my neck during most of the performance, I felt that this woman was perhaps one of the people he saw when he was not with me, especially after the performance, when she and a male escort and another couple had a snack together with us. As we were leaving the restaurant, Len stayed behind for a few minutes to talk to her privately. We drove home in a taxi, all jammed in together, and I couldn't believe it—Len dropped me off at my apartment and he went on with them!

I was now getting angry as well as feeling increasingly humiliated in this situation. High anxiety about what was happening to me continued.

Once, during one of our telephone chats on a Friday when he had failed to ask me out for either Friday or Saturday, I asked him what he was doing over the weekend. He told me he was going away with "a friend."

"Len," I blurted out, "tell me the truth. Are you seeing someone else?"

"I'm not seeing anyone," he said. He emphasized the word "seeing."

"I guess that means you aren't seeing me either," I said. He didn't answer. "Call you Monday," he said lightly, and hung up.

Not long after that, I went into the hospital. I needed serious surgery. Len called me immediately after the operation to find out how I was. He seemed genuinely concerned. He visited me regularly at the hospital. I realized during those visits how very uncomfortable this whole relationship had become for me. I pictured him leaving me and going off to see some other woman. Feeling vulnerable, realizing he was bad for my health at a time when I needed to recuperate, I decided I could not let this go on any longer. Two weeks after I left the hospital, I called Len up and invited him to lunch. I explained during the meal that I wanted to end our relationship. He most certainly was seeing other women, and that wasn't what I wanted.

At one point I said, "You must have had many conversations like this in your life." He smiled knowingly, an acknowledgment that I was right. He insisted we remain "friends." I pictured myself as one of those "friends" he talked about to the current woman—or women—in his life. I declined.

A few months later, at Christmastime, I received a card from him. On it he had scrawled, "Now that time has passed and the hurt and anger have dissipated, maybe we can be friends."

I never replied to the card.

Within months I ran into another woman who I discovered had also once been involved with him. (Over the years I have met many of his ex-lovers.) At that point I was still ignorant of the full extent of Len's womanizing. She filled me in. She had been with him much longer, for over three years. Len and I had lasted a little over six months.

When she talked about him, it was obvious to me that she was not completely over the hurtful experience, even though many years had gone by. She told me of Len's habit of picking women up on street corners, at museums, wherever he happened to be. He had consistently lied to her. He had once given her crab lice he'd picked up from one of his other women, and then lied about that, too, claiming, preposterously, that he had caught them from sitting on the beach. An attractive, impossible man, we both sighed, ending our conversation about Len.

Many years had passed when I ran into Len acciden-tally a while ago. I was with my second husband. Since our romance had been over for such a long time, the anger and humiliation Len had caused me were long gone. I was able to greet him pleasantly and even feel rather friendly toward him. He wasn't *all* bad. He was still funny and bright, and he actually could be a loyal friend. He had been the emotional mainstay of a sick ex-girlfriend for years. I kidded, saying that maybe he was the cause of her illness, but in truth, Len is a mixed bag, as are many of the men who can't be faithful. Not all bad, but bad for *you*.

Len may have been the first of this kind of man whom I encountered after my first marriage folded, but he was not the last. The second was Dan, who cheated on me from the day we met at a political fund-raiser. He moved in on me right away. Two minutes after we were introduced, he was asking me to have dinner with him afterward. I explained that I was already invited to a dinner party. He wanted to come along. I told him it was impossible; the host was not prepared for an extra guest. Dan then pressed to meet me for a drink after the dinner party. He was a very good-looking, well-dressed, well-spoken man, with an air of distinction. He ran in a very sophisticated circle. I thought he was worth exploring, so I agreed to the late-evening drink, which ultimately started a romance that lasted nine months. I only found out much later, after the affair was over, that when I had left the fund-raiser to go to my dinner party, Dan started talking to another woman at the same function and persuaded her to come home with him. He had sex with this woman while I was dining with my friends, then got rid of her and came to meet me at the appointed hour.

Unlike Len, Dan wanted to see a great deal of me, and consistently. From the beginning, we were together every weekend until Sunday night, as well as a couple of times during the week. I found out later that he often had dates with other women on Sunday nights after I had departed, and that even with our busy schedule together, Dan managed to pick up other women at the many art gallery openings and cocktail parties he attended. He would bed these women one, two, or three times before dumping them. He considered me his "main squeeze," and in his fashion he was being faithful to me; the other women, who were as necessary to him as breathing, were generally limited to one-night stands, or to a few encounters at most.

I had a certain amount of suspicion of Dan all along—Len had sensitized me. Dan, too, lived in a world full of women. The walls over the bar in his living room were full of affectionately inscribed photos of ex-lovers. I refused to give him the photo of me he requested. I did not want to be part of that gallery.

We would walk down Madison Avenue together, and we would frequently meet attractive women he knew. He would talk about this old girlfriend and that one. The real moment of truth came one day when I went to make a call from the phone in his office at home and found his datebook lying open in front of the telephone. Each week, in two or three of those seven days on the pages facing me, there were initials penciled in, with zeros next to them. I couldn't help myself. Curious, I turned the pages back in time. The initials and zeros appeared regularly every week. I figured the zeros might represent the number of times he and the initials had made love. Sometimes there was one zero, sometimes two, sometimes three, with an exclamation point following if it was a trio of zeros. I wasn't sure if my conclusions were exactly on target, but my instincts told me it was a sexual score of some kind.

When I returned to the living room where Dan was waiting, he noticed I seemed upset. He asked me if anything was wrong. I confronted him with what I had seen in the datebook on his desk. I'll give him credit; at least he didn't try to lie. I was right. It was a sexual code, a record of his casual conquests. He admitted everything. Our affair was over.

By the time I said good-bye to Dan, I had become more aware that these two experiences of mine were not isolated incidents, or even exceptions to the rule of dating—the world today is full of men who can't be faithful.

The amount of infidelity in our time, and the misery it causes women, became more and more apparent to me over the years, not only personally but professionally. I touched on the subject in some of my previous books, particularly *The Love Crisis*, but also in *Is There Sex After Marriage?* Among the letters I received from readers of these books were many that moved me with their stories about unfaithful partners. Women kept bringing up the issue of infidelity with regularity in question-and-answer sessions after my lectures. I could see the pain on these women's faces. In my workshops for people who wanted to improve their relationships, I found distraught women grappling with husbands in affairs and with unfaithful boyfriends. And, as an advice columnist, with each new batch of mail that arrives, I am reminded again and again of the extent of male infidelity and the hell it puts women through. Many of the letters I receive are from women who are hurt, puzzled, and profoundly shaken by men who aren't faithful.

It finally came to the point where I felt this emotion-laden topic deserved a book; I had to talk to the huge population of women out there who were not just devastated, but also desperately seeking answers. They did not know how to cope with unfaithful men. If you are reading this book, I presume you are among them. I decided to write *Men Who Can't Be Faithful* to give you answers to the question of why a man cheats in the first place, and to tell you what you can do about it when infidelity shakes up your life.

I used case histories from my professional and personal experiences and drew on the letters written to me, as well as scholarly papers and surveys and the best current thinking among clinicians in the field of marriage therapy about infidelity. Most important to the book, and most revealing, were my interviews with seventy-six brave men and women who told me what it felt like to cheat and be cheated on.

Of course, the stereotype of the man who cheats in our society is the straying husband, and this book is about them and for the wives who must cope with their infidelities. But men who can't be faithful can be single as well as married, and I write for the unmarried women as well.

Infidelity in the singles population is a neglected subject. As a result, there is a paucity of statistics, but, judging from the complaints of unmarried women, as well as clinical evidence from therapists' practices, there is a plethora of single men who practice infidelity today.

The extramarital activity of husbands is better documented. In 1948, Alfred Kinsey shocked the world when he reported that 50 percent of American husbands had been unfaithful. Later surveys indicate that this number has increased. For example, Dr. Bernard Greene, drawing on 750 case histories of married men, stated that 60 percent of his subjects had been unfaithful. Shere Hite, in her study of the sexuality of 7,239 males, claimed that 72 percent of men married more than two years had cheated.

Youth and income seem to contribute to increased

infidelity. Husbands today have affairs at younger ages than in the past, and when annual income tops $60,000, the incidence of infidelity leaps to a whopping 70 percent.

Seventy percent of the men under forty queried in a national survey of 4,066 men by Dr. Anthony Pietropinto and Jacqueline Simenauer thought that they would have an extramarital relationship.

Research shows a strong correlation between permissive attitudes about sex as a single person and subsequent adultery in marriage. This fact, coupled with the loosening of sexual morals and mores that has occurred in the intervening years, and findings from the later surveys, makes it safe to assume that Kinsey's 50-percent figure is somewhat outdated.

I tend to go along with the numbers put forth by two reliable, noted sex researchers. Dr. Paul Gebhard, one of the coauthors of the original Kinsey Report, has estimated that 60 percent of husbands commit adultery. Wardell Pomeroy, another Kinsey coauthor, gives 60 to 65 percent as his estimate.

This means that *most* wives—at least 35 million women—will share, at some time, the heartbreaking experience of having been sexually betrayed by their husbands—some of them repeatedly. Surveys indicate that the number of extramarital partners for men has escalated over the years.

The figures on adultery, of course, don't account for the additional millions and millions among the 41 million single women today who also have to cope with men who can't be faithful.

Some indication of the amount of infidelity in the world of the unmarried can be gleaned from the survey *Singles: The New Americans* by Jacqueline Simenauer and David Carroll. One out of four—more than twice as many single men as women—preferred nonmonogamous sex to fidelity. Simenauer and Carroll discovered, too, that women, during the years they are single, have far fewer sexual partners than men—from one to nine was the female average. Twenty percent of single men have anywhere from twenty to forty-nine sexual partners, while one out of ten claim over one hundred partners. "Despite sexual liberation," conclude the authors, "women are still far more reluctant than men to take on many sexual partners."

A recent survey of college students by Gary Hansen, published in *Archives of Sexual Behavior*, found that 70 percent of the young men surveyed had relations with someone other than their steady dating partners, even though they were moderately opposed to nonmonogamous relationships. (Women college students were strongly opposed to such relationships.)

Live-in lovers, who fall in an emotional zone somewhere between married and single, are well represented in the world of unfaithful men, too. Simenauer and Carroll found that single men who cohabited with women were twice as likely to approve of casual sex and one-night stands as those who lived alone.

Philip Blumstein and Pepper Schwartz, in the survey *American Couples*, discovered that one-third of cohabiting males were unfaithful. Sixty-four percent of them had repeated outside sexual encounters, with almost half reporting between two to five partners. A minority of these live-in lovers were wildly nonmonogamous, having up to twenty bedmates. In this same survey, which also covered married couples, even more of the husbands (71 percent!) philandered repeatedly: 42 percent had between two and five extramarital partners; 22 percent had sex with from six to twenty women.

It must be concluded from these surveys and other statistics gathered over the years that men, as a group, not only cheat more than women do, but they cheat with more partners.

Is AIDS Slowing Things Down?

From my interviews, I know that AIDS is certainly on men's minds, but men's behavior does not always match their mental attitudes. Respected national surveys show that the majority of husbands disapprove of adultery. And yet, as we know, the majority of husbands engage in it.

I have talked to husbands for whom AIDS *is* a deterrent. They admit they might try some hanky-panky if they weren't so scared. In one case a man broke off his affair with a woman known for her sexual adventures.

But a much larger number have created all kinds of rationales for feeling safe while remaining adulterous even in the age of AIDS. For example, one man says he has changed his sex habits—he now only sleeps with married women whose husbands are workaholics. He figures they are safe—they have been in monogamous relationships and their husbands are too busy with career matters to play around. I disabused him of that notion, since I have interviewed plenty of workaholics who manage to have quickies. This revelation did not alter his behavior.

Another husband has cut down on the number of his extramarital partners. He now sticks with one woman with whom he feels safe because she was willing to be tested for AIDS. Interestingly, he did not get himself tested. With his history of philandering, she should have insisted on the same thing.

Some married men have had one lover for years, so they feel out of danger. One man has had the same mistress for about fifteen years. He sees her almost every day in the afternoon. They have lunch together. He takes long trips with her. He recently hosted her fiftieth birthday party. He has something like a second marriage with her, so AIDS doesn't bother him.

Single men are scared, but as one told me, echoing the viewpoint of others, "That doesn't mean I'm going to stop having sex."

Many men, single and married, say they are being more careful about choosing sex partners. They claim they can tell which women are safe—as if some infallible sixth sense will protect them. Only a very small number are relying on a less magical and surer method—condoms. The use of condoms as protection against AIDS has largely become the responsibility of women, just as birth-control methods have always been. Heterosexual men today rarely insist they want to wear them. Indeed, they often insist they don't, even when the woman thinks they should.

A man on the West Coast says he now only has oral sex, figuring that this is safer. A few husbands have always limited their extramarital encounters to oral sex because, in their crazy logic, they do not consider this to be infidelity. Sometimes they don't even consider it real sex. One woman remembers definitively refusing to have intercourse with a man. "Then if you won't, will you go down on me?" he asked.

Some men have worked out elaborate systems based on statistics to counter fears. For example, they have somehow calculated that it is safer to have sex with someone than to get in an airplane or cross a traffic-filled street.

Men who are compulsive about sex; who are trying to solve problems in their marriages; who depend on conquest to shore up shaky self-esteem; who are intensely afraid of intimacy; who can never remain satisfied with a woman because they are narcissists; or who are very macho: all of these are still having affairs, as far as I can determine. If AIDS has really cut down on adultery in a significant way, or whether it will as the epidemic broadens, remains to be seen. There are no comprehensive surveys to tell us as yet.

Although AIDS may eventually lower the statistics, certain other things in our society have raised them. For one thing, consequences have lessened. With no-fault divorce, adultery is no longer grounds for divorce. The breach-of-promise suit that sometimes resulted when a man left a woman after promising marriage (often getting her into bed that way) is a quaint, faintly remembered custom of the past. In addition, in recent years, more wives faced with adultery are staying in marriages and trying to work things out.

Research has shown opportunity to be a prime determinant in whether a man will stray or not, and opportunities have increased in our world. More liberal sexual attitudes, and the larger number of women in the work force, have put men into contact with a greater number of women who are already sexually experienced and therefore more apt to respond to their advances. Even in the work world of the eighties, men persist in eroticizing their contacts and relationships with women.

The increased number of unmarried women, and their ratio to available men in our population, makes a certain amount of man-sharing (voluntary or involuntary) inevitable. There are not enough men to go around. Married men tend to get involved with single women, and there are more single, lonely women today who are vulnerable to these illicit romances than there were in the past.

There is also more of a population of women for single men to choose from. Since they no longer have to marry for sex or respectability, there are more men staying footloose and fancy-free, going from one available woman to another.

Because I am concentrating on male infidelity does not mean I don't recognize that there is a jump in the number of women who are having affairs, too. But that is a separate subject and another book. The women who have affairs today do so out of greater unhappiness in their relationships than do men, and with more emotional involvement. Statistically, they remain in the minority. It is the *majority* of men who are unfaithful. In that sense it is the male norm and has been for a long time.

Who Are These Men?

There is no single profile of a man who can't be faithful. Unfaithful men can be young, middle-aged, and even elderly. The press recently reported a rupture in the marriage of the cosmetics tycoon Martin Revson and his wife of eighteen years, Eleanor. She claimed that Revson, at age seventy-seven, was involved with a younger woman. Another man, a seventy-four-year-old, considers this millionaire lucky. He, who had been an active womanizer all his life, told me how frustrated and saddened he was because although his spirit was still willing, his body wasn't—he simply couldn't get it up the way he had in the past for extramarital flings. His wife, who had suffered through his repeated infidelities, had an opposite reaction to his. She, of course, was delighted.

Unfaithful men can be rich, poor, and everything in between, but rich seems to help (remember the leap to 70 percent when income exceeds $60,000). Money is a turn-on for both men and women. It also affords the man resources to carry on a romance with less guilt. One of the things that preys on an unfaithful husband's conscience if he isn't well off is the family money being squandered on the other woman.

These men can be highly educated or quite un-educated, celebrities—like Gary Hart, John F. Kennedy, Steve McQueen, or Richard Burton—or unknown. They can live in small towns or large cities. Although some earlier studies indicated that men who were religious were more likely to remain monogamous, other, more recent ones have shown that religious men are as apt to have affairs as those who never enter a house of worship. That goes for some religious leaders, too.

The Reverend Jim Bakker's television ministry collapsed because of his sexual escapades. Jimmy Swaggart's patronage of prostitutes is public knowledge. There are many more anonymous ministers of all denominations who are womanizers. Like college professors, who are in a similar position of authority with their students, religious leaders are in an ideal situation to carry on if they want to. Women still respond to men in authority—be they bosses, doctors, or clergymen—as sexy. One Protestant minister in the Midwest whom I interviewed has three current girlfriends and several ex-lovers among his parishioners. Each of the women he has been involved with is under the illusion that she is the only one with whom he has ever strayed—they feel special because of his attentions and don't think of him as the womanizer he is. The following letter appeared in a recent Ann Landers column:

Dear Ann Landers:
    I was disappointed with your advice to the bride who said she had slept with five men in the wedding party, including the minister. You advised, "Keep your mouth shut. The minister does not need the publicity."
    I say the minister also does not need to remain in a position where he can continue his hypocrisy and wreak emotional havoc on those who trust him.
    For thirty-two years I was married to a minister who was protected by people who also kept their mouths shut. In the meantime, my husband was taking advantage of young women to whom he should have been ministering.
    If people had not remained silent, he would have been removed from his job. The net result was that he caused irreparable harm to all of those who believed he was a servant of God, including his wife and children.

                    *   *   *

Unfaithful men need not be handsome. A recent *New York Times* review of a biography of the noted French existentialist author and philosopher, Jean-Paul Sartre underscored this: "The fact that he was short, unattractive, and startlingly cross-eyed in no way hampered his amorous conquests. . . ." The journalist Carl Bernstein, whose adultery was publicized in *Heartburn*, the thinly disguised autobiographical novel Nora Ephron wrote about their marriage, is not considered a handsome man.

The temperaments of men who have affairs range from sweet and sincere to boastful and manipulative. There are bastards who are monogamous and nice guys who stray. According to a study done by sex researcher H. J. Eysenck, extroverts may be more prone to infidelity; he found they have more sexual partners than introverted men, and start premarital and extramarital intercourse earlier in life.

Another study conducted by Drs. Josef Schenk and Horst Pfrang corroborated this tendency among single men, but they dispute whether the same dynamics apply to husbands. They may be right. Many a wife has found out that her quiet, low-key husband was involved with another woman. "My husband is so shy. Who would have believed it!" exclaimed one wife who recently discovered that her husband and a secretary in his company were carrying on.

Even though there are certain neurotic types—for example, narcissistic, hysterical, and obsessive men—who are drawn to infidelity and are, among others, examined in this book, the psychological makeup of unfaithful men can vary greatly, as can the nature of their affairs, from brief encounters to long, involved relationships.

There *is* one thing that all men who cheat share, however, and that is the ability to make women miserable and to wreak havoc in their relationships.

Among men as a society, this is rarely taken into account. There is no censure from other males for infidelity. Quite the contrary: it often raises a man's stock among men. Not only are no points given for good monogamous sex, but it may even be regarded with derision. By remaining true, you aren't being one of the boys. One man remembered being looked at with suspicion when he refused to go with a call girl who had been hired for him by a business associate.

The pressure in male society is toward infidelity rather than away from it. A man excites secret envy among his peers when he is perceived as a successful stud. Gary Hart and Warren Beatty, for example, were once overheard discussing other men's sexual scores. Hart is reported to have shown admiration for another senator who would line up five or six girls in New York and, according to Hart, "Have himself a weekend."

In addition, men cooperate in other men's sexual escapades. Single men, for example, sometimes serve as "beards"—they pretend to be the dates of women their married friends are seeing, so that the illicit lovers can go out in public together, or, in certain instances, even attend parties in the married man's home. A male friend, divorced at the time, served that function for a well-known New York politician. The friend was always in tow when this politician wanted to take his actress mistress out to a public restaurant.

When a woman accidentally bumps into a friend's "steady" or husband with another woman, and an involvement seems clear, there is always agony about whether to tell or not. Men generally experience no such conflict when they stumble onto a friend's affair. They know they will keep quiet.

Women understand each other's pain in these circumstances. Whether married or single, it is the rare woman who can accept a man's sexual betrayal without severe rumblings in her psyche. If a woman discovers her man's secret and doesn't get upset, it is generally a sign that something, apart from infidelity, has already rotted away the relationship in her eyes.

Philip Blumstein and Pepper Schwartz concluded from the results of their survey that the wives who did not react to a husband's affair as a catastrophe felt that the relationship was doomed anyway. David Moultrap, a marriage therapist and expert on affairs, feels that a cool reaction to infidelity bodes poorly for the future of the couple—the less anxiety a spouse feels in reaction to an affair, the higher the probability that the marriage will be terminated.

It is for women, married or single, who are not cool, but instead are stunned, hurt, and angered by sexual betrayal and are not sure what to do about it, that this book is written. Like millions and millions of other women, I have been there.

TWO

How You Can Tell If He Is Unfaithful

PRISCILLA'S HUSBAND USED TO BADGER HER TO BECOME MORE sexy. He blamed their poor sex life on her. If only she would be more responsive, he complained, they would make love more often. As it stood, they were down to practically zero. Priscilla didn't feel right about never having sex with her husband. She accepted the blame. After all, she had become less interested in sex since the children arrived, and she had refused him many times in the past. Priscilla went to see a sex therapist. The therapist asked to see Priscilla's husband too. When he came, he repeated his charges. They never had sex because Priscilla was not much interested in it.

In the course of treatment, the therapist taught Priscilla to think more positively about sex, and to become more sexual with her husband. Priscilla began to be more amorous at home, and she looked better than she had in years. Today she is a woman who likes sex, but now that she is interested, he isn't. Sex has stopped altogether. Priscilla has begun to wonder if her husband is having affairs.

A woman I'll call Anne is bothered by the same worry. In a letter to me, she explained:

"My husband often comes home from work, eats, takes a shower, and then, about eight or nine o'clock, he'll fix his hair, put on cologne and his best clothes, and say he is going to a friend's house. He doesn't come home until

18

between two and five A.M. If I ask him where he's been so late and what he did, he'll say, 'We'll talk about it tomorrow.' He always finds ways to keep from explaining.

"Am I insecure or childish?" she asks. "Or is my husband having an affair?"

For the past six months Helene has found her husband distant and uncommunicative. She knows something is wrong but she can't put her finger on it. She dares not think it, but sometimes the question "Is there another woman?" surfaces. She shoves the thought away time and time again.

Greta has been going with Al for two years. She can't say exactly why, but she thinks he may sneak in affairs with other women on his nights out. Is he doing it or isn't he? she wonders.

If you are reading this book, you may understand what agony these women are going through. Right now you too may be pondering the painful question, "Is he, or isn't he?" Or perhaps you have lived with such anguished doubts in the past. Maybe many times, with many men. Or you may worry about the future. Will he always remain faithful to you? Living with the thought of infidelity is an extremely common experience. There are millions of women like Priscilla, Anne, Helene, Greta—and you— who, feeling upset or vaguely troubled, would like to know the best way to tell if a man is being unfaithful.

Of course, the most obvious and best way to find out is to ask a man directly. But if you are like most women, you won't. You are afraid he might say yes. And then what? The thought sends a wave of fear shuddering through you.

The truth is you can't count on him telling the truth, anyway. Unless they are caught red-handed, a large proportion of men who cheat will deny everything.

How, then, can you tell, when you are afraid to ask or want to be on firmer ground before you do. How can you double-check if your man is telling you there's no one else but you think he may be lying?

Take this quiz. It will tip you off to what is going on now and what you should watch for in the future.

		Yes	No
1.	Are your instincts telling you something?	/	
2.	Is he acting differently lately?		
3.	Have his habits changed?		
4.	Are you feeling anxious?		
5.	Does he look different?		
6.	Is sex different?		
7.	Have you found a tangible clue?		
8.	Are there strange phone calls?		
9.	Is he suddenly encouraging you to take trips or vacations alone?		
10.	Are there signs that your home was invaded while you were away?		
11.	Do you suspect that a woman he invites over is more than a friend?		
12.	Are others suspicious?		
13.	Have there been accidental slips or disclosures?		

1. Are Your Instincts Telling You Something?

The most important thing to pay attention to is what women often refuse to heed—their own intuition. You can't put your finger on it, but you *feel* something is wrong or strange. If this kind of creepy feeling is nagging at you, listen to it! Your intuition is telling you something. Unfortunately, what it is telling you, you may not really want to know. Women frequently ignore or discount a persistent or recurring inner sense that all is not as it should be. Generally, women deny their own feelings because they can't face up to the fact that their man is not being faithful. It is just too painful, frightening, or wounding to their own sense of self-esteem, or maybe it is too reminiscent of past injuries, perhaps a father who seemed to reject them. Or the thought of a break in the relationship is more than they can bear. They can't imagine life without him—they feel they would be lost emotionally or economically.

They prefer not knowing to having to take action, which acknowledging the possibility of an affair implies. It is important to understand that for many of you there may be a tendency to deny your own gut feelings—but that doesn't mean that your intuitions aren't tipping you off. They are whispering in your ear but you are just refusing to listen.

2. Is He Acting Differently Lately?

Another thing to pay attention to is change.

What about your partner's attitude? Does he suddenly seem more emotionally detached or withdrawn at home or on a date? Does he seem to be lost in daydreams? Is he unusually preoccupied? Do you feel somehow shut out? One woman said the first sign that made her take notice was that her husband stopped talking to her. Many men do this. They are carrying around a secret, and unconsciously, since they are afraid of letting you in on it, they clam up altogether.

James Vaughan, in *Beyond Affairs*, a book about his own infidelity, written with his wife, Peggy, explained how this worked for him:

"In essence, I was withdrawing from Peggy—putting distance between us by setting new boundaries around what I was willing to discuss with her. I wanted to avoid getting into any discussion which might even remotely relate to my affair with Linda."

Other men stop communicating at home because their inner absorption with the affair, or even their own warring emotions, have made them turn inward.

Some men become evasive or touchy and defensive. Interestingly, others who may have been moody or taciturn previously may suddenly seem happier or friendlier once an affair begins. There are men who, in trying to cover their tracks, or because they are truly feeling guilty or even more content, actually become more attentive to a woman while an affair with someone else is going on. Some men become more polite, or start to do things for you or the children that they ordinarily wouldn't. Over all, the thing to watch for is a marked difference in mood, no matter what it is.

3. Have His Habits Changed?

Change of habits is another important clue. He may suddenly need to work later more often, to go away more, to attend more conferences, to entertain more clients. His business trips may get longer. It is common for men to tack on a day either before or after a business trip to be with a lover. The result of all this is that he just isn't around as much as he used to be. He may start to explain how he's using his time more than he did before. For example, he may say he was with Jack or Bill when he comes home late, when he never went into explanations in the past.

You also may not find him where he is supposed to be if you happen to try to reach him. One woman whose suspicions were beginning to be aroused wondered why the phone was always busy when she was away and trying to reach him from a pay phone. This man called his mistress whenever his wife left their home.

If you are a single woman in a relationship, your man may stop calling you every day the way he used to. He may surreptitiously check his phone messages on the machine with the door shut when you are there, and you may hear the faint sound of a recorded female voice. He may mention a play he saw and suddenly realize you didn't see it with him. He may go away for the weekend without you, with the plea that he needs some space. He may say he can't see you as much because he is overwhelmed with work or needs time alone. In general, he may ask you out less often, or have to rush away suspiciously on Sunday, for example, when he used to linger on.

One woman recalls that, at breakfast on a Sunday morning after she had slept over at her boyfriend's house, she suddenly grew suspicious when he told her he had to meet his mother at one that afternoon. "He didn't even like his mother!" she remarked.

Another woman figured something was up because her lover got all dressed up in his best new suit, supposedly to meet a male buddy who had just flown into town. "He was just paying too much attention to his appearance," she said.

Dressing up in an unhabitual way before supposedly going to work on some papers at the office, or for an evening with the boys or anywhere else without you is frequently a signal of infidelity. One woman wrote to Ann Landers:

> When my husband and I go out for an evening, it's in a dirty car, any old shirt will do, his patched slacks are good enough, and his running shoes "feel great."
>
> Where does he take me for dinner? Either to a greasy spoon or some joint on the edge of town that the truckers think is terrific.
>
> When he goes out with the boys on Friday nights, he dresses up to the nines, puts lifts in his shoes to appear taller, and wears a man's girdle to pull in his gut. He sprays himself with cologne till I could gag, then heads for the car wash before meeting the guys.
>
> Mr. Hot Shot rolls in about 3:00 A.M., looking very rumpled, and he's exhausted. I think I smell a rat. What say you?

Ann Landers thought she smelled a skunk.

4. Are You Feeling Anxious?

The feeling that any or all of this creates in you is anxiety. Pay attention to anxiety. If you are single, you anxiously await his phone calls, wondering more and more when he will call. You anxiously await his invitations to see you, never sure anymore when he will. You anxiously wonder if perhaps you have done something wrong. Out of anxiety, you may try harder when you are with him, to no avail. He still seems less available than before.

A married woman, feeling anxious, may worry about her weight, her ability as a sexual partner, and her loss of attractiveness due to aging, which may make her either go on diets or eat even more, depending on the woman. She may fuss more with hair and makeup. She may start to study sex manuals, buy sexy nightgowns, and work more energetically at being a good sex partner—again without any effect. Her partner still stays out late or remains less interested in sex. He seems not to notice her efforts.

Finally, anxiety makes some women start drinking too much. No matter what goes on, don't take to the bottle. Look what happened to Joan Kennedy.

5. Does He Look Different?

A new interest in his appearance is a strong clue from a man that some hanky-panky is going on. A husband may finally lose weight, start working out with a vengeance, buy a new wardrobe, start to dress in younger-style clothing, get new underwear, change from baggy boxers to sleek, colored bikinis, start plastering a hank of hair from the side of his head over his bald spot, decide to touch up the gray in his hair, switch from sober, horn-rimmed glasses to fashionable tinted lenses. You have lived with him or accepted him the way he is for a long time, so it is generally not for you that this overhaul is going on.

The sudden disappearance of the wedding ring on his

finger can be an alarm bell, as in the case of this woman who complained to Ann Landers:

> A few years ago, my husband removed his wedding ring from his finger, saying it could be a hazard on his job. (He works in the construction field.) Finally he stopped wearing it altogether.
>
> Last Christmas he came home from the company Christmas party wearing a very expensive gold initial ring, which he said was a gift from "Lyn," a young woman who works for the company. The ring has not been off his finger since the day he got it.
>
> Yes, I asked him how come this ring isn't hazardous on his job. He said in case he ran into Lyn, he doesn't want to offend her by not wearing her gift.

Most men are not so crude or stupid. If they are pretending to be single with other women, they may take off the ring while they are out, but they are sure to put it back on before returning home. A few unfortunate men have lost their rings when they fell out of a pocket during their escapades. One desperate husband in Manhattan spent hours trying to fish his ring out from under a subway grating where it had fallen while he was putting it back on before going home.

6. Is Sex Different?

A change in sexual habits is another clue. It could go either way. There may be bouts of impotence when he never had any trouble before. He may suddenly try out new tricks in bed—things he has learned from someone else. His desire for sex with you may dwindle markedly, and you may have sex much less often than in the past, leaving you to wonder what the matter is. He may try to avoid you, and suddenly become a night owl, staying up later than you and crawling into bed only after he thinks you are safely asleep. Some men stop having sex with their regular partners out of a strange sense of loyalty to their new lovers. Others simply transfer their erotic interest elsewhere. An outside involvement, however, sometimes works as a general aphrodisiac for a man, and he actually may have sex with you more often and perhaps with renewed interest, which can make you feel that an affair at that time is out of the question. One man confessed, "I often go straight from my lover's bed to my wife's. It's a real turn-on for me to have been with someone else and make love to my wife when I get home."

Sometimes the change in the bedroom is more ephemeral—you just get a strange feeling that while your husband or boyfriend is making love to you, he is mentally somewhere else, more distant than before. Men for whom sex is like clockwork are the hardest to spot a change in, at least sexually, because their habits don't vary. A woman recently wrote to me, saying her husband made love to her every night with total predictability, and that therefore, since he continued to do so, she hadn't the faintest idea that he had had two affairs within a period of five years.

Finally, if your man has been badgering you for years to try oral sex, some other variations, or some kink, and you have consistently refused him, or he has been pressuring you to have sex more often than you want to, and suddenly he doesn't bother you anymore, he may have found the solution to his desires with someone else.

Single men who are spreading their sexual favors around may find ways to keep you dangling while conserving their physical resources. One woman said one of the first signs that he was sleeping with others—which he was—was that her boyfriend suddenly found excuses to leave without having sex with her at the end of some evenings. When she mentioned that they had not slept together in more than two weeks, her boyfriend feigned surprise and pleaded stress at work, but since he wanted to keep her around, he immediately made a date with her that would include lovemaking. One of his other women was put on hold.

A man who regularly juggles more than one woman admitted to me that he substitutes intimate phone calls for dates sometimes, or lunch for dinner. This, he knows, will keep a woman feeling he is still interested and give him the time and energy he needs to romance someone else. Another busy lover told me that he sometimes avoids sex in the morning with a girlfriend who has slept over when he knows he is going to see another woman later that same day. Of course, this is not a problem for every man who has multiple love affairs. "It is particularly exciting to me to know that I have slept with one woman in the morning and another one that night—it makes me feel like a teenager again!" explained one thirty-eight-year-old bachelor.

7. Have You Found a Tangible Clue?

Physical clues to affairs include unfamiliar smells and scents on your man's body or clothes when he comes home. The opposite can also be a sign. Beware of a man who arrives home after a long day at work, or an evening out with clients, smelling daisy-fresh—as if he had just stepped out of a shower.

Other typical signs: matchbooks from unfamiliar restaurants, night spots, or hotels; incriminating scratches; black-and-blue marks; a hair clip on the floor of his car; a lipstick or makeup stain; a note; a piece of paper with an address or phone number on it; an envelope with a strange postmark or no return address; a receipt from a motel; unexplained florist bills; or expenses at fancy stores on his credit card bill. A woman found a package of condoms hidden between volumes on her boyfriend's bookshelf. She said nothing at first and just counted how many were missing from the pack each time she came to his apartment. Only then did she confront him.

When Jacqueline Onassis was married to Jack Kennedy, she found a pair of women's panties stuffed into her pillowcase at the White House. This may not have been accidental, at least as far as the other woman was concerned. One experienced womanizer I have talked to is extremely vigilant because he is convinced that there is a tendency on the part of some women to leave their mark in the form of something tangible, such as a forgotten comb or a left-behind scarf. A woman who lived for two years with an artist who worked at home gradually came to recognize that he was leading a secret life while she was at work. She would spot a bobby pin on the bathroom floor, a hair on the sink. "While I was actually holding the evidence in my hand, he had the nerve to vehemently deny everything," she remembered.

8. Are There Strange Phone Calls?

You may have a problem if you are at your boyfriend's apartment and the phone rings and he picks up the receiver and says, "I have to call you back," too many times. Or if he goes into the next room to continue his conversation behind a shut door.

Married men who are cheating can be even more outrageous. Many more husbands than you would imagine, considering the danger, regularly call their lovers from their own homes. Any new pattern of telephone conversations in a low voice or behind closed doors, or at odd hours, or calls that are broken off rather abruptly the minute you enter the room, may be clues that an affair is in progress.

A woman in New York City figured something strange was going on when, one weekend morning after her boyfriend went down to get the Sunday newspaper, she, too, decided to leave her apartment to go to the supermarket to get something and discovered him at the pay phone on the corner, deep in conversation. Some husbands take off from their families at a table in a restaurant to make their calls to the other woman from the pay phone near the men's room.

Many of the married men who like the thrill, comfort, or contrast of talking to their lovers from their own homes devise all kinds of ruses to make their conversations appear legitimate. A husband, for example, may tell his wife that there is a project in progress that must keep him in constant contact with a co-worker—and the colleague is, of course, female. Or he may let his wife know that pressure at work makes his secretary have to contact him at home after hours.

A forty-three-year-old accountant told me that his wife found out about his philandering when she accidentally picked up a telephone extension upstairs and found him talking, in an incriminating way, to her best friend from the phone downstairs. His wife wasn't the only one incensed by the discovery. Since this man was active with several women in his town at the same time, when his wife separated from him, telling everyone why, four of his other girlfriends—who, until that moment, thought they were his one and only "other woman"—were furious at him as well.

9. Is He Suddenly Encouraging You to Take Trips or Vacations Alone?

One husband in San Francisco, having an affair after many years of marriage, suggested that his wife take a trip to Europe that she had been asking for, but without him. He pleaded that he couldn't accompany her because of his business. She went, and he then was free to see his mistress as much as he liked and even sleep over at her apartment while his wife traveled.

Men in similar situations are often eager to have their wives visit relatives out of town (especially if the wives take the kids). A favorite ploy is to have the wife stay at the beach or in the mountains all summer because it is "better" for her and the kids, while he toils in the city. The "summer bachelor" is a familiar figure in large metropolises. These husbands parade around with other women quite openly all summer long, often calling the unsuspecting spouse nightly to check in.

10. Are There Signs That Your Home Was Invaded While You Were Away?

It is particularly enraging to a woman if she finds out, but it is quite common for an unfaithful man to invite his lover to his home, and often into the bed he shares with you. Most frequently, of course, this happens when the wife or live-in girlfriend is out of town. John F. Kennedy's mistress Judith Exner says that she and he used the bed that Kennedy shared with his wife, Jacqueline, in their Georgetown home. We all know, too, how this practice led to the downfall of Gary Hart. In cases like this, it is more frequently a snooping neighbor than the press who tips a wife off. Soiled sheets, perfume on the pillowcase, or something left behind have all raised suspicions, but men in such situations are not all oblivious to the danger of this—many have told me of carefully laundering the bedding before the wife returned. The smell of freshly laundered sheets could be a tip-off, particularly for a man who generally lets you do the laundry.

A business consultant who had been living with his girlfriend for three years avoided the whole problem with linens by carefully spreading a sheet out on the floor so that he and another woman he saw on the sly could make love on it and thus leave the bed he shared with his live-in love untouched. This same man, in a subsequent marriage, invited another other woman to visit him while he was at home recuperating from a serious illness. He introduced her to his wife as an old friend and persuaded her to take time off as his nurse to go to a movie. He assured her the "friend" would look after him in her absence. Soon after his wife's departure, he persuaded the "friend" to perform oral sex on him, which, as he joked to a male friend later, speeded his recuperation enormously. One man told me of frantically scrubbing away at a bloodstain on the sheet (his girlfriend's period had begun unexpectedly), while watching the clock for his wife's imminent return.

11. Do You Suspect That a Woman He Invites Over Is More Than a Friend?

Some men find ways to invite their lovers to their homes, generally to parties and gatherings, when the wife is present. Your instincts often tell you that something is fishy. Listen to them.

"My wife knew I liked the girl," a man in Connecticut told me, talking about his mistress, "so I decided to invite her to a party at the house. I thought that would stop my wife's suspicions. It didn't. She went right for her."

An advertising executive on the West Coast has always, since the beginning of their long marriage, kept his wife informed about his large number of female "friends." He receives calls from them at home, and they are sometimes invited to his home. Almost all of these friends are either former lovers or current ones—something he, of course, has not revealed to his wife.

In my interviews with men, I heard many stories of husbands kissing or fondling or even making love to a mistress in one part of the house while the wife was in another. Some men find this a particular thrill.

One husband told me how he discovered the excitement of this. He remembered arriving home after an evening of dancing with another couple. His wife, pregnant at the time, went upstairs to bed. The husband of the other woman was having a drink in the living room. "She was coming out of the bathroom. I was passing by in the hallway. She made a grab for me. I went through the ceiling."

Joseph Kennedy had no compunction about inviting one of his mistresses, Gloria Swanson, to his home, with his wife, Rose, acting as hostess. A woman told me of receiving evidence of her husband's affair in a devastating manner when her young son came into the kitchen while a dinner party was in progress and asked, "Mommy, why is Daddy holding that woman's hand under the table?"

12. Are Others Suspicious?

It is not uncommon for friends, children, and other relatives to become suspicious or to know some telling details about an affair before a woman does. But unless a woman is prepared to receive the news, she may continue to deny the possibility that he is carrying on.

Rose Kennedy was one of the queens of denial. Even after Joseph Kennedy had petitioned church leaders in Boston for permission to live with Gloria Swanson, she refused to admit that an affair existed. "You know," she told one interviewer in regard to Swanson, "they talked about Mr. Kennedy and me in the early years of our marriage. But I paid no attention to it. Neither did Joe. We were in love long before we were married and forever after."

Her blind spot did not apply to her sons, however. She was acutely aware of her sons' sexual liaisons. She managed to find out the name of every woman Ted

Kennedy was involved with, which was more than his wife, Joan, did.

After Joan finally left Ted and was living in Boston while Ted stayed in the family home in Virginia, Rose was asked by Kennedy biographer, Lester David, if the marriage was breaking up. "I don't know," she said.

"Then why," David asked, "has Joan gone to live in Boston while Ted remains in Virginia?"

Rose, close to ninety years old at the time, had impaired hearing. "Virginia?" she asked. "Who's Virginia? I never heard of *that* one!"

A woman in Philadelphia remembered receiving a phone call from a friend, telling her that her husband had something going with his secretary. Because she was still unable to accept the fact of her husband's infidelity at that point—even though he was coming home in the wee hours more and more often—she became angry at the friend rather than at the husband. She later divorced this man, who had continued to deceive her with a series of women.

Another wife I interviewed who already knew about her husband's affair received an anonymous phone call telling her that her husband was seen with another woman in a well-known Florida resort. She interpreted this as backbiting and hostility from the informant, but I am not so sure. Women often feel a kind of sisterhood in regard to male infidelity; they think it is their duty to warn another woman of what is happening. In this way they are different from men, who tend to shield and alibi, or at least keep quiet for one another. James Vaughan, in *Beyond Affairs*, talks about running into a friend while he was with the "other woman." He was worried about the consequences, but soon found out he didn't have to be: "I would learn that most men can be trusted in this way, whether or not they have had an affair."

Sometimes it is grown-up children who become suspicious. The daughter of one woman, whose husband had been mysteriously disappearing into a nearby town one day a week for the past four years, demanded to know from her mother, "What does Daddy *do* there every Tuesday?" Her mother, who had not said anything about her suspicions until that point, answered within earshot of her husband, "I think your father is having an affair with a woman there." The man, a swift thinker, turned her accusation into a joke by saying, "Oh yes, I'm meeting Joan Collins, who flies in every week from Hollywood, and she is fabulous!"

13. Have There Been Accidental Slips or Disclosures?

Not uncommon are the "accidents" that often, in effect, amount to full disclosures. Liberace described walking into a theater when he was a young man and finding his father there with a strange woman.

A twenty-seven-year-old who works with his father, the owner of a large company, recently overheard a phone conversation in his father's office and blew the whistle to his mother, telling her there was another woman. This ended the double life his father was leading with a young woman who had a son by him and whom he was supporting lavishly.

A husband was horrified recently when, while burning a bunch of old checks in his den's fireplace, one, by chance, blew away, dropping at the foot of his wife, who looked at it and demanded to know who the woman was to whom the check was made out. He lied his way out of it, but it was a birthday present to the man's girlfriend.

Accidental disclosures may include slips of the tongue when a man calls you by the wrong name, pieces of paper left lying about with phone numbers or names and addresses on them, receipts from hotel rooms that are accidentally found, or phone bills you happen to see, with repeated calls to strange phone numbers. A clothing buyer for a department store found out that her boyfriend was cheating when she discovered a vibrator in his night-table drawer. They never used a vibrator together.

Mrs. Andy Capasso went to a restaurant one evening and accidentally ran into her husband, who was having dinner with his lover, Bess Myerson.

In a few cases, wives have found out about infidelity through calls from hospitals or the police. There was the physical accident of a heart attack while a man was in a lover's bed; a fatal heart attack tipped Happy Rockefeller off that her husband, Nelson, had been playing around. It is a statistical fact that people with weak hearts are more prone to cardiac problems during extramarital sex than when they are making love to wives. There is more anxiety, often coupled with heavy eating and drinking as a prelude.

A wife of twenty-two years accidentally found out about her husband's recent series of affairs that kept him hopping around the country when she called him at an out-of-town hotel where he was supposed to be on business, and the operator asked whether she wished to speak to Mr. or Mrs. ————.

Sometimes the accident of fate occurs when a man is carrying on with someone else's wife and her husband finds out. It is not uncommon for the injured spouse to call the wife of the man who is cuckolding him to tell her what is going on. It was Eddie Fisher, then married to Elizabeth Taylor, who called Richard Burton's wife at the time, Sybil Burton, to inform her about the escalating affair between their respecive mates.

Occasionally the other woman will call to break the news. In one case it was blackmail. She wanted money to leave the wealthy husband alone. More often this happens out of vengeance, either because a man refuses to leave the wife or because he has already broken off the affair. This is the cheating man's nightmare. So is venereal disease, another "accident" that reveals infidelity, despite his desperate protests that it came from a towel or a toilet seat, or out of thin air. A man may pass on to his partner syphilis, chlamydia, crabs, gonorrhea, herpes, various vaginal infections, and the most frightening sexually transmitted disease of all these days—AIDS.

A gynecologist who has as patients both the wife and the mistress of one man finds that he is constantly treating both women for the same thing.

One "other woman" reported that she wondered why she was getting so many repeated vaginal infections until she found out her married man lover had a stable of women besides her.

What These Questions Are All About

Obviously, the more you have answered "yes" to the questions above, the more probable it is that your man is cheating. But the real purpose of the questions in this section is not to tell you whether your man is unfaithful. If he is, it is likely that you already know. You just haven't admitted it to yourself. Look at Anne, the woman whose letter I printed at the beginning of this section. Even though her husband disappears almost every night, all dressed up and smelling good, and doesn't return until between 2:00 and 5:00 A.M., she hasn't come to the obvious conclusion that he is definitely fooling around. Anne only thinks he *may* be, and wonders if, instead, her suspicions are the result of her being childish and insecure.

Many women are like Anne. They refuse to believe fully what their guts are telling them, and look the other way when confronted by behavior that is, at best, odd and uncharacteristic, and at worst, very incriminating.

The purpose, then, of the quiz you have taken is really to make you think more specifically about a question that you may keep dodging, and, if necessary, to make you face facts.

No one says that knowing about your partner's infidelity is pleasant. But deliberately not knowing is not pleasant either. It has a psychic cost. You may get angry, for example, at trivial things, instead of at what is bothering you—his infidelity.

One woman whose husband was a notorious womanizer would get blazingly furious at him and create scenes when she noticed him just looking at a pretty woman in public. She never admitted to herself or to him that he was repeatedly unfaithful. As a result of suppressing the facts, she was walking around with a great deal of bottled-up fury. Her scenes when he was simply looking was the way she vented her fury indirectly.

You may develop a stress-related illness from all you are keeping inside. You may have crying jags for no reason. You may become depressed.

Worst of all, since you aren't dealing with the issue of his infidelity, you allow it to continue, and you become, in effect, a collaborator in his affair.

Finally, it is imperative to confront his infidelity these days because of AIDS. Your partner may unwittingly be sleeping with someone who is carrying the virus. Infidelity has become a mortal danger to your health, a fact you cannot overlook.

What you don't know *can* hurt you, both physically and mentally. And what you don't deal with can hurt the relationship, as well. Once an affair is brought out in the open, believe it or not, it often improves a relationship (see Chapter 14). But ignoring ongoing infidelity widens the gap between partners.

Now this doesn't mean that in a few instances suspicion isn't unfounded. Of course there are women who are pathologically jealous. They go crazy and start imagining things if their man wants to pursue any interests, even innocent ones, on his own. They mistakenly think of love as fusing with another, as two becoming one. Women like this react to any solitary activity on a man's part with jealousy. Unfounded jealousy can also haunt an extremely insecure woman whose poor self-esteem makes her imagine that her husband must always be after other women, because she is so undesirable.

It is easy to figure out if you are just being neurotic. Irrational jealousy is a continuing problem in a woman's life. The green-eyed monster reappears in every important relationship with a man. If you don't have this kind of history with men, chances are your suspicions have some grounds, at least enough to make you want to keep your eyes wide open.

I want to insert one caution before I leave the subject of clues to infidelity: suspicious behavior occasionally is caused by something other than an affair.

Let me give you an example. Geraldine called her husband, Thomas, at the hotel he was staying in while on a business trip. The hotel said he had checked out the day before. Since he hadn't returned home that night, Geraldine jumped to the conclusion that he must be having an affair.

It turned out that Thomas, who was unhappy in the relationship, was preparing to leave Geraldine. He had rented an apartment for himself in a nearby city. There was no other woman. He had gone there to be by himself and fix things up. The situation was actually worse than Geraldine imagined. But because she confronted Thomas about her suspicions, she was able to persuade him to go into therapy with her. Today they are working as a couple on the issues that were causing the rift. Thomas is no longer so sure he is going to leave Geraldine. He has given up his apartment. Geraldine has given up her suspicions, something she could not have done if she had not confronted Thomas about his deception. She did not let suspicion linger on, poisoning her own mind and the relationship. Her marriage was saved because she brought the matter out into the open. Let that be a lesson to you.

THREE

Will He Cheat in the Future?

LESS OBVIOUS THAN THE SIGNS THAT A MAN IS ACTUALLY having an affair are the clues that tell you if a man is likely to be unfaithful in the future. Here are thirty-four important things to watch for, based on studies, surveys, and findings from sociologists, therapists, and other mental-health professionals.

1. He has a background of cheating. His history counts. For example:

- If a man was unfaithful to you while you were courting, he is more likely to do the same thing after you are married.
- A man who has been unfaithful in his first marriage is a good candidate for an affair in his second (even if he left his first marriage for you). In second marriages, in general, there is a higher infidelity rate.
- If your husband has already had one affair, it makes him statistically more apt to repeat the experience.
- The single man who has a history of seeing more than one woman at a time is a bad bet for monogamy.

2. His father had affairs. A man like Jack Kennedy, whose father had affairs, or Marlon Brando, whose father was a womanizer, is very likely to repeat this pattern in his own life.

Interestingly, even men who are not consciously aware of a father's infidelity may know subliminally and ape his actions. One man who entered couples therapy as the result of a crisis brought about by his wife's discovery of an affair claimed that his father had never played around. One day he received a call from a woman who had been born out of wedlock and adopted. She was looking for the man who she had found out was her father. It turned out that this woman was his father's daughter. Unconsciously, he knew about his father's infidelity all along. In retrospect he remembered his mother saying, "In those days we put up with everything."

A salesman in Denver who has had affairs since day one of his marriage thinks it may be in his genes. He denies ever knowing about his father's affairs until late in life, although he does remember answering a strange call when he was about ten. It was from a woman from another city who was trying to get in touch with his father. He also remembers his father telling him how his grandfather would seduce the family servants and other women in town.

Occasionally a father, particularly in very macho ethnic groups, will even go so far as to introduce a girlfriend to his son. One man in therapy recalled his father proudly introducing him and his brother to his pretty mistress when he was fifteen.

It adds to the possibility of infidelity if a man's mother tolerated her husband's adultery. He often expects that the woman in his life will do the same.

3. Your father cheated on your mother. Your own history counts as much as his. A woman who grew up with a father who was a womanizer often unconsciously chooses a man who will repeat this pattern in her own relationships. Since her father was one of the most notorious womanizers of his day, it is no accident that Jacqueline Kennedy Onassis had two husbands, John Kennedy and Aristotle Onassis, who had affairs.

4. He had a lot of sexual experience before marriage. Various studies, including a survey conducted by *Psychology Today*, reveal that men who have engaged in a lot of premarital sex are more likely to indulge in extensive extramarital sex.

5. *His schedule gives him unaccounted-for time.* Phil, who works in a business in which his girlfriend is an active participant, has far fewer opportunities to meet someone to play around with than George, who disappears into an environment in which he interacts among strangers during the business day.

Harry, who works at a routine, strictly nine-to-five job, has much less opportunity to get involved than does Cliff, who regularly has to work late, John, who travels a lot, or Arnold, whose executive job allows him largely to create his own schedule.

Ralph is like Harry. He is supervised all day on his job and is strictly accountable for his time to a boss. This cuts down opportunities for an affair.

In contrast, Andy, a salesman who is always out making calls; Frank, a business owner; and Claude, a self-employed professional, are three men who can make their own time to a great extent. It is easier for them to squeeze in affairs during the work day. Frank and Andy often dally on long lunch hours (a common trysting time). Claude frequently knocks off early, meets someone, and is still home in time for dinner (another common tactic).

When their work schedule allows it, many men conduct their affairs during daylight hours in an effort to leave their mates in the dark.

6. *He has opportunities for affairs.* Several studies have shown that opportunity, in general, plays a crucial part in determining whether a man will cheat or not.

In a survey of four thousand men by Anthony Pietropinto, M.D., and Jacqueline Simenauer, nearly two-thirds said they would have an affair if the opportunity and circumstances were right.

In another study, by Robert Whitehurst, 41 percent of the subjects claimed that the critical factor in their infidelity was the place and people they were with, which presented the opportunity for extramarital sex.

John Edwards, in a study of extramarital involvement published in the *Journal of Sex Research*, states that in 40 percent of the marriages where perceived opportunities for extramarital sex existed, affairs actually occurred.

Commonly reported "opportunities" are:

• Parties where people dress seductively, flirt with members of the opposite sex, and drink—temptation in the making.
• When a wife or girlfriend goes out of town.
• When a man is traveling alone.
• When an aggressive woman makes the first move. Certain men would never start an affair themselves, but they will respond if a woman takes the initiative. They feel absolved of responsibility: "It isn't my fault—she started it." Other men, perhaps out of kindness or believing that masculinity requires that they seize sex when it is offered, are unfaithful simply because they don't know how to say no. (A certain number of these, because they are doing it without real desire on their part, find themselves impotent.)
• When a man finds himself unexpectedly alone with an attractive woman. One Seattle consultant who works from home while his girlfriend goes to an office found himself alone during the day with a friend of hers who was using the couple's guest room during a visit from out of town. Guess what happened.

Another man told of spending time, at his wife's urging, with the recent widow of a close friend. He would drop by her house to ask if there were things she needed fixed and inquire about her well-being. "One day she started telling me how grateful she was to me. She came close and put her hand on my arm. I found myself aroused. I liked her. I felt sorry for her. We ended up making love. It was just a couple of times. I didn't have it on my mind when I started going over to her house." This man concluded his story with a phrase I have heard over and over again: "It just happened." Many men who have affairs because of a chance opportunity have not planned to be unfaithful.

7. *He has close contacts with other women.* A secretary, a co-worker, a woman's best friend, or a man's female friend are all more likely sexual rivals than a complete stranger. Studies have shown proximity to be a big factor in whether a man will have an affair or not.

"It's often purely a matter of availability," says David Moulton, a Boston family therapist and expert on affairs.

He characterizes paramours as usually "best friends or co-workers or business acquaintances."

Lyn Atwater, in a study of forty women, found that a sizable proportion of the women who become partners in extramarital affairs started out as casual friends of the man.

Laurel Richardson, in *The New Other Woman*, a study of liaisons between married men and single women, tells of many women who described their original interaction as friendship. She makes the point, however, that these women may have been slow to recognize the married man's sexual intentions.

If a man has a close friendship with a woman, it does not necessarily mean they have a sexual relationship, but the closer the relationship, the greater the odds it will happen. In relationships like this, "sexual relations may become inevitable," writes Gerald Neubeck, an expert on extramarital problems, "not necessarily because one 'lusts' sexually after the 'outsider,' but because one believes sex belongs in the relationship."

A woman explained this progression in her relationship with a happily married father of two: "We've been good friends for three years, but just recently confessed to each other that we both have close feelings for the other. Neither of us wants to end our friendship. I'm afraid that sooner or later our feelings will overpower our sensibilities and we will have an affair."

A married man who has had a series of affairs during his marriage told me, "All the relations I ever had just came about. They were people I had known for years, women I had regard for. There was only one I ever thought about primarily sexually. The others I didn't think of in terms of sex. We were originally friends."

John Edwards, in his investigation of sexual behavior in and out of marriage, mentioned friendships between couples, in which the husband confides in the other woman, as a common starting point for infidelity.

8. *He feels alienated.* One well-known study by Robert Whitehurst pointed up the fact that men who feel alienated, estranged from their environment, and powerless had more short and transient affairs than did other men.

Highly alienated men accounted for 80 percent of the infidelity among Whitehurst's subjects.

Some people believe that alienation is something that grows in a man as he ages. Emotional detachment, cynicism, and disenchantment are fostered in many cases by the behavior he has to engage in and is witness to in the business world.

9. He is unconventional. Researchers Gerald Neubeck and Vera Schletzer found a correlation between unconventionality—a disregard for social mores—and infidelity. Nonconformists refuse to follow rules, in or out of marriage.

10. He really doesn't believe in monogamy. Many women have never talked directly about monogamy with their partners. They simply assume that it's part of the package—that a man expects to be faithful once he starts to go with you, or if he moves in or marries you. Don't assume anything. There are many men who have affairs simply because they don't believe in monogamy. They may have had parents who didn't practice it. They may come from an ethnic group in which infidelity is assumed to be a male prerogative. They may even think of monogamy as something that is outdated. These men, if they marry, never intend *not* to fool around. Affairs, for them, are predictable. They are acting in a way that is consistent with their beliefs.

11. He thrives on adventure. A man who has searched for exciting experiences all his life may be predisposed to affairs. In our society, according to the psychologist Albert Ellis, "one of the few remaining areas in which they can frequently find real excitement and novelty of a general as well as a specifically sexual nature is in the area of sex-love affairs."

12. He is searching for self-fulfillment. Infidelity can be part of a philosophical search for self-fulfillment. This attitude, particularly prevalent in the late 1960s, considers monogamy to be restricting, and experimentation with multiple partners an attempt to express oneself fully. There are far fewer people in the eighties who consider complete sexual freedom to be a sign of humanism, but some leftovers still exist.

13. He never feels guilty about anything he does. It stands to reason, but one study by Gerald Neubeck and Vera Schletter corroborated that individuals who possess few guilt feelings about any of their actions are poor prospects for monogamous relationships.

14. He is very jealous. Irrational jealous outbursts in which a man unjustly accuses his partner of being interested in other men or of having an affair may be an indication that he is the guilty party; *he* is playing around, or seriously wants to. Therapists call this projection—a process in which one person accuses another of doing something he himself is thinking about or is actually doing. Studies have found that jealous males are *more* likely to be involved in outside relationships, while jealous women are *less* likely to be involved with a third party.

15. You have been married close to fifteen years. Although infidelity can and does occur at any stage in relationships, certain times in life spawn affairs. At greatest risk are men in and around the fourteenth year of marriage, when most affairs occur, according to the marriage therapist David Moulton. Baby-boomers should pay particular attention to this fact. This period in marriage is occurring for many of that generation right now.

16. He is nearing an end-of-decade birthday. Age thirty, forty, fifty, and so on are times of summing up when a man may feel he needs more closeness, more freedom, more or better sex and searches for it elsewhere. Or he may decide things about you or his relationship don't quite suit him, so he wants to try other partners. He may also become very conscious of the shortening of time and want to make up for missed experiences before it is too late. Talking about one end-of-decade birthday (age thirty), Dr. Harold Lief, professor of psychiatry at the University of Pennsylvania Medical School, and a specialist in marital and sex therapy, comments, "We find a lot of extramarital sex going on at this time, almost as if people are testing themselves in other relationships that would give them more pleasure; they wonder if somebody else will be a better companion, as well as a lover."

17. He is in his thirties. This is the decade of greatest danger for a man. David Moulton pins down thirty-seven to thirty-nine as the most statistically probable ages for an affair.

18. You are pregnant. Another period when affairs are common is during pregnancy. Masters and Johnson revealed that many of the men they studied started affairs at this time.

Some prospective fathers react to the changed appearance of their pregnant wives. Some begin to identify the wife as a mother at this time, and as a result no longer respond to her as a sexy woman. Others feel more trapped and committed by the pregnancy and unconsciously seek to escape via an affair.

Rock star Rod Stewart had an affair with a twenty-two-year-old model while his live-in lover of three years, Kelly Emberg, was pregnant with their baby. "To go off with another woman while I was pregnant was the lowest thing he could have done," exclaimed the irate Miss Emberg, who echoed the feelings of many women in similar circumstances.

19. You have just had a child. Fatherhood also is a well-known starting point for extracurricular sex. Peter's reactions are typical. He had looked forward to the birth of his first child, but after his son Jonathan arrived, he began to feel neglected. He felt his wife was no longer focusing on him as she used to, and was now lavishing all her attention on the baby. Feeling hurt and deprived, he started a brief affair with a co-worker.

Affairs at this time are also often a reaction to anxieties produced by the new responsibilities of fatherhood.

20. One of his parents has just died. Another time of great risk is when a man's parent dies. A fling can be a reaffirmation of life in the face of death. Sometimes it is the disappearance of the restraining force that previously held him back. A mother or father who would have disapproved is no longer around, so he feels free to play around. Harvey's reactions are another explanation for affairs during bereavement. He felt his wife wasn't offering the kind of sympathy and support he needed. An ex-girlfriend who had contacted him when she heard of his mother's death soon became his lover.

21. He is feeling unsuccessful. A man who is not doing well in the work world may try to buoy up his failing sense of masculine pride by taking a lover of either sex. It is not uncommon for a man who feels in trouble in the work world to have a homosexual relationship. Lack of success in a career can make a man feel powerless, while the ability to conquer another woman (or man) often produces a sense of power.

The affair may actually be a displaced way of acting out business competition with other men. Here, from an interview, is an example of this from a husband talking about a time in his life when he felt he was failing:

"My income was very low and I was kind of jealous of some of the husbands in our community for the money they were making, and their good jobs. I went for their wives—women who had a lot of money, lots of help in their homes, and great social standing in the community. In a way I was getting back at the men, and while I had their wives I would insist on real dirty sex. I wanted a whore in the bedroom—that is what I made of them. I didn't want to talk about anything except sex. I would make them get into sexual positions that were almost ridiculous."

22. He has become very successful. In contrast, a man who has made it big often feels that one of the rewards of his success is a mistress. Darryl Zanuck, one of the great moguls at the height of the Hollywood studio system, used to insist on having one of his stars or starlets or another female studio employee into his office every afternoon at four for sex.

Some men who reach success in the business world have a hidden fear of success; they cannot stand being a winner in all areas of their lives. It terrifies them. On an unconscious level they fear retribution from jealous gods for their good fortune. Many more men than you would imagine screw up their domestic lives once they become successful in the business world. There are many ways of doing this—turning off sexually to a mate, becoming indifferent to a mate—but a very effective method is to start an affair with someone else and then have their wives find out about it. The unhappiness that ensues in one area of their lives makes them able to tolerate happiness and success in the other. In the obscure underground logic of fear of success, their domestic intranquility buys off the wrath of the gods.

23. He is part of the corporate world. Some business environments encourage extramarital involvements. "There has never been any attempt to hide the fact that corporate men expect sex as a natural reward for business success," writes the psychiatrist Robert Seidenberg in his book, *Corporate Wives—Corporate Casualties.* He goes on to say that it is used as a payoff, as well. "Our largest American companies have admitted that female entertainers are often used to help land prospective customers. . . ."

Many men have to travel on business in our country. Dr. Seidenberg describes the temptations in their path: "Conventions, national meetings, and the required business trips are conducive to errant sex for the husband. At such places the ordinary restraints of home and community are absent; he has the freedom of anonymity, which is often enough to overcome the inhibiting code of fidelity and familial responsibility. Many men feel they deserve a good time as a reward for hard work and extraordinary effort."

One of the things that gets overlooked when a man has sexual encounters out of town is the possibility of loneliness, especially if he is particularly dependent and used to living with a woman. The psychologist David Klimek explains this phenomenon in his book, *Beneath Mate Selection and Marriage:* "Away from home many traveling salesmen, businessmen, and conventioneers find themselves flirting with women they usually would not have noticed in order to reduce massive separation anxiety. Even ordinarily faithful husbands surprise themselves with their urge to become involved with someone when they are in unfamiliar and possibly frightening surroundings."

Affairs do not generally hinder a man's career. Quite the opposite. According to Dr. Seidenberg, "a man's sexual activity . . . if done with discretion—may actually enhance his image of power (potency) in accordance with *machismo* expectations. A sexually chaste male, married or not, is under suspicion of lacking virility and adventuresomeness."

24. He is a workaholic who can't stand emotions. Men who live for work and find the emotional side of life bothersome may find extramarital sex attractive. Dr. Frank S. Pittman, a psychiatrist who treats couples in Atlanta, explains that men like this "may like sex, or consider it healthy, but women just don't matter to them. Emotions of any sort are to be overcome or ignored—emotions don't fit into the equation. And they can get their sex less emotionally away from home."

25. He knows men who are playing around. Several studies have corroborated that knowing people who are unfaithful can give you ideas of your own, which you eventually act on.

A successful businessman in the West told me how he started on a round of affairs—the first in his eight-year marriage—after he moved to a new community where he fell in with a bunch of married businessmen who went to bars together to pick up women. He accompanied them and soon he was having sexual adventures, too. In the book *Beyond Affairs*, James Vaughan describes how he started to think about having an affair only after a married friend introduced him to his mistress.

26. He drinks or uses drugs. Men who drink or take drugs have a very high rate of infidelity. Inhibitions fall when they are binging or drugged. Over 90 percent of men who are addicted to sexual conquest of one kind or another also have drug or alcohol dependencies.

27. He is going through an anxious period. Many men use sex like Valium—for stress reduction at selected times when life becomes uncertain or frightening. Anxiety often gets translated into sexual tension, and during a crisis these men have to go out and find a woman. Common stress points that produce affairs, besides births and deaths, are geographical moves, role changes in a relationship (e.g., wife takes a job, husband is asked to help out more at home), children leaving home, career changes, retirement.

For other men, using affairs to deal with stress is simply part of a well-entrenched, lifelong pattern and not necessarily dependent on a crisis. These men are used to calming any kind of anxiety with sex, and they use it the way other men take a drink or get high. Something minor upsets them, and they go out and score.

28. You are very overweight. Your worst fears may be justified. Ralph Johnson studied sixty case histories from the Family Service Agency and found that one of the leading reasons given for cheating was that "the spouse was extremely obese or 'too fat.'" It isn't only your appearance. Many men get angry at a woman who gains weight after marriage. They feel betrayed—this wasn't the way you were when they married you.

29. He seems depressed. Therapists find that depressed men sometimes start a round of almost frantic womanizing. Although they don't know on a conscious level what they are doing, their affairs are an attempt to out-sprint the blues.

30. Your marriage has become unhappy or you have lost touch with each other. Probably the most important clue as to whether your husband will have an affair or not is the current climate within your relationship. A marriage filled with constant strife and unhappiness, or made sterile by an inability to communicate, is the perfect environment to sprout an affair.

Whether it is a product of his projection or based on real qualities in the woman, when a man feels genuinely deprived because he feels you are always criticizing or belittling him, or that you are so self-absorbed that you aren't really interested in him or his needs, or that you're superficial, valuing only material things rather than human values, or that you and he clash about everything, he is ripe for a sexual adventure.

Dissatisfaction on his part, however, may start only after an affair is already in progress. When this happens, unhappiness is being used as an excuse. The man starts to look for things to make him unhappy in order to justify his infidelity.

As a general rule, unhappiness and incompatability have to be great to cause philandering. If the man is dwelling on minor disagreements, he may simply want to bed someone else with a clear conscience.

31. One of you has threatened to leave. If fights have led to screams for separation in the heat of the moment, by either party, whether you meant it or not, watch out! One study noted a remarkable jump in affairs when altercations between partners led to one or the other saying, "I am going to leave you."

32. He wants out. Sometimes a man will have an affair and manage to get caught because he really wants to end the relationship, but he can't make the first move in that direction. He is trying to get the woman to say, "It's over," or "Get out!"

33. You have stopped being romantic together. A *Psychology Today* survey uncovered a link between high romance and monogamy. If romance has endured in your relationship, you may have a built-in deterrent to cheating. High romantics in marriage were found to be less likely to have had extramarital sexual experiences than others. Morton Hunt made the point in his study, *The Affair*, that a search for lost romance was often the motivatation for involvements with others.

34. You are in a happy marriage. This, too, may come as a surprise, but contentment is not an absolute guarantee of monogamy. Various studies show that men have affairs even when they think their wives and marriages are great. Morton Hunt found that 50 percent of adulterous husbands considered their marriages to be happy. A study, published in the *American Journal of Sociology*, of married men involved in casual sexual relationships with single women whom they met in a cocktail lounge, found these men to be committed to their families. They described their marriages as happy. Shirley Glass and Thomas Wright, in a 1985 study of extramarital affairs, reported that 56 percent of the men who had engaged in extramarital intercourse thought they had happy marriages.

If you are the wife of a man who feels he is content, it may be particularly hard for you to understand why he had an affair. Women can't comprehend just how shallow and detached a man can be in sexual encounters. They find it difficult to believe that a husband can play around and not think it has anything to do with his existence as a husband. That, however, is genuinely the way many happily married men think.

As all of the above indicates, in certain ways men are different from women. Next I'm going to show you why he may baffle you—how you and he may look at your relationship and sex through very different eyes.

FOUR

The Differences Between Men and Women

"IT'S THE WAY MEN ARE, YOU KNOW? WE NEED A LITTLE variety." A thirty-two-year-old policeman, who has had three affairs since his marriage six years ago, was trying to explain the reasons for his actions.

A lot of men feel the way he does—that the urge to stray is built into masculinity.

Is it really?

I hate to say this, but it's possible. I know I found this concept of programmed infidelity hard to swallow, and you may, too, because women think so differently, so before we go any further, let us look closely at what science tells us about the difference between you, as a woman, and him, as a man.

THE URGE TO STRAY:
WHAT SCIENCE HAS UNCOVERED

One team of researchers, R. P. Michael and D. Zumpe, who studied the mating habits of rhesus monkeys found some basis, at least among our animal ancestors, for the male propensity to stray sexually. They paired a male monkey with the same female for a period of three and a half years. Each year that Mr. Monkey lived with his mate, sexual frequency declined more and more. When, however, at the end of this period his female partner was removed and a new mate was introduced to Mr. Monkey, copulation increased dramatically. When the new mate was replaced by the old one again, sexual activity took another big dive.

Similar results were found in experiments with rodents and dogs. In addition, in experiments with rats, the female nature showed itself. In contrast to males, females tended to return to the sexual mates with whom they were familiar. Lady rats also preferred spending more time near the odor of males they had experience with, rather than nosing out strangers on the rat scene.

Now, human beings are not apes, rats, mice, or dogs. Our minds, for one thing, influence how we feel about sex as much as, if not more than, our bodies do. One can't be certain from these experiments with primates and rodents that desire for novelty is built into males (which creates infidelity), while females more naturally prefer what is familiar (which reinforces monogamy).

However, another experiment with human beings tends to point more clearly to an innate difference between the sexes.

In 1986, researchers in the department of psychology at the State University of New York at Albany tested the ways in which males and females responded to repeated exposure to the same sexually titillating film, then to new films of this genre. They found that the sexual arousal that occurred during initial viewings declined after repeated exposure to the same film for men and women alike. However, when new erotic material was introduced in the form of two fresh films, one showing the same actors from the first movie performing different sexual acts, the other featuring different actors, a marked gender disparity showed up. Men responded with greater excitement to the *new* partners, while women's excitement escalated when they saw the same, by now familiar, actors in new films.

Of course, some of the differences between the sexes are culturally induced. In our society, women are devalued by both sexes if they sleep around too much, while the man who is known to be a womanizer is often regarded as a sexy guy by both men and women.

The messages men and women receive from the media are different, too. Women's magazines are always telling women how to fix the relationship they are in or how to achieve a committed one. In contrast, men's magazines send out messages to readers that the best thing a man can do for his image and self-esteem is to be a successful stud.

The strong preference for monogamy by women may also stem from the fact that women bear children. They need to know who their child's father is, since they often rely on the man for protection and support.

It really doesn't matter much whether the difference is biological or culturally induced, or both; the fact remains that men and women *are* different. Because of this, the sexes have a hard time understanding one another. Women are often mystified by men's ability to enjoy sex with strangers, while men are equally baffled by women's tendency to mix up sex with emotions. This was encapsulated in the words of a young man in Chicago: "When I start sleeping with a woman, it's like she starts to own me. I haven't promised her anything, but she becomes upset if she thinks I'm seeing someone else. Sex, for a lot of women, is the same thing as commitment. You sleep with a woman and she wants you to be monogamous. A woman can't understand that she may be a guy's main squeeze but he still might want to go to bed, very casually, with other women he meets."

From women, the tone is in direct contrast to the casual tone of men like the one quoted above, when they talk of their affairs. The female cry is one of deep betrayal. "I put my emotions into sleeping with a man. I don't know why men can't understand that. I don't sleep with a man only for sexual satisfaction. I have sex with a guy because I like him. If I find out he is making out with another woman I feel personally rejected," explained a twenty-eight-year-old woman.

Another young woman told me, "I absolutely could not understand it when I found out that Ronald had been having sex with a woman in his office. How could he say, 'It doesn't mean anything'? To me it meant I wasn't satisfying him completely, that she had something I didn't. I was totally devastated, and there he was saying, 'It didn't mean anything to me.'"

If you are like most women, your reaction may be similar to that of the woman above. He may feel he got involved with someone else to satisfy a passing itch, but you feel diminished by the fact that he took another woman to bed. You imagine that his lover must have a better body, be prettier, sexier, more desirable.

It doesn't matter how good looking you are yourself. The beautiful TV personality Cindy Garvey, who had to cope with the infidelity of her husband, Steve Garvey of the Los Angeles Dodgers, admits, "You automatically compare yourself to the other person."

"When I found out about the other woman," a thirty-four-year-old woman confided, "I kicked Clyde out. But I spent months of agony wondering what she looked like, what was better about her than me. I pictured her as having these wonderful, full breasts, so much nicer than mine."

"She was fifteen years younger than me," one middle-aged wife told me. "I kept staring in the mirror, studying every sag, every wrinkle, kicking myself for not having gotten a facelift."

"I wondered about her all the time," said another woman. "I thought she must be gorgeous. I knew I wasn't."

To feel yourself inferior to another woman in this way is a bitter, humiliating experience that many women endure, so you are not alone if you are going through this.

Men, Women, and Closeness

The different ways men and women tend to react to intimacy creates another problem between the sexes. Although there are some women who have problems dealing with intimacy too, on the whole women have less trouble joining sex with closeness, love, or commitment than men do. Women often become sexier and more comfortable with a man with whom they feel an emotional bond. In contrast, when a man starts feeling close to a woman it may produce hidden anxiety. He may begin to feel trapped, stifled, controlled, vulnerable, too dependent. He may fear that he will lose his independence and identity in the relationship, or he may just feel slightly uncomfortable or vaguely itchy without knowing exactly why. The relationship has become too hot for him to handle emotionally, although he may not recognize this consciously.

A man experiencing this hidden anxiety will unconsciously find ways to cool off the relationship to restore his comfort. He may find fault with his partner, drop her altogether, get into an argument with her, feel a loss of sexual desire for her, or get interested in another woman.

One man who had been married just a month was recently caught red-handed by his bride, who discovered an incriminating note from another woman. He entered therapy at his wife's insistence and was able to locate his problem for the therapist: "I felt absolutely trapped, squeezed into a box," he said, explaining his reaction to his marriage, which was essentially a very happy one for him.

A casual affair can be very hot and sexy for a man simply because it is more emotionally shallow or time-limited. His sexuality flows more freely when he is less involved with or committed to the woman. This male dynamic is not universal, but it is very common and it truly baffles women who don't understand that, for a lot of men, sex and love or commitment don't go well together.

Trouble handling intimacy accounts for men withdrawing emotionally or getting involved with someone else just when things seem to be going great between you. It accounts for the habit of many men who refuse to allow themselves to get involved beyond a certain point with their dating or extramarital partners. They think they are protecting their independence or marriages in this way. What they don't realize is that they often are protecting their sexuality in the relationship, as well. It would cool if they allowed themselves to feel closer to the woman.

The underlying differences in approach to sex constitute one important reason for the tension that exists between men and women in our society today. Men have their guard up about women wanting to "possess" them once sex enters the picture, while women are wary because they feel that men don't regard sex in their relationships as a sign that something important is going on the way they do.

It wasn't always this way. Before the sexual liberation of the 1960s, sex with women was taken more seriously by men. Of course, there were always seducers in our society—the Don Juans and Casanovas of their particular communities—but when women were expected to remain virgins until marriage, the majority of men knew that a tremendous favor was being granted to them if a woman gave in to sex. It was generally understood by men as a sign of her great love that she would do such a thing. Men used to feel a lot of responsibility to a "nice" woman who finally had sex with them. This sense of responsibility sometimes even made them refuse sex.

One man remembered a young woman he met when he was stationed in another country during World War II. "She came from a very good family. We started going out. I saw a great deal of her for almost a year. She was beautiful and a lovely person. We fooled around a little. I think she would have gone all the way with me. But she was going to marry this guy from her own class. It had been arranged by her family when she was a little girl. She was expected to be a virgin. I just couldn't do that to her. I liked her too much. I knew I would be gone in a few months. So I kept things in check."

With sexual liberation, sex in relationships became devalued by men. It no longer meant that something important was being given to them; it was now expected in the relationship. As a result, the sense of obligation to sex partners disappeared. Sexual liberation allowed the innate male "roaming" tendency to come fully to the fore.

The same devaluation of sex in relationships did not occur for women. Maybe they no longer were expected to be virgins. They had sex earlier and more easily. But the emotional investment continued. Even if caring was not part of the original game plan, women found themselves becoming attached once sex began. The innate female nature asserted itself, and because sex made them feel attached, women wanted their bed partners to be monogamous once intercourse became part of the relationship. Since sex in itself didn't work the same kind of attachment magic for males, many men resented the pressure for monogamy that they kept experiencing from women early in relationships. And women were repeatedly disappointed in men who dodged the emotional commitment they desired.

Lack of understanding of where each gender was coming from in sexual relationships created a certain amount of hard feelings and lingering resentment on both sides of the singles scene in the post-liberation era.

Male and Female Sexuality

There are intrinsic differences, as well, in how males and females function sexually.

On the whole, to feel sexual, women need more romance and buildup than men do. Women like affection—nice things said to them, hugs, and kisses—to feel aroused. Men's sexuality is more tied into fantasy and visual stimulation. The sight of a pretty woman, an attractive nude body, or an erotic daydream may be all a young man needs to feel charged up and able to function.

Some men find it difficult to understand why women are always hankering after romancing and affectionate extended foreplay as a prelude to intercourse, while women often can't understand how a man can just want to jump right into sex.

In marriage, the tie-in of men's sexuality to visual stimulation often creates an erotic crisis if a wife gains too much weight.

Women, whose sexuality is not so visually oriented, can often stay turned on to a man who becomes flabby, but a recent study of over one thousand married people by the sociologist Lynn White proved that it was much more important to men that their spouses stay slim. Dr. White found that marriages were more apt to run into sexual problems when the wife gained weight.

This is a matter you have to take seriously, because research shows that when husbands judge the quality of their marriages, they place greater importance on sex than wives do. If they don't like what's going on in the bedroom, they often consider themselves to be unhappy. Women, in contrast, put more stress on the emotional and affectional aspects of the relationship. When, for example, your husband doesn't talk or want to listen to you, or doesn't display affection, you may consider your marriage less than ideal.

The reasons that men and women give for their affairs reflect this difference in what each considers most important. When men are asked why they have been unfaithful, they most commonly cite sex. Women say they commit adultery for the satisfaction of emotional needs. In various studies, men have characterized their extramarital affairs as more sexual than emotional, while women have depicted their affairs as more emotional than sexual. The extramarital activities of men and women parallel their interactions as single people: men, in dating relationships, can have sex and remain emotionally aloof, while single women generally get more emotionally involved.

The differences between the sexes are consistent and significant both before and after marriage.

WHAT HOLDS MEN BACK

If it weren't for women, many more men than now do would cheat. They may not understand why, they may not like it, but men certainly recognize that women want fidelity. Of course, for some men, monogamy is a matter of honor, but for most, more than ethics, it is the fear of losing women who are important to them, or of terrible repercussions in the relationship, that keeps them on the straight and narrow.

When you look at the behavior of men unfettered by women—males in gay relationships—the amount of infidelity is phenomenal. Results of the *American Couples* survey done by Philip Blumstein and Pepper Schwartz show that 90 percent of gay partners have affairs between the second and the tenth year of established relationships. In the same way that male homosexual behavior reflects the tendencies of the general male population, lesbian relationships reflect the female disposition: monogamy is prized and most frequently practiced.

Kinsey wrote in his famous report that "most males can immediately understand why most males want extramarital coitus. . . ." Blumstein and Schwartz, going along the same track, theorize that infidelity is so rampant in the male homosexual population because males understand one another's natures and allow some straying. They are not held back by the single strongest barrier to infidelity in heterosexual relationships—women.

IT'S EVERY MAN'S DREAM

All heterosexual men—whether monogamous or not—fantasize about sex with other women, so that even if they are monogamous in fact, they are unfaithful countless times in their reveries. Women fantasize too, but they tend to daydream about romance rather than hone in on raw sex, the way men do. Character has little to do with it. A study by Gerald Neubeck found that fantasy involvements were as high among men with strong consciences as among those with weak ones. Men's magazines, with their centerfolds, cater to these fantasies.

Although the basic message of the girlie magazines encourages infidelity, the centerfolds may do the opposite for part of the male population. Many men use these photographs of nude females to restrain themselves; they get enough of a secret thrill, masturbating while thinking of a woman in a picture, to be able to remain faithful to wives and girlfriends in the real world. Like it or not, women have to understand that masturbation is part of most men's lives, whether they are single, living with a woman, or married, and it is quite normal for men to use fantasies, often featuring "other" women, to create their climaxes.

The noted sex researcher John Gagnon blames the early pattern of masturbation, as males mature, for their ability to separate sex from relationships. He notes that "masturbation is for most adolescent boys the major sexual activity, and they engage in it fairly frequently. It is an extremely positive and gratifying experience to them. Such an introduction to sexuality can lead to a capacity for detached sex activity—activity whose only sustaining motive is sexual. This may be the hallmark of male sexuality in our society."

THE STRONG MALE DRIVE TOWARD MONOGAMY

When men are monogamous, it is because they choose to check the detached, roving side of their nature, and discipline themselves for the sake of a relationship with a particular woman. They are able to accept the restrictions of monogamy because it ensures the satisfaction of other needs—*needs that are just as important as sex to the majority of men.* Most of the same men who are turned on by the thought of sexual variety also have a basic and deep need for security, comfort, the cushion of a home life. These two clashing needs—for the soothing reliability of domesticity on one hand and the excitement of an unrestrained sexual life on the other—are always at war within men. Under ideal conditions, men would choose to have both, and if it weren't for their women, most would take both. However, having both does not mean uncontrolled womanizing. Two women—for example, a wife and a mistress—would satisfy a lot of men. Some think they can reconcile the duality of their natures by secretly cheating; others think the risks to their home lives, to their standing in the community, or even to their jobs are too great.

AIDS, of course, has added a new peril to playing around—and is causing even the most unrepentent womanizing man at least to think twice about his life-style. But when the style is based on a lot more than the occasional itch that most men feel—when sex becomes a compulsion; an expression of unfinished business from the past, based on childhood psychological injuries; a way to reduce stress from nonsexual sources; a reaction to a troubled relationship; or many of the other reasons why men philander—then it can be hard to be monogamous, no matter what perils are involved.

Let us look at some of the men who live in the shadowy world of affairs, multiple relationships, deceit. Who are these men who can't be faithful? What motivates the chronic womanizers among them, and the others who don't fool around all the time, but instead may get involved in an occasional stray affair or find themselves embroiled in long-lasting, more emotional love affairs?

In the chapters that follow, you will find the psychological reasons why your husband or boyfriend has cheated. In Chapter 8 you will discover the special situations that create infidelity.

If you can recognize your man among those I describe, you'll get clues as to whether he is apt to repeat his infidelities, based on what drives him. You'll discover, too, in Chapter 10, that you may unconsciously have a bigger role in his infidelity than you imagine.

I'll start by giving you a glimpse of a married man and a single man, both of whom live a life-style based on infidelity.

FIVE

Compulsive Men

IT WAS FIVE O'CLOCK ON A FRIDAY AFTERNOON IN JULY. BERT was on his way to his summer house in the country. In a plastic bag slung on his wrist were presents for his two children, aged eight and six. His wife, Doris, would be meeting him in an hour and a half at the train station. Bert looked forward to the weekend with his family. It had been a frantic week in his business and he was tired. He figured he could spend the long train trip resting. He chose a seat next to the window and had started to open his newspaper when he was stopped short by the woman who was about to sit down next to him. Before she plopped down with a weary sigh, he had noticed her figure—it was slim but rounded. Her legs, as she crossed them, made him look twice. He turned toward her as the train pulled out and he saw wonderful blue eyes crinkle from a smile, as she responded to a crack he made about the unknown adventure they were about to embark on. Service on this particular train line was the butt of many jokes, and the woman answered with a crack of her own. She was on her way to a town one stop farther than Bert's destination, and within a half hour, Bert and his seatmate were joking together like old friends.

When Bert emerged from the train to greet his wife with a warm and sincere kiss, and to hug his kids, he had in his pocket the woman's phone number. He would be having lunch with her the following week, and within two weeks he and she would be sharing a bed in her apartment on a Thursday evening when he was supposed to be entertaining clients. Was this the beginning of a big romance that would cause Bert, a devoted family man, anguish because it imperiled his marriage? No. Bert enjoyed the woman and loved the sex with her, but after two or three trysts he never saw her again. It was against his policy to get "involved." Bert, the genuinely warm family man, had been having adventures like this since the first year of his marriage.

It is Monday and Ben is looking at his telephone. Whom should he call? He had seen Myra on Friday night, Debbie on Saturday. He decided to call Glenda. When she picked up the phone, he noticed that she sounded glad to hear from him. "Hi," he began, "how ya been?" "What did you do over the weekend?" she asked. Ben didn't like questions like that. "I didn't ask you what *you* did," he bantered, throwing the conversation back in her court. "What *did* you do?"

She began a recital about her sister and her sister's kids being in town that bored Ben, but he hoped that he had gotten her off the subject of where he had been that weekend. "I only have a minute. Busy here at the office," he interrupted. "I wanted to know what you're doing Wednesday."

"I have to work a little late," she explained, "but I should be able to get away by nine-ish."

"Well, why don't we make it for lunch instead," he said.

"Okay," she agreed, but he noticed a slight disappointment in her voice.

"Gotta rush. Let's make it for one on Wednesday. I'll call you in the morning to tell you where." That took care of Glenda for the week. He decided to call Lily, an old girlfriend. He hadn't seen her in a while. Maybe he could have lunch with her. Lily was delighted to accept his invitation. Ben next called Myra, then Debbie, to tell them what a nice time he had had on Friday and Saturday respectively. Then, after noticing the new girl in the office, he returned to the papers on his desk.

Ben is a compulsive woman-chaser. Wherever he goes, he always has one eye out for an attractive female. His life revolves around an always-changing group of women with whom he is romantically involved. Although some stay on, some drop out, to be replaced by other women. Those who

continue with Ben have generally gone through the
following process: At the beginning of a relationship, Ben
treats women with great interest. He comes on with
intensity. His actions are genuine—he really is very
interested. He calls them every day on the telephone. He
sees them regularly. Soon, the women Ben chooses to
concentrate on begin to fall for him. After all, he is quite
charming, very intelligent, good looking in a sexy sort of
way, and he has a sense of humor. In one way or another,
they let Ben know that they like him a lot. That, unfortunately, is the beginning of the end.

As Ben becomes more secure about a woman, his
feelings imperceptibly change. He starts to feel a little
edgy or anxious without knowing exactly why. He starts to
see a flaw here, an imperfection there he hasn't noticed
before. By chance, he meets another woman at a party, in
an elevator, on a plane—wherever he finds himself at that
particular juncture in the relationship. He starts to see
this other woman. He may also call an old girlfriend or
two whom he has been neglecting. The original steadiness
and intensity of his courtship stops, although he continues
with the relationship and acts as if nothing is different.

A week may go by now without his asking her out,
then maybe two weeks are skipped, although he may meet
her for a quick drink or lunch. His phone calls become
erratic. The woman becomes increasingly anxious, never
knowing when or if he will call. She sometimes doesn't
hear from him for a day at first, then two days, then
sometimes three or four. Then he will turn up again. He
will not comment on his absence. He still acts interested
when he is with her, but now the woman wonders more
and more if he is sleeping with others. She thinks he is.
She begins to obsess about it.

She finally asks him what he does with his time away
from her. He gives her evasive answers. If she persists in
questioning him, he may become annoyed. One of his
women who often saw him on Fridays but never on
Saturday nights finally asked him why they never saw
each other on Saturdays. He didn't answer the question
directly. Instead, he said, "Well, if you want to see me
Saturday, we can see each other then." He started asking
her out on Saturdays. Initially she regarded this as a

triumph, until she realized that now she no longer saw him on Fridays.

Frustration and confusion multiply week by week for a woman involved with Ben. She suspects more and more that he isn't being quite honest and that he is seeing other women. She begins to complain about him to her friends. She starts to feel rotten about the relationship and finally about herself, because she feels she has failed somehow in the competition with other women whom she imagines he favors.

At this point, either she decides that the whole thing has become too painful or that there is no future in the relationship, and she stops going out with Ben. Or she hangs around, knowing, and deciding to accept the fact that she is not the only one in his life. She settles for the good times they have together. The worst possible scenario is that she will unrealistically keep on hoping he will change. Or she may abandon such hopes and start to date others herself. Another possibility is that she decides to stop sleeping with Ben because she cannot stand a nonmonogamous sexual relationship but she is able to continue in his life as a platonic friend. Ben has many women friends who are ex-lovers. For all of his roaming, he has a hard time giving up a woman altogether. Ben likes women. He doesn't much care for men. "Men are too competitive," he claims.

Ben is the pseudonym of a real man who one day entered therapy because at age thirty-seven he began to realize something was wrong—he had never really been close to any woman for long.

What came out over the months in his therapy sessions was an inward feeling you would never guess at if you judged Ben by the externals—he was good looking, well dressed, and appeared sure of himself. But behind Ben's great exterior hid another Ben—the real Ben—who did not think he was so great. In fact, Ben did not believe he was really attractive and desirable. Feeling inferior to other men, he avoided relationships with them. Feeling flawed, he sidestepped really close relationships with women who he feared would recognize his imperfections. Ben needed the steady stream of new sexual conquests to give him an ego boost he sorely needed. Each new woman in his life gave Ben a lift like nothing else could. If a woman became his sexual and emotional conquest, he felt on top of the world—attractive, desirable, powerful, manly.

Unfortunately, these feelings lasted only a little while. Then Ben started feeling unsure of himself again and in need of fresh validation that he was adequate, or even terrific, as some of his women made him feel—at first. No matter how much he may have liked a particular woman—and he did have favorites over the years—he became restless. She could not, over the long haul, give him the sense of validation that only a fresh conquest could provide.

Besides pepping up his self-image, having more than one woman around at all times took care of a deep-rooted fear of rejection. Unconsciously, Ben played the "backup" game, a common one among womanizers. If one woman told him to buzz off, or rejected him in favor of another suitor, there was always another around as insurance that he would not be left all alone in the world. The fear of abandonment and loneliness haunted Ben subliminally.

The motivating forces behind Ben's actions are typical of many womanizers. They search for a sense of adequacy and insure themselves against the pain of rejection through multiple relationships. If you are involved with a man like this, you find he can infuriate you as well as devastate you. After all, you may have a fragile ego yourself and you feel his infidelities as personal rejections. However, if you could think more objectively about what drives men like Ben (and Bert) to womanize, you could begin to realize that it is really quite sad that they feel so inwardly weak, bruised, and fearful.

For many of these men, womanizing is not even a choice. It is an addiction. Because women are able to give them a rush of good feelings time and time again, sexual conquest has become, for them, the equivalent of liquor for an alcoholic, or narcotics for a drug addict. These men need women—new women—in a way that makes it very hard, if not impossible, for them to give up their habit.

One charming West Coast man of thirty-six told me that he had been sleeping with a string of women all his adult life. His job put him in contact with many young, pretty females, so his life-style was very easy to maintain until he really fell for a beautiful tall blonde.

"I have a weakness for blondes," he admitted, his blue eyes twinkling. She and he maintained a serious relationship for two years, until she left him because of his sexual activity with others. He really loved her and begged her to come back. He promised he would be monogamous from then on. He meant it.

"I really tried," he explained, "but then another pretty blonde came along. That time she left me for good. . . . I'm looking for the woman who can make me be monogamous," he says quite sincerely. This is not an uncommon fantasy among single men who can't be faithful. They think that somewhere in the world is a woman who is so beautiful, sexy, or whatever that they will no longer be attracted to others. They fail to realize that monogamy is not something that happens to you magically from the outside; it comes from your own inner desire and ability to discipline yourself against the attractions felt by everyone who is sexually alive.

Of course, the fragile sense of self-esteem, the fear of rejection, and the addictive quality behind their lives with women are generally not recognized consciously by these men. They rationalize their motives by saying, "I enjoy playing the field," or "I just like women, what's so terrible about that?"

Time and again I have heard men like this say, "I have a very high sex drive," without realizing that it isn't sex at all that is driving them. They are using sex to obtain emotional gratification that has little to do with erotic pleasure, although that may be one of the by-products of their life-style.

It is amazing, considering the dynamics, that some extraordinarily desirable men are compulsive womanizers. Warren Beatty is known in Hollywood for going through women like a hurricane in the tropics, despite the presence of significant long-term partners in his life. Marlon Brando, Richard Burton, Frank Sinatra, Steve McQueen, Clark Gable, John Barrymore, and Errol Flynn are other examples of the many well-documented Don Juans of Hollywood. Although the glamour of Hollywood stars makes it easy for the womanizers among them to find women willing to succumb to their blandishments, every town has its polished seducers who practice their craft successfully. Many of these are married men like Bert, who picked up a woman on a train in the story at the beginning of this chapter.

Married men who are womanizers often have had a premarital history of infidelity with their wives. Bert, for example, when he was going out with Doris, was secretly seeing other women, too. At the time he rationalized his behavior by claiming the other women were "just for sex" because Doris was still a virgin and refused to go all the way before marriage. Within a year after the wedding, however, Bert was stepping out on Doris again.

Some men start their infidelities on the honeymoon. An architect told me of going on a honeymoon cruise with his bride. One day, while she was on one deck, he was on another, making out with a passenger he had just met.

George, a businessman in Toledo, waited longer, however. It wasn't until the tenth year of his marriage that he started a series of brief affairs. George, who, like Ben, finally entered therapy to straighten out his life with women, told me his story.

"I had been concentrating on my career more than anything until then," he explained. "Sex wasn't terrific, but I didn't think much about it. I was doing what everyone was supposed to do. I was married and having kids. We had moved to Arizona and were living in our own house. There was a divorcée living next door. My wife and I used to have cocktails with her in the evening. Then my wife took the kids for a week's visit to her parents, in Maine. The divorcée and I continued to have cocktails together and one night we ended up in bed. I didn't set out to seduce her. It wasn't something in my head. I had never been unfaithful before—it just happened. I believed in monogamy in marriage enough not to do it any other way. But sex with my wife was infrequent. It was something she seemed to put up with. We always did it one way. She never wanted the lights on. After the experience with the divorcée, I said, "Gee, sex can really be fun!" She was much freer than my wife. From that time on I started actively seeking out affairs. Whenever I had an opportunity with someone in, say, a business situation, I would make advances.

"Very soon after that we moved to another state. For three months I was there without my wife before we sold our old house. I was staying in a company apartment. I started running out with a lot of women. I met some men who became my buddies. They were all married, too. The first acquaintance was a real-estate guy who was showing me houses. We went out drinking. The first time we did this we met a woman, and she and I and this guy, the three of us, made it. Then I made it with her alone several times and it started snowballing. I kept meeting other women. I always had an eye out. It didn't matter much what she was like—more that she was sexually available. The men I was hanging around with were promiscuous and there were a lot of available women there. As I started getting into it, sex became more and more important. I started spending more and more time looking for it and getting involved with it."

Some woman-chasers, like bachelor Ben, are able to sustain some long simultaneous relationships along with other shorter ones, if a woman will put up with it. There are two women like this in Ben's life now. Men like George and Bert, however, limit themselves to quick encounters, and very brief relationships. Other men are happy with just two sexual partners and can carry on with both of them for long periods of time. Still others think the more the merrier and keep adding to their ranks. Some men who find monogamy impossible are honest with the women in their lives; they tell them straight out that sexual fidelity is not for them. One bachelor who tells his dates he has multiple relationships has seen one woman regularly for five years—along with others. She doesn't like sharing him, but is willing to accept the limitations of the relationship. Others are quite dishonest. They make each woman feel as if she were the one and only. They lie with regularity.

Most men who have multiple relationships fall somewhere in between. They neither lie nor tell the truth. They evade. A bachelor of twenty-eight echoed the words of many other unattached men I spoke to: "It's the sin of ommission," he explained. "I don't tell a woman I am going to date others, or that I've been with someone else. I try to avoid it. But she knows I wasn't with her. It's up to her, really. I won't volunteer the information, but if she asked right out what I did at some specific time, I would probably tell her."

The odds favor brief relationships of little substance if a compulsive womanizer is married. Married men like to feel they are protecting their marriages by having their flings "just for sex." These men divide their lives in two. They lead comparatively normal, conventional existences with their wives. They may be good fathers, even church-goers with their families. But away from home they are always on the prowl, ready to spot a potential bed partner no matter where they are. They go through a predictable ritual of engaging her attention, becoming seductive, getting her into bed, then disengaging.

Compulsive men are mentally obsessed with sex. Dr. Patrick Carnes, a specialist in sexually dependent personalities, calls them hostages to their own thoughts. "Every passerby, every relationship, and every introduction to someone passes through the sexually obsessive filter," he explains.

"I think I overthink sex," Bert remarked. "I'm always looking for a new sexual challenge, a new scene that I might want to try."

In the business world these men are generally as hardworking and conventional as anyone else. The secret they keep from their wives may be open knowledge at the office, however. A man's secretary, for example, may realize what's going on because other women call him or he calls them on the office phone. Some men have reputations as company lotharios.

Many womanizers pride themselves on the fact that they can always balance their work with their busy love lives. George says of his promiscuity during his marriage, "It never interfered. It was something that was always underlying—I flirted a lot. But I could always take ten minutes out and flirt if I met a woman who seemed available through business—and then make a date for later on."

Many married men are also proud that they give their families priority. "I have never, ever let it get in the way of my home life," Bert explained. "If I have a date, it is on the way home from work. At least in the beginning it was pure, unadulterated quickies. Or, if I have a date and something comes up at home, I will cancel the date. I have my own standards. The family comes first."

However, to do this, may of these men establish, from the earliest days of their marriages, work patterns that habituate the wife to nights when her husband will work late or entertain clients.

Clark Gable is an excellent example of a compulsive womanizer, judging by the details in Jane Ellen Wayne's book, *Gable's Women.* He lost his mother at the age of seven months. Until the age of five, when he remarried, his father left him to be raised by his grandparents. Clark's stepmother, a loving woman, tried to get him interested in the finer things in life—reading, music, dancing. His father, a tough oil rigger, spent Sundays, his one day at home with his son, trying to make sure he wasn't a "sissy." Until his dying day his father castigated his son for being unmasculine: "Actors are sissies," he said even when Clark Gable had already become a legendary superstar who radiated a supermasculine image on screen. Clark admitted he hated his father.

This background—early abandonment by the father, the lack of a masculine presence at home much of the time, and the fears that were transmitted by the father when he was there—succeeded in making Clark Gable forever insecure about his masculine identity, no matter how virile he appeared and acted. The "sissy" legacy from his father lingered somewhere in Clark's soul. His sexual problems were alluded to by many women he had bedded who found him irresistible anyway. "He had more magnetism than any man on earth. But he wasn't a satisfying lover," said Joan Crawford. When she became engaged to Gable, Carole Lombard told friends: "He's a lousy lay, but I adore him!"

His womanizing—the classic case of an insecure man trying to prove his virility to himself and the world—was legendary. He was known for one-nighters. He frequented a high-class whore house near the MGM lot. He had numerous affairs with actresses like Loretta Young, as well as with lesser known women. One of his favorite and frequent bed companions was a rather plain-looking writer in Hollywood.

Once when he was shown a picture of a lineup of all

the MGM female stars, Clark smiled, "They're all beautiful. I've had every one of them."

He had an affair with Joan Crawford that started
when he was newly arrived in Hollywood and lasted thirty
years, through all four of his marriages, and her marriages
as well.

Crawford confirmed the fact that he had a weak ego
and that he womanized compulsively: ". . . even when he
was married to Carole [Lombard], whom he loved more
than his career, he was always in bed with someone else.
Very few women got past him."

Clark Gable could love women like Crawford and
Carole Lombard but he could not be faithful to anyone.

"I Wish I Could Stop"

There is a group among compulsive womanizers
whose behavior has become a real and conscious problem
for them. These are the men now known in mental-health
circles as sex addicts. They feel their lives have gotten out
of control. These men may be ashamed of certain aspects
of their lives. They may not like their habit of lying to
women, for example, to get them into bed. Or they may
have been caught by their wives, who threaten to leave
them, but they feel compelled to have affairs anyway.
They may patronize prostitutes, or have to leave a job
because of a sexual liaison or scandal. They may find
themselves repeatedly involved in a series of sexual
relationships with people they don't really like. These men
realize they may be imperiling their jobs, their marriages
or other love relationships, their standing in the community, even their health or that of their wives, but they
continue to act the same way, feeling helpless to change.

A letter to Dr. Joyce Brothers illustrates this kind of
out-of-control behavior.

"Why does this man say he loves me when often on the
same night he makes love to me, he moves on and I'm sure
makes love to other women?

"He tells his mother he wants to marry me and wants
me to bear his children. I believe him and yet why is he so

promiscuous if he loves me? He tells me he doesn't love these others but he can't stop himself."

While many other womanizing men manage to conduct their lives with only a modicum of guilt, or none at all, severe sexual addiction is characterized by guilt, shame, and feelings of powerlessness to end what they consider to be destructive or shameful behavior.

Even when their behavior is relatively controlled, compulsive womanizers may have some negative feelings about what they are doing. Bert confided, "It's always been that the chase is better than the culmination. Not that the sex wasn't good, but the challenge was always better. I'd walk away from some of these women, saying, "What the hell am I doing here?" Sometimes it happened beforehand—as I was beginning to make out I would say to myself, 'This is ridiculous.'"

A Chicago man remembered feeling bad about lying. "One time I was with a woman who exuded sex. I got caught up in the biggest bunch of lies with her. Instead of saying I was married, I went through the whole separation story bullshit. It got blown up all out of proportion. . . . She wanted me to meet her family. I said to myself, 'It is not worth it just to get into her body.' That was in the second year of my marriage, and it started me on the straight and narrow. From then on, I never lied about my situation."

Another man told of being trapped in a crazy, rather shameful episode. He had gotten up in the middle of the night from the bed he was sharing with a woman he was seeing regularly to sneak off to see another woman. Pulling his car out of her driveway, he accidentally ran over her dog. He felt he had to come back inside the house to wake his girlfriend up and tell her the dog was dead. Given the situation, he could see no other way out; he confessed what he had been up to. His girlfriend now had two reasons to become overwrought—his treachery, and the death of her pet.

Men bothered by their behavior but unable to make changes are much like alcoholics or drug addicts who are always trying to break their habits. They swear time and again to give up the woman-chasing, but find they can't.

OBSESSIVE COMPULSIVES

There is another kind of man who may become a compulsive sexualizer. He suffers from an obsessive-compulsive personality disorder. His commitment to everything, including women, is always conditional. He is a man who always harbors a multitude of doubts and uncertainties, and his waverings extend to his relationships. He can never be absolutely certain you are the ideal woman for him. Dr. Leon Salzman, an expert on obsessive-compulsive personalities, describes them as having great difficulty with fidelity because they cannot pass up opportunities. "For such personalities, infidelity is commonplace and fidelity is a rarity, if not impossible," he concludes.

You can recognize an obsessive man by the rigidity of his habits. He may insist on sleeping on the same side of the bed, having dinner at exactly the same hour, eating only food he is familiar with, adding exactly two and one-half level teaspoons of sugar to his coffee. Obsessives tend to be very neat, freaking out when they find things in disarray or in unfamiliar places. They rely on rituals of all kinds to create a sense of control. Taking charge is the only way they feel safe in this world. Control is so important to these men that they generally need to dominate the women with whom they have relationships.

Whenever anxiety arises, an obsessive resorts to one of his big or little rituals to calm himself. He may smoke, eat, straighten up his desk. Sex often becomes one of the rituals he relies on as a tranquilizer. When the obsessive man starts to feel uptight, he may go out and score, which will make him feel in charge of his life, and therefore safe once more.

A variation of the obsessive-compulsive type is the man who, after many years of being a monogamous, solid citizen, suddenly starts playing around. He is invariably very hardworking, conscientious, and orderly. Frequently he is a superachiever. In the process of reaching his work goals he suppresses his erotic drives and fantasies. However, after decades of being a good workhorse with blinders on, a man like this may suddenly go wild. This was the case with Harold. Married twenty-three years and the father of three children, Harold was a model conventional citizen.

One day he met an attractive young woman, the daughter of a client. He soon found himself involved in a passionate affair with her. Its force took him by surprise. She ended the affair and he followed it with two other passionate liaisons. Harold could not understand the surge of sexual feelings he was in the grip of. He was bewildered by what was happening to him. He did not love these women, he still loved his wife. The tremendous wave of passion that Harold was experiencing was the result of having suppressed his desires and erotic impulses for so long. When they finally rose to the surface they erupted in an uncontrollable way.

SIX

Other Womanizers

THE PEDESTAL/GUTTER SYNDROME

FOR MANY MEN, WOMANIZING IS THE RESULT OF LOOKING AT women as either pure beings or whores. The Pedestal/ Gutter Syndrome they suffer from accompanies many other psychological motivations for infidelity. For men with this mind-set, women are divided into two classes— you are either good (on a pedestal) or bad (in the gutter). If you are thought of as the "good" woman, you are admired, but not thought of as sexual. Bad women, whom these men look down upon either consciously or unconsciously, are the erotically alluring ones. An example of this is one man who came into couples therapy with his wife as the result of an affair. He described the other woman in his life as cheap, vulgar, kind of dumb. When asked why, if he felt this way, he found her so attractive, he replied, "She's sexy." For some men, because of religious teachings or the way they were brought up by their parents, any woman, no matter how elegant, can be thought of as bad simply because she is having sex outside of marriage—only bad girls do that!

When a man is single, he may take a woman out for a long time but never try to sleep with her. But he has an active sex life on the side with women he thinks are sluts, or he may even patronize prostitutes. Or he may be able to be highly sexual with a woman as long as he isn't committed to her, but the minute he cares for her or moves in with her, for example, or becomes engaged to her

77

or marries her, sex disintegrates because she suddenly becomes the good, pure woman in his eyes and is therefore asexual.

Elvis Presley suffered from the Pedestal/Gutter Syndrome. He valued the fact that his wife, Priscilla, was an unsullied virgin when he met her. Soon after he married her he lost sexual interest in her and started sleeping with other women whom he didn't respect as much as Priscilla, but who were able to excite his sexual interest.

It can take a woman by surprise when the same man who started out having a torrid love affair with her (before she became the "good" woman) suddenly cools down markedly in sexual interest once the commitment is made. As soon as this kind of man moves in with, gets married to, or even just starts feeling more committed to the woman in his life, he is apt to start eyeing other women and having affairs to recapture sexual thrills.

This way of thinking about women is often evident in subtle forms all through a man's life. For example, George told me about his dating habits in high school and college, when he would often secretly go with girls from the "wrong side of the tracks, girls not from my own social class." He would have sex with them while also dating and taking to proms and parties girls he described as being "from my own clique." The girls from his own group he considered off limits—he never even tried to have intercourse with them.

This division in his mind between what bad girls do and good girls don't do carried over into a date that momentarily confused him. "There was this girl I thought of as one of my crowd, who showed signs of wanting to have sex. It seemed like she wanted to go further and further. But I couldn't really believe it, so I didn't follow through." When, after a decade of monogamy but infrequent sex with his wife, his period of extramarital promiscuity began, George's partners were often, as he described them, "high school graduates"; his crowd had all gone to college. He admitted preferring young women like this to those from his own social set: "They were exciting!"

Some of the men who operate according to good girl/ bad girl categories emphasize the split between the good women they form relationships with, whom they often like in a nonsexual way, and the women they relegate to affairs, by keeping the sex in their affairs "dirty"—having the women talk obscenely during the sex act, for example, or dress up in sluttish outfits. Or they may engage in "kink," doing things they wouldn't dream of with their wives—using costumes, having threesomes, even engaging in sadomasochistic playacting. One notorious womanizer, a married celebrity whose indiscreet infidelities have embarrassed his wife, who is also well-known, had one of his girlfriends of the moment join him in making love while another couple watched. As an example of the kind of contempt he had for his extramarital partners, when this same woman met him a few months later at a party in New York, he refused even to say hello.

An engineer told me that he regularly went after kink in his many affairs. "I started it to ease my conscience," he explained. "I would fool around when it offered me things that intrigued me, like bondage—tying the woman up—no pain, no heavy stuff. I figured I wasn't doing that at home, anyway, so it was okay."

The fact emerged, in my talks with this man, that he actually preferred that his wife not engage in the kinds of acts that turned him on, even though he lamented that she wouldn't. He told a story of being invited to the home of a couple who lived next door. They started the evening by showing a porn movie on a home screen. It soon became obvious that the couple was trying to lure this man and his wife into mate-swapping. "I pulled my wife out of there so fast," he said, "I didn't give her a chance to tell me whether she wanted to or not!"

It is difficult for a married man who suffers from the Pedestal/Gutter Syndrome to remain faithful, because the wife either loses erotic interest in his eyes, or he arrives at the same place through a different unconscious maneuver. He chooses for a wife someone who conforms to the "good girl" image by not being very interested in sex. Either way, he feels that he is forced to look elsewhere for what he needs, often blaming it on the wife.

"ME" MEN

Christopher Lasch, in his best-selling book *The Culture of Narcissism*, made the public aware of a new man proliferating in our society—the narcissist. Narcissism is a personality disorder that accounts for the womanizing of many single and married men.

Many narcissistic men hide their basic problem with relationships behind glitzy exteriors. Their personalities can be dynamic and winning. They often operate well in the social world. Because they lust for power, money, and prestige, many of them are quite successful.

What their smooth persona hides, however, is a shallowness, and an inability to relate to others except in a very limited way.

All relationships, for the narcissistic man, are based on self-interest. He is a taker. He doesn't even understand what the word *give* means. You listen to him, he never listens to you. Because he regards others as satellites to himself, rather than as individuals in their own right, he cannot recognize that you have needs too. Unable to put himself in other people's shoes, he has no empathy for your feelings, or anybody else's, for that matter. He reacts very badly to the merest hint of criticism.

The narcissistic man has a grandiose image of himself that is really a defense against lurking, deep-down feelings of insecurity, low self-esteem, and inner emptiness. Since he judges himself by how he appears to others, the narcissistic man has an inordinate need to be admired. This makes infidelity a given. If he doesn't have a constant supply of new admirers, his underlying feelings of emptiness, restlessness, and boredom overtake him.

Since narcissistic men regard the women in their lives as extensions of themselves, many of them like to be seen with beauties or women of status who will reflect glory upon them.

Unfortunately, the moment a narcissistic man possesses you, he devalues you, no matter how much he may have admired you during courtship. An example of this is a man who met a woman he thought was extremely beautiful, intelligent, and lively. He idolized her, fell in love with her, and finally married her. Now that she was his, however, he suddenly found her boring. His feelings for her were extinguished. Sex, which had been exciting, suddenly became dull and mechanical. This led him to seek out other women for affairs.

For single men, the process of devaluation that takes place once they have conquered a woman leads them to go from woman to woman. For married men this means marrying, becoming disappointed in the wife, and then going on to have affairs.

Conquest by itself feels good to the narcissist because it gives him a feeling of power and creates a sense of control over women whom subliminally he may fear, envy, and hate. Narcissists often have an unconscious view of women as larger than life, controlling and capable of devouring them.

Here is how this view of women operates for a minister in the Midwest. He has had many affairs with the women in his congregation. He picks weak women who are looking for a fatherly authoritative figure. He courts them by listening to their troubles, giving them advice, and being friendly and helpful. Along with his advice he may touch a little, then kiss, then pet, and finally, by the fourth time he sees a woman, he will take her to bed. By that time the woman has fallen in love with him. She thinks the affair is just beginning, but to her dismay he suddenly withdraws. He is no longer friendly or helpful or even interested in sex with her again. He has emptied the woman of what he sought from her—admiration. She has served her purpose and he no longer needs her. Also, he is terrified of her love because he thinks she will make demands on him. His underlying fear of women as voracious creatures has been invoked by her affection, and so, frightened, he disappears from the relationship.

Another reason monogamy is foreign to the narcissistic man's nature is that he feels he is entitled to take whatever he wants without constraints. In addition, he is in terror of being dependent on anyone, which leads him to avoid full commitment to you, even if he marries you.

Since he places such value on physical attractiveness, he also may lose interest in you as you age, and turn to other, younger women for sexual gratification.

In relationships, narcissistic men see you as either all good or all bad—either you are idolized or you are seen as being rotten. Most people have good and bad traits, but the narcissist does not understand this notion. They can either love you or hate you, but they can't do both. To be able to love, a person must be able to tolerate feelings of hate and love toward the same person. Narcissists cannot do this. When warts or imperfections appear, they turn off. As a result, these men often feel justified in philandering because they view you as so defective.

Splitting—the mechanism by which a man looks for pieces of what he needs in different women, rather than finding it in one woman—is another important ingredient in the makeup of the narcissist as a man who not only can't be faithful but often is quite promiscuous.

Gary Hart exhibits many symptoms of narcissism.

To begin with, Hart had the kind of mother who often creates narcissistic children. Nina Hartpence was cold: Gary Hart told journalist Gail Sheehy in "The Road to Bimini," an article published by *Vanity Fair*, that his mother was an undemonstrative woman. She was also self-centered and unable to view a child as an individual with needs distinct from her own. Strict, controlling, and determined to inculcate in her family the dogma of a stern fundamentalist religion, Mrs. Hartpence insisted that Gary meet *her* standards of perfection.

Narcissism is an identity impairment and it often occurs when a child is treated the way Gary was—as an extension of the mother—and is not allowed to develop his own inner self.

As a child Gary Hart already showed signs of the basically aloof personality that characterizes narcissists. When Gail Sheehy went back to the town where Gary Hart grew up she interviewed his schoolmates. She discovered that he was not close with any of them. He never brought friends home.

At a class reunion in 1984 one friend said he was as detached as he had always been.

In addition, when it came time for Gary Hart to choose a wife, he did what narcissists often do. They pick women who will reflect glory upon them through either beauty or status. Lee was probably considered a catch for a guy like Gary when he met her at college. She was good-looking and her family was several rungs higher on the social ladder.

Initially, Gary regarded Lee as a challenge and wooed her ardently, but soon after he conquered and wed her he began wondering about what he had done. This turnabout tactic is typical of narcissists. They often initially idealize a woman, just as Gary did Lee. Once the woman is won, however, a rapid disenchantment sets in and a need for other females who will supply fresh admiration grows. Reports indicate that Hart's womanizing began early in his marriage. A neighbor who observed his behavior said: "Lee would leave for Kansas or Nebraska to visit her family, and he would mind John and Andrea. They were toddlers at the time, but no sooner did Lee walk out the door than young women would start tramping in one at a time. Fifteen minutes before Lee was due home the last lady would be out the door."

Gary Hart has the charisma that is common to narcissists and he uses it in a typical way with women. He automatically turns on great, persuasive charm at first, but then he abruptly withdraws emotionally. Some of his female conquests have related how intense he was while pursuing them and how completely inaccessible he became immediately afterward. Political workers say that he seduced and spent the weekend with many women on the campaign trail. Gail Sheehy reports that when some of these women would show up, enamored, in Washington to work for him, Hart would walk by their desks without any sign of recognition, reducing them to tears. This is not unusual behavior for narcissists for whom others become non-persons—they literally cease to exist in their minds—once they have stopped being useful.

The narcissist's utilitarian approach to people extends to his wife. Gary Hart patched his marriage up for political reasons, but he often forgot to introduce his wife, and on the campaign trail aides had to remind him to kiss or even touch Lee.

The lack of empathy that is characteristic of narcissists seems to be part of Gary Hart's personality, as well. Gail Sheehy says he was unable to connect the emotional or moral expectations of those around him with their instrumental value to him. "He balked at having to phone potential supporters, and he rarely thanked people who had given up months and years of their own careers for him." Perhaps the ultimate proof of Hart's intrinsic inability to understand how others feel is the fact that he was startled to learn from his wife that his children were devastated by the Donna Rice scandal.

Finally, the sense of grandiosity that is so central to a narcissist's personality seems abundantly clear in Gary Hart's character.

Larry Smith, an administrative assistant for Hart during the early 1980s, was so disturbed by his grandiosity that he quit as Hart prepared to run for the presidency. Smith later told staff members that one of the major reasons he left was because he had become convinced that Hart had a dangerous sense of being "divine and above the rules."

This is an accurate description of narcissists, who see themselves as above others, feel entitled to whatever they want, and operate as if they can get away with anything because of a characterological blind spot—they can't connect what they do with its possible effect on others.

The sense of superiority and the blindness of narcissism were proven again many weeks after Hart reentered the race for the Democratic nomination. He was asked why he spent the weekend with Miss Rice despite the fact that aides had warned him he could be under surveillance. Although his showings in the primaries were dismal by then, Hart remained unable to recognize his defective judgment. Instead, he assumed a posture of moral superiority by stating, "I have the same rights as any other American citizen, and I can have whoever I want in my house. It is a matter of principle with me." The right Hart invoked does not extend to those who aim to be president, but Hart still appears unable to make that connection.

Narcissism seems to be the real reason for Gary Hart's ultimate downfall. Promiscuity is part of the narcissistic pattern, but that is not the whole picture. Hart played around despite the warnings of those around him that the press might no longer stay silent, and he foolishly invited reporters to follow him because he truly could not gauge the consequences of his actions. It was not stupidity, nor was it a death wish as some have surmised. It was the narcissist's inability to connect his actions with their effect on other human beings that destroyed Gary Hart as a serious presidential candidate.

HE-MEN

There are some unfaithful men who think that sexual conquest and having affairs is merely appropriate behavior for their gender. In their mind, either consciously or unconsciously, womanizing is what real men do, and what real women don't. The double standard is alive and well for men like this.

Brutes

Macho men, when they are "brutes," frequently also drink, smoke, and hang out with the guys (often at bars), assuming this to be a natural part of masculine life. They possess a feeling of camaraderie with other men, and their talk of women may sound as if they are referring to a strange group of creatures from another race; it is patronizing, indulgent, or, depending on the man, either openly or subtly hostile. Some of these men set out to hunt women with one or more buddies.

Sometimes buddies cover for each other. They feel free to use an alibi—"I'm going out with Bill," or "I was with Harry"—to disguise affairs. In one instance, a buddy was given the task of hatchet man. He had to tell a married man's "other" woman, who kept calling him, that she shouldn't bother the guy anymore—the affair was over.

Often, current conquests are paraded before buddies as a way of showing off to the guys. These men want the admiration, respect, and, whenever possible, envy of fellow males. They worry about how they look in the eyes of other men.

One twenty-four-year-old husband told me why he let his male friends know about his girlfriends. "When I have something that is good I like to show it off," he explained. "A girl comes under the same category as a house or a car. It is to show that I am successful."

Women are regarded by these men largely as creatures who exist to serve them. This means wives and girlfriends are expected to please them, and not bug them too much. They may refuse to tell you where they have been all night, or rely on their standard excuse of being with the boys and assume you will accept it. If you object to his coming home in the wee hours, or even the next morning, you are regarded as a pain in the neck. If a man is single and you want to see him more, you may be labeled "demanding." If you raise a fuss about other females in his life, you may be considered "possessive," something to which men like this react as if to poison. They fear being "pussy-whipped"—having to answer to women—more than anything else in the world. To them, independence is interpreted as masculine, and independence means they can do anything they like, and the women in their lives should accept it. Men like this often had mothers and grandmothers who put up with their husbands' affairs, which adds to their expectations that you will too. They may grouse loudly about women's liberation if they have a wife who won't stay true to form.

The one-night stands, pickups, and other female figures who float through their lives are seen purely as vessels to serve their sexual needs of the moment. The way they often refer to women as "pussy" or "pieces of ass" among themselves quite specifically describes their function. Sex is often accompanied by, or is the result of, a lot of drinking.

Frank Sinatra is a classic example of a macho man. When he cheated throughout his first marriage, to Nancy Sinatra, she was expected to put up with it.

Sinatra's callous treatment of women, so typical of macho men, is well known. Like many machos, once he had conquered them sexually, he treated many women with contempt. In *His Way: The Unauthorized Biography of Frank Sinatra* by Kitty Kelley, a woman who knows him reports the details of this kind of behavior on Sinatra's part: "It was really something to see. Frank would bring someone to the desert for the weekend. . . . I saw a lot of what I'd call Frank's 'before-and-after' treatment. Before bed, he would be charming. The girl was 'mademoiselle this,' 'darling that,' and 'my sweet baby'. . . . It was the next day that we'd always find the other Frank, the one who wouldn't speak to the girl who had been the most beautiful woman in the world the night before. . . . The minute the conquest was achieved, kaput. The girl could pack her bags. I saw many of them leave his house in tears."

Like most macho men, Sinatra is constantly surrounded by male cronies, and his sexual conquests are often shown off to them.

The macho man's need to dominate the women in his life is typified by Sinatra's treatment not only of his first wife, but of subsequent ones as well. When he was married to Mia Farrow, he was increasingly upset when she had to be away from him and work in movies. He wanted to control which films she worked on. David Susskind recalls in the Kitty Kelley biography that midway through the production of a TV movie Mia was appearing in, she failed to show up. "I started to worry because we had only a week or so to go before airing and I needed to make a decision about replacing her, so I flew out to the Coast and she showed up for work with black welts all over her body. . . . I sat down with her and said, 'Mia dear, I don't think someone wants you to do this role.' She lowered her eyes and said she still wanted to do it."

Sophisticated Sportsmen

Some of the more sophisticated men among the machos don't come on as crudely as the brutes. To women, they may not even appear obviously macho. There are many men like this among today's crop of bachelors. They may be work-oriented—even workaholics. Instead of hanging out at bars, their male bonding may take the form of playing tennis, going sailing, or working out at the gym with other guys. They may seem to treat women kindly, but although they may have a more polished manner, their point of view inwardly is similar to the others'— women are frequently regarded as conveniences and/or ornaments who will give them "points" in the eyes of other men. An article by Marcelle Clements in *New York Woman* magazine describes athletes today who use the term "table pussy" to describe a women who is regarded primarily as a "bimbo"—for decoration and sex—but who is presentable enough to bring out to dinner with one's friends.

A bachelor in San Diego told me, "Right now I am going out with three women. I'm not interested in any of them, but it's somebody for companionship on weekends, or someone to have dinner with, or go to a film or play with during the week. I don't think about them during the daytime. I can barely remember their phone numbers when it comes time to call them. It's just somebody to do something with."

Another man, in Chicago, remarked, "I go with a lot of women who are not the brightest. But they look good. They fill a need when I want to go someplace and be seen with somebody who looks right. The men I know all go to the same places—the same trendy discos, the same vacation spots. It's sort of competitive. We all try to establish an image. We want to look like successes to each other. Part of the image is to be seen with the right kind of woman." The terms he used in the following statement confirmed my feeling that women are seen as male commodities more than as individuals: "We have a code of ethics," he explained. "If someone is seeing a woman, hands off. And no used merchandise, either. You don't go out with a friend's former girlfriend. It's an unwritten code of the locker room."

WOMAN-HATERS

The hostile male goes far beyond macho attitudes. He really hates women and is downright sadistic. Sometimes men like this have been emotionally abused as children, often they were frightened of one or more parents. Many, early in life, learned to release hostility by making someone weaker suffer. This brought them temporary relief from the anxiety, confusion, rejection, and fear that permeated their childhoods. If their problem was with their mothers, they learned, as they matured, how to take out their hostility toward their mothers on all women. They may do it sexually—men like this often use their penises as a weapon. They conquer women as a form of aggression, and their aim is to hurt women emotionally. As single men they often engage in one-night stands and enjoy wounding women by their rejection in this way. Or they may carry on the relationship to the point where a woman begins to care for them, if they are able, then reject her. Or, frequently, they openly carry on with other women, in essence flaunting them in your face.

A successful businessman in Denver simply announced one day to his wife that he was having an affair and would continue to do so, and she could either take it or leave it. He knew his woman—these men often have excellent instincts, and with a lot of practice this makes them excellent judges of what other people will tolerate for a variety of reasons. This wife stayed with her husband and, after initial fury, learned to live with the situation. The security her marriage gave her was more important to her than his infidelity.

When they are involved in marriage or other long-term relationships, these men are often mean to women with whom they have relationships in other ways than overt womanizing. He may humiliate you, insult you, take your money, or refuse to share his wealth with you. Some even rough up women. Often, however, they know when a woman is fed up and ready to call it quits. They will then be nice for a while, or put on the charm, which is how women stay hooked to this kind of man, whose infidelities are but one weapon in an arsenal of hateful behavior.

IMPULSIVES

Oscar Wilde once said, "I can resist everything but temptation." Some men who are involved in a series of relationships with women are like this—in the face of temptation, they always give in. These are the impulsives of the world.

Basically, impulsives are all very immature. However, in their immaturity, some are more grown-up than others. The semi-grownups can hold down good jobs and act responsibly in their careers. However, in other areas of their lives they are like little kids. When they see something they want, whether it is a new gadget or a woman, they must have it. If a woman catches their attention, they want her and they take her. It doesn't matter to them whether they are already in a relationship or a marriage. They don't even consider it. Firmly rooted in the moment, they just go ahead and act on their attractions. Life, for impulsives, is experienced as a series of immediate opportunities and temptations. They operate on whim and instant impressions. Since their attention wanders and gets caught again elsewhere quite easily, fidelity is rare, promiscuity quite predictable.

Marcello Mastroianni, who has been married to the same woman since 1950, has had close friendships with many beautiful actresses and has lived openly with both Faye Dunaway and Catherine Deneuve. Known as a great lover of women off-screen as well as on, he admits, talking about his many affairs, "What else could I have done? I'm immature. I was born this way . . . I can't govern myself . . . Sunday morning, at the beach in Ostia, I see these pretty girls in bathing suits and I go crazy."

The most infantile among impulsive men, since they are given to quick action without thinking of consequences, can be oblivious to complications or drawbacks that would make another person stop and think. As a result, occasionally they can find themselves caught in strange, embarrassing, or uncomfortable situations. For example, one woman told me about meeting a man at work and becoming friendly with him. She started talking to him, she said, "Because he looked sad. I asked him why he looked unhappy. He explained that he had just broken up with his girlfriend."

He started coming over to this woman's house supposedly to talk about his problems, and soon they became lovers. He told her he had been married but was separated from his wife, but that he had given his wife the woman's phone number in case she needed him for their child. Soon she found, on her phone answering machine, messages from the wife, calling her all sorts of names. She discovered that not only was her lover still seeing the girlfriend he had claimed to have broken up with, but he wasn't really separated from his wife, either. Unlike other unfaithful men, for whom such an action would be insanity, he gave the wife the phone number, not taking into account the possible consequences. In this case the woman called the wife and they became allies pitted against the man.

Sometimes impulsiveness can result in callousness, as in the following case of a woman with her lover:

She and he were waiting on a street corner for a cab to take her home, when he caught sight of an attractive oriental woman sitting in a parked car across the street. Without thinking, he said, looking at the woman, "A Chinese woman. I've never had a Chinese woman." A cab stopped in front of them at that moment. She, infuriated, said, "So go have her." She got in the cab and slammed the door. As the cab sped away, she saw him heading toward the woman in the car.

Infantile impulsives can be just as impulsive and irresponsible in other areas of their lives as they are with women. They may quit a job abruptly because they feel frustrated one day, forgetting all the other benefits attached to work, or the consequences for their families or life-styles. They may always be getting into trouble of one kind or another because they can't control themselves. They can't set goals or make long-range plans, so they may go from job to job, instead of climbing their way up a career ladder. And since they can't plan or organize, there is often a drifting or even a chaotic quality to their lives.

Men with poor impulse control frequently use drugs and alcohol with as little restraint as they exercise in the rest of their lives.

They have no moral values, so they feel free to do whatever they want without guilt. Moral values require abstract thinking and a distance from the immediate. The impulsive man is incapable.

Operators

Most impulsive men are like mindless children, hopping from one event to another. But there is one group who are real "operators." They are quick to seize opportunities, figuring out instant angles in situations to see how there can be some immediate practical gain or advantage for them. They focus quickly on what works.

With a woman, this means such a man can be totally insincere. He will lie to his wife and say to another woman, "I love you," "You're beautiful," "I think we have a future," "I'm about to leave my wife"—whatever he thinks is needed to get her into bed. He is not interested in the woman per se, but only in the possibilities of making out with her.

Actors

A final kind of impulsive man has a hysterical personality. Life is an ongoing drama for him. Lively and very expressive, his emotions run high and he gets carried away by his feelings. He is easily distracted. He is the kind of man who can fall rapturously in love every two minutes and cannot be faithful for very long to anyone. He exists for the highs of high romance, and has no tolerance for the simmering-down that is normal in all relationships. When this happens, it's all over as far as he is concerned. If the hysterical man is married, he can't be in love with his wife. He has known her too long for her to be the object of his passions, which feed on newness, excitement, and drama, even though he may depend on a less emotional wife to provide an anchor in his otherwise tempestuous existence.

HOPPED-UP MEN

This kind of man gets involved in a series of affairs only when he is going through a period of manic behavior—days or weeks of wild euphoria. You can recognize him because he becomes supercharged, hyperactive, hopped-up, and giddy. Speech may quicken. He may become extremely talkative, to the point where he spews forth an unending stream of words and wild ideas on disconnected topics. You feel that his mind is literally racing.

During a manic period it is typical for a man to get involved in too many things all at once. To the casual observer he may appear infectiously upbeat and cheerful, but if you know him well, you may feel he is frantic and disorganized.

He may want to be with people all the time. Friends and acquaintances may be subjected to telephone calls at all hours of the day or night. Although others may perceive him at this time as intrusive or demanding, the man in a manic period is not aware of his effect. He feels on top of the world, self-confident, capable of doing anything.

Hypersexuality is a common symptom. A man may go through a series of casual sexual encounters and/or may place inordinate sexual demands on a regular partner. Need for sleep is markedly decreased, and so sexual and other escapades can keep him busy long past the hour when he would normally be in bed. The lack of judgment typical of people who are manic often makes them exceptionally indiscreet, with the consequence that a partner may become aware of one or more sexual infidelities. A crisis in the relationship often results.

There are some men who suffer from a milder form of mania that is chronic. They are always slightly souped up. Most go through bouts of mania when they are up and often also suffer from periods of depression when they are down. Clinically such people are called manic-depressives. It is believed that they suffer from a chemical imbalance that produces their wide mood swings. The drug Lithium, administered by psychiatrists, helps control the mood swings of these men.

PRINCES

A man who is a Prince is the product of his mother—a woman who frequently was deeply dissatisfied with her husband, who she felt could not meet many of her needs. Often the husband is a good workhorse but is regarded as lacking sensitivity, culture, or the ability to communicate or express emotions.

When her son was born, this wife treated him like a messiah and diverted all her love and attention to him.

Anything he wanted he got, and only the best was for him. She became his servant and he became overly dependent on her. All through life, mother and son remain emotionally enmeshed.

Because the mother regarded her son as her salvation, he came to see himself as God's gift to women. And because his mother gave him everything, no woman in his later life can live up to her performance. You can never recognize his true worth or give him as much as he deserves.

A Prince's needs for attention and affection are inordinate. Since no one woman can fill up his bottomless pit, he often tries to get satisfaction by doubling up—by always having one or two affairs going. In this way the Prince feels he almost gets enough attention and loving to get by. A Prince may play around a lot as a single man, but marriage is generally considered to be a goal, since it was something Mother instilled in him as part of his future. Fidelity is another of the values that was stressed by Mother.

A Prince, therefore, may start out being faithful to you in a relationship as a single man, because of his beliefs, but soon he may feel, for one reason or another, that you are not worthy of him, and so he drops you or starts seeing other women.

Eventually, often later rather than sooner, a Prince carries out his mother's mandate and marries. If a Prince manages to be faithful to you as a husband, it is becaues he puts all of his effort into making himself into a big success in the business world and sublimates his sexual drive. Just as often, the Prince as a husband begins to feel unappreciated by his wife, and in today's world he assuages himself with affairs. Not without a price, however. Since he is going against the values instilled in him, he feels guilty. In his fantasies, a Prince thinks the answer would be to have you agree to his affairs. But since he generally marries the kind of traditional woman for whom this would be impossible, he usually doesn't even broach the subject. Instead, he carries on surreptitiously, grappling with a conscience that bothers him from time to time.

TRIANGLE-MAKERS

Tug-of-warriors

Some men thrive when two women are fighting over them. They may moan and groan while they are caught in such situations, but they feel their absolute best in the middle of the heat of a triangle. Secret infidelity does not last long for men hooked on triangles. Either they manage to be found out, or they let you know directly that a rival exists, because the whole purpose of cheating is not sex, not love, not romance, but the tug-of-war that ensues.

Men like this often grew up in a situation where a triangle existed—his mother and father may have vied to show him that each loved him more than the other. Or two significant women who were somewhat competitive may have raised him—a maiden aunt and his mother, for example, or a grandmother and his mother.

Being involved in a competition between two women also imparts a great sense of power to a man who may feel somewhat inadequate.

To keep the triangle going, these men often flip-flop back and forth between two women, never quite making up their minds. They may decide to leave you for the other woman one day, then change their minds, and come back to you, then do the same thing all over again.

Generally the triangle ends because either you or his lover gets fed up and leaves him, or orders him out. If it was up to the man, he could keep the triangle going forever. Some of the more determined and kinky triangulators do keep it going forever by getting two women to agree to a ménage à trois.

If one triangle ends, men like this inevitably find another. If they marry, they will soon be heavily involved with another woman. If single or divorced, they will start a new romance once they win you, and the whole game gets played out again. For a man to be a true triangle specialist, it has to be a recurring situation in his life, rather than a once-in-a-lifetime event.

Duelists

A second kind of triangle is formed by the man who habitually fights an emotional duel for a woman with another man on the field of love. This man has a habit of starting relationships with a woman who is married, going with, or committed to someone else when he meets her. He likes taking a woman away from another man. The name of his game is not the woman in question but the man. He gets charged up by the competition. What keeps him glued to the relationship has less to do with his interest in your qualities than with his need to win out over the other man.

If he does triumph and you become his, suddenly his ardor will dim. You are no longer as exciting as you were. You can bet he will soon dump you or take another lover, throwing you, who gave up another man for him, into a total tizzy.

His new love is likely to be yet another married or committed woman, which puts him once more in a position where his passion boils—he is pitted against another man.

The roots of this kind of obsession are in the oedipal stage of childhood, in which this kind of man is emotionally stuck. Around the age of five or six, a boy is normally infatuated with his mother and fantasizes about taking her away from his father. That, in essence, is what he keeps trying to do in his triangles—he is symbolically winning Mom from Dad.

Like the triangle-makers, the next type of man we'll examine is reacting to you as his mother. However, unlike many of the triangle-makers, whose drama is really with the other man, he is playing out his role directly with you.

SEVEN

Making You Mom

BABIES

THERE IS A WHOLE GROUP OF MEN WHO CAN'T WALK ACROSS the street without a woman along. A man like this will often have a series of lovers who will fill in when you are away, busy, or sick, when they find themselves with a day off or a few hours in the afternoon with nothing to do. If they travel alone, they find it so uncomfortable that they cruise the nearest bar to pick up a woman. If his wife goes to visit a relative out of town, such a man will always pick up the phone to try to get one of his lovers to come over.

Brian is one example of a Baby. Brian moved to New York City from a small town in Minnesota a year ago. He has a steady girlfriend in New York, one in his hometown when he visits, and another in Chicago, where he travels on business frequently.

Gerard is another illustration of a Baby at work. Gerard is a high school principal in a suburban town in the South. He is married. Through the school, Gerard has the opportunity to meet many women who are teachers, school counselors, school nurses, or the mothers of students. He generally has a string of two or three lovers picked from among the women he meets. Some are married women, but in his stable there is always at least one single female. Gerard realizes there are times a married woman will not be available. Since Gerard spends a lot of time seducing a woman, and because he is a good talker, many of his conquests fall in love with him.

Gerard, however, remains emotionally unavailable to them once the seduction has taken place. Gerard needs these women, but they are, in essence, interchangeable. He just wants them when he needs to keep from feeling alone.

Recently, Gerard's wife went out of town for the weekend. He decided to call a woman who hadn't heard from him in months. He begged her to come over. She refused, saying, "You only want sex." He said, "I only want to talk." He persuaded her to come over and talk. Once she arrived, Gerard kept trying to get her into bed. She decided to leave. Gerard could not understand her argument; she wanted more than sex from him. As she went out the door, Gerard burst into tears.

To Gerard, and men like him, all women are really mothers. He acts with them like a baby who expects his mother to feed him instantly when he cries with hunger. Gerard regards women as breasts with milk. He expects women to accommodate him when he needs their nurturance, which he takes through sex. Men like Gerard are completely selfish and self-centered, just as a baby is. Men who are Babies have no notion that women have lives or needs of their own. Babies are incapable of fidelity because, in their infantile way, they feel they must have a string of women on call to feed them.

THE BAD MOMMY SYNDROME

Soon after they marry or become committed to you, or start living with you, many men start to react to you in the way they related to their own mothers as children. Initially, these men think you are wonderful—they often look at you in an idealized way, imagining that you have the qualities they feel Mother lacked. But soon after commitment, reality starts to intrude. They begin to see little faults that deviate from the ideal image. Although some people can adjust to this inevitable recognition of faults in a partner, a man like this cannot. He goes into reverse. Now, instead of being this wonderful woman who is everything Mother was not, you become just like her in his eyes. He starts to think of you as having the same traits that he disliked so much in a parent. Let's see how this works.

Arthur grew up with a mother who he felt suffocated him with her demands. When he met Francine, who was soft-spoken and sweet, he thought she was the answer to his dreams of a woman who would be the opposite of his mother—easygoing and compliant. Soon he was in love with Francine, and a year after meeting, they were married. A few months into the marriage he began to see that Francine was different from his picture of her. She wasn't domineering, but she liked to express her opinions about things. Arthur overreacted. Gone was his idealized picture of Francine as sweet and gentle, replaced by an image of her that matched the way he felt about his mother. He saw her as demanding, domineering, and controlling. He switched from an all-good image to an all-bad one, which is very characteristic of men who are destined by their inner psychological workings to see wives as "bad mothers." The man who suffers from the Bad Mommy Syndrome does this only with his wife, in contrast to the narcissist, who splits everyone into all-good or all-bad categories.

No matter what specific characteristics from the past are assigned to the woman, the picture they paint of her in their disappointment is almost always antierotic in nature. The woman is seen as punishing, demanding, controlling, frustrating, disapproving, or even castrating. The result? The man feels turned off and seeks sexual excitement with someone else.

The appeal of an affair is built into situations where the Bad Mommy Syndrome is operating. The same projection of negative traits onto a partner does not occur with a lover. That is why affairs can be so enticing. It isn't the other woman who is really so alluring. The irresistible quality is that the affair seems like a relief from the repetition of old frustrations and conflicts that occur when a man projects qualities from a person in his childhood onto his adult partner.

The Good Mommy Syndrome

Another kind of unfaithful man who turns you into a mother is actually searching for a nurturer. A single man like this generally gets the right vibes from a woman who will, perhaps, make all the arrangements for a vacation, because he is so busy, or will like to cook for him rather than go out to dinner—a nurturer. This type of man may even select you as a mate because he thinks you will be a good mother to his future children. He may want someone who will be the mother he never had, if, for example, his mother died when he was young. More often, these men want a duplicate of their own involved, nurturing mothers. Their instincts for choosing such women are excellent.

Jim, a businessman in Chicago, grew up with a mother who did everything for him. She made his bed all through childhood and adolescence, she helped select his clothing, she gave him frequent advice, she helped him choose a college and a career. When he married Jeanne, she took up where Jim's mother left off. She did everything for him. She paid the bills, took things to the post office and the cleaners, cooked elaborate meals for him, and made sure he went to the doctor and dentist for regular visits. Jim loved and truly appreciated his wife, but soon he didn't feel turned on by her. He started having brief affairs with women he met through work who seemed to lack his wife's qualities as a person, but to whom he was more physically attracted.

Men like Jim generally respect or even adore the women they are attached to. The only problem is that they have identified her so much as a mother that the incest taboo is invoked and sexual feelings disappear. They have to turn to other women to feel erotically charged up.

When a married man like this has affairs, he generally makes it quite clear to the other woman that sex with his wife may not be great, but she is a wonderful woman and he has no intention of ever leaving her. Such men often feel guilty about cheating on their loyal, helpful wives. One way they learn to live with their guilt is by keeping outside encounters "just for sex."

REBELS

Another type of man who obliquely casts his woman in the role of mother is the fellow who uses infidelity as a means of rebelling. He sees a committed relationship as restricting and suffocating, and he often views the partner as a monitor—grading his behavior, always ready to disapprove. Emotionally, he responds to you as a controlling parent. Feeling hemmed in and controlled, a man like this reacts like an adolescent. To escape from what he sees as a demanding relationship, he has affairs that he sees, in contrast, as play and freedom—islands of bliss, excitement, and abandon.

In essence, rebels are acting like bad boys, and like a lot of bad boys they really want to return home to mama. Therefore, they either confess or manage in one way or another to get caught by the partner, punished, and, inevitably, taken back into the fold.

Other rebels have become trapped in a rigid stereotype in marriage. For example, they may have assumed the role of the sober, rational, dependable partner in the relationship. Since they shut out the playful side of their nature in their role of family man, they may rebel at some time and become the opposite—they enter into an affair in which they can allow themselves to be fun-loving, more emotionally expressive, or even irresponsible. It's a way of breaking out of a very restrictive pattern of behavior vis-à-vis a mate.

Many rebels are actually extremely dependent in their relationships. However, they may interpret dependency as shameful or anti-masculine, and they embark on a path of infidelity to proclaim their independence and/or affirm their masculinity. They are saying through an affair, "See, I don't need her that much." But they do, and so they, too, frequently arrange to be found out.

THE EROTICISM OF SECRECY

Before I leave the subject of infidelity caused by men relating to women as their mothers, I want to point out another, connected phenomenon concerning affairs. Many men get charged up by secrecy. The fact that they are doing something secret with a woman is just as erotic to them as the actual sex.

A man who has repeatedly been unfaithful told me, "To me, the greatest turn-on is sharing a secret nobody else knows—just being together with a woman when my wife and the woman's husband don't know about it."

Three things are behind this sexualizing of secrecy: first, the man may feel he is keeping something hidden from his mommy—you—and as with many little boys, this gives him a particular thrill; it is an assertion of furtive independence when he feels dependent on you. Second, secrecy is connected to the erotic pleasures obtained from masturbation. In masturbatory acts, intense erotic pleasure is often mingled with guilt—the same combination of feelings that frequently exists in illicit affairs. Third, since many children wonder what their parents are doing behind closed doors, sexuality, for them, becomes connected with something hidden and wondered about—and perhaps it is what little boys wish they could do with Mommy during the oedipal period, around the age of five or six. A love affair in secret puts the man behind those closed doors, in a symbolic sense, and this secret thrill can be very powerful and alluring because it is based on very early, primitive sexual feelings for a close relative.

A MAN CAN BE A COMBINATION OF VARIOUS TYPES

Although I have described the dynamics of unfaithful men under separate headings, you may recognize traits of your man in more than one of the previous sections. That's because, although one type is usually predominant, many men are a combination of two or more of the categories of unfaithful men I have told you about.

For example, the actor Steve McQueen combined traits of four kinds of unfaithful men. He was, first of all, a compulsive womanizer, one of the greatest philanderers that Hollywood—a town noted for its infidelity—has ever known. His compulsive life-style with women documented in Penina Spiegal's biography, *McQueen*, was based on the profound inner insecurity so common among these womanizers. According to Spiegal, his father had abandoned him at six months. His mother abandoned him repeatedly. She would disappear, leaving him with his grandparents, come back periodically promising to be with him forever more, then shortly dump him again back home with the grandparents. Steve always felt it was somehow his fault.

His monumental womanizing started long before he became famous. As a struggling unknown actor in New York he was a king of one-nighters. He also had some steady girlfriends but was unable to be faithful to any one of them. The reminiscences of an important girlfriend from those early days, in *McQueen*, describe exactly the behavior of compulsive womanizers: "Steven had floods of women. He was always looking for the next pleasure, the next conquest." Penina Spiegel writes, "Sex became mechanical for Steve. He used women briefly and then discarded them."

Like many compulsive womanizers, Steve McQueen was very attached to the home life he had with his first wife, Neile, despite his extramarital affairs. In a characteristic rationale employed by compulsive womanizers, McQueen felt that as long as he didn't get emotionally attached to any of his sexual conquests, he was being loyal to his wife.

As mid-life approached, he worried about aging, as do many compulsive womanizers, and the number of women in his life increased even more.

It was at this stage in his life that McQueen showed signs, always lurking in his personality, that he was also a Rebel.

He began to feel that his wife was restricting his freedom, and although he had been discreet before, he now began flaunting his affairs by taking his women out to public places frequented by people who knew the McQueens. At this point, his wife could no longer tolerate it and she sued for divorce, which devastated the actor. Like many Rebels he was really very dependent on the person he was rebelling against.

McQueen was also a He-man. In typical macho fashion, he always surrounded himself with a coterie of male friends. With them he shared typical macho activities: adventures on motorcycles and in cars, barroom brawls and sexual escapades. When one of these friends dropped out of the crowd at the behest of his wife, who heard rumors of the sexualizing, McQueen accused him of being "pussy-whipped."

Like many macho men, McQueen would show off his conquests to his friends. At times this even seemed to be the point of what he was doing. A good buddy of his reported that often, once McQueen knew that a woman would be willing to sleep with him, he would turn to his friend and say, "The hell with her. Let's you and I go somewhere."

The actor seemed to believe that women should be "barefoot and pregnant." He made his first wife quit a very successful career in the theater to devote herself to him. In his second marriage, to the actress Ali MacGraw, he and she became reclusive to the apparent detriment of her career. He also played what appeared to be domination games with her, publicly ordering her around. A friend recalled: "She'd start to say something and he'd say, 'Leave the room' or 'Sit down' or 'Get me a beer and don't open your mouth.'"

McQueen often crossed over the borders of machismo to become one of the Hostile Men I have described. He hated his mother and, while driving cars at high speed, would often treat friends to a stream of malevolent remarks about her. He seemed to take out his bad feelings toward his mother on women in general. His first wife, who stayed close to McQueen all his life, has said, "Steve hated women." His daughter, Terry, has stated, "My father hated all women but me." McQueen put Ali MacGraw down, openly making fun of her body.

So you see how traits from many different types can come together in one man. In Steve McQueen's case the

Compulsive, the He Man, the Hostile Man, and the Rebel coexisted.

Thus far I have talked about men who have individual psychological problems that lead to affairs. The seeds of the behavior were there before the man entered any adult relationship with a woman, predetermined by an individual family history that may have left him insecure, immature, frightened, and full of rage at women, or filled with myths about how men and women behave.

But as the next chapter explains, many affairs have their roots in other issues, and infidelity is caused by more immediate situations.

EIGHT

Special Situations that Make Men Cheat

WHAT ARE THE KINDS OF SPECIAL SITUATIONS IN LIFE THAT promote infidelity? Sexual problems, revenge for injuries in a relationship, emotional deprivation, power struggles, midlife *angst*, divorce, and ambiguous sexual orientation all can play their part. Let us start by looking at the one that is most commonly cited by men themselves for their infidelity—problems with sex.

TRYING TO SOLVE SEXUAL PROBLEMS

"I'll Look for It Elsewhere"

Gregg, forty-two, is telling me about his wife. "She happens to be a terrific woman, but she feels she is a very asexual individual. She thinks she has always been like that, but she was not. When we first got married, on a scale of one to ten she was a five, which was all right. But now she is at zero and I want her to move to one or two and she doesn't understand that. She has absolutely no desire for sex, so, rather than fight for it, I have sex elsewhere. I have pretty much fooled around during our entire marriage." Greg has been married for twelve years. He started his affairs in the seventh month after the wedding.

Lester, a man of fifty-four, is talking: "Let me tell you what happens. A woman has a baby. That is what she has been taught to do in life. She is supposed to get married and have kids. So she has the child and her mission is fulfilled. She feels she doesn't have to have sex anymore. Now she can devote her time to the children. You buy a piano so the kids can have lessons, and she turns away at night. You stop having sex with your wife, so you go out and find it with someone else.

"There's a whole generation of these women. They were brought up not to screw around. They didn't like sex. And the men became like animals anytime the wife rejected them and turned away."

Eric, forty-eight, is telling me his story: "In those days there were still double standards. You asked your wife to do certain things, and if she didn't do them, you went elsewhere. I sometimes wonder if I couldn't have nurtured it out of her. She has done oral sex twice in our twenty years. She finds it abhorrent. I took the easy way out. Women always liked me. Because women were so accessible to me, I thought, 'If she doesn't want to, if it is going to be a hassle, I'll just do it elsewhere.'"

Although two of these men talk about it as a generational thing, disparities in sex drives and tastes exist in marriages of all ages. Several studies have all come to the same conclusion: one of the leading reasons for affairs is infrequent and/or poor sex. Shere Hite, in her report on male sexuality, found that most men said they had affairs because sex at home was unsatisfactory and usually too infrequent. She noted that they complained of being more highly sexed than their wives. In the Simenauer and Pietropinto survey of four thousand men, 32 percent of the husbands cited unsatisfactory sex at home as a primary reason for cheating.

Men have affairs to get more sex if a wife's sex drive is significantly lower than theirs; they do it to obtain certain sex acts, such as oral sex, that a wife refuses to do; and they do it when they have lost all desire for their wives.

Sexual disparities, such as markedly different sexual appetites or opposite temperaments (e.g., an inhibited prude paired with a sexual adventurer), can be legitimate problems that lead to affairs, but loss of desire has to be looked at more closely. Turning off in a committed relationship does lead certain men into affairs, but the loss of desire on a man's part is often a symptom of other nonsexual problems such as the good-girl/bad-girl split (see pages 77–79), turning a wife into a bad or good mother (see pages 98–101), suppressed anger at a partner, or intimacy problems (see Chapter 9). A combination of these factors often operates subliminally in sexually incompatible couples.

No matter what its cause, when there is a wide disparity in sex drive, with the husband desiring more frequent intercourse, many men feel that outside sex is remedial—it takes the heat off the marriage.

One man explained, "I've tried stopping the affairs. I'd like to get it all together. I'm at a point where I would rather not be fooling around. But I can go for about two or three months, and then I explode about the sex. We end up having terrible fights. So I have one relationship now with a nice woman who doesn't expect much from me, and it keeps the pressure off the wife."

"I play around a little," an economist confessed. "If you don't get it inside, you get it outside. But it's difficult. I feel guilty, I worry I'll catch something, or that I'll get involved."

"Maybe I'll Find Someone Who Can Help Me"

Male sexual dysfunctions, such as prolonged impotence with a steady partner, can also lead a man to try it out with someone else.

A single woman described her experiences with Murray, a divorced lawyer: "He was a charming, articulate guy—very successful. He came on hot and heavy, like he couldn't wait to get me into bed. On our third date he did. He could get it up at first, but he couldn't keep it up. I was sympathetic. I told him not to worry, that a lot of men have trouble the first time. We went to bed again about a week later. The same thing happened. I was still soothing. I know how upset guys can get about this. I kept telling him it was nothing to worry about. The next week we tried again. The same thing. He stopped calling. We hang around in the same circles, and I knew he was seeing a lot of other women. He never saw anyone more than three weeks or so. About a year after our affair, I got a call out of the blue from Murray. He wanted to see me. I said sure. He came on like the first time, unable to keep his hands off me. He told me he had been in therapy. I thought maybe he had been cured. At the end of the evening we got undressed. It was the same scene all over again. He couldn't keep his erection. I never heard fom him again."

A lot of single men with sexual problems are like Murray. They keep going from woman to woman, hoping for the magic vagina that will cure them.

If a man is married and impotent, a new partner sometimes works like magic, but just as often these men are impotent with the new woman too. A few hop from woman to woman in these circumstances, just as single men do—in search of a woman who will be the cure. The majority, too humiliated by the failure, stop.

"The Fire Always Goes Out"

Some men hide a great deal of insecurity about their sexual adequacy from you. Men like this are great at the beginning of an affair. The need to prove themselves to women initially outweighs their sexual anxieties, and at first they can even be firebrands, intense and passionate. But once a relationship continues beyond the opening stages, or culminates in marriage, this kind of man peters out. The old anxieties come to the fore again. The man becomes afraid that his sexual inadequacy will become evident to you, and he backs off. He either disappears from the relationship or, more frequently, continues it, but sex becomes sparse, leaving you puzzled about what has happened.

Sexual neglect often activates your own insecurities and you may blame your looks, your shape—whatever you feel isn't up to par. Because a man like this is so terrific at the start of a relationship, he often gets involved in a series of beginnings—short affairs, which can drive you, the primary woman in his life, even crazier. Not understanding his dynamics, you become even more sure that other women are simply more attractive to him then you are. He may even become convinced of it, too, since a lot of his behavior is based on unconscious motivations.

GETTING BACK AT YOU

Frank was shocked to discover that his wife, Mary, had been having an affair with an old boyfriend who had moved back into town. He felt angry and betrayed. His wife gave up her romance but Frank still brooded about her infidelity. One day, while having a drink with a man who worked in his office, he started talking to a woman who was sipping a drink by herself at the next table. His co-worker left for home and Frank moved over and sat next to her, where they drank, joked, and chatted for another hour. She invited him to her nearby apartment for another drink before he returned home. Frank and this woman ended up as lovers.

It was not a very happy affair for anyone involved. Frank was not all that crazy about the woman and he upset his wife. He managed to leave the woman's name on a slip of paper, and his wife found it. When she accused him of being a lying cheat, he shouted back, "How dare you complain, after what you did to me?" He soon broke off the affair, and he and his wife finally went into couples therapy to get their relationship straightened out. Frank had had a revenge affair.

"The spouse having an affair with someone else" was among the nine most common reasons given for affairs in a survey of clients of the Family Service Agency. The psychiatrist Bernard Greene, in his study of unfaithful spouses, reported that 40 percent cited revenge as the motive.

Revenge affairs are not limited to marriage. Men and women who live together often do the same thing. And it can happen to couples just going together, when one sneaks in a quickie with someone else and the other retaliates. Because the motivation is anger, hurt, and malice, as well as the need to prove that you are still attractive in the face of the mate's straying, these affairs are generally unsatisfying and may even leave the perpetrator feeling slightly ill, albeit momentarily triumphant.

Sometimes your affair is just what he has been waiting for. It gives him permission to go out and play.

If you are a woman whose crime is being repaid in kind, you may find yourself in an awkward position. You may feel just as hurt and betrayed as you would have if you had not had an affair yourself, but you feel that your right to get furious is severely curtailed. How can you carry on when, in your eyes as well as in his, his affair was justified? Sometimes revenge affairs start a vicious cycle of tit-for-tat, so that both partners find themselves involved in a never-ending cycle of "I'll show you" infidelities, which seriously erode the chances of putting the relationship back together.

Another kind of revenge affair pays a woman back for nonsexual crimes. He may feel that you care about him only for his money. He may find you a critical bitch. Perhaps he is angry because you are sloppy and don't care what you look like around him. Maybe you fight all the time or you put him down in public.

A husband in Minnesota, married to an alcoholic, put up with her binges and the emotional turmoil in which she kept the whole household for fifteen years. He had remained monogamous throughout it all. When he met a woman at a party that his wife couldn't attend with him because she was home drunk, he felt justified in starting an affair that lasted two years. He felt, on an emotional level, that he deserved to have a little fun in return for all that his wife had put him through over the years.

HE'S TELLING YOU SOMETHING

Many times an affair is really a message. For example, one woman business executive recalled a time when she had become so absorbed in her career that she spent most of her time working. She came home mainly to sleep. Her husband, understandably, felt neglected. He started an affair, she found out, and when the two of them talked the whole matter out with a therapist, she realized the affair was really a way for her husband to tell her, "Please pay more attention to me and stop taking me for granted." She listened, cut back on her hours, and soon the marriage was back on course.

Another woman was back in school, earning her law degree. Her husband missed her. She spent long hours studying. He started flirting with a woman he met at work. On evenings when he would take this woman out for a drink, he noticed that his wife never even asked where he had been; she was too absorbed in what she was doing. This made him feel angry, and soon afterwards he started sleeping with the woman he had merely been flirting with before. He came home even later now. Still his wife didn't notice. His anger grew and so did the affair.

In a few months he thought he was in love with the other woman who lavished attention upon him. He told his wife about the affair and said he wanted to leave her to be with his new love. The wife finally opened her eyes to what was going on, and she was understandably upset. However, he insisted that he loved the other woman, so she let him go. The man started living with the other woman, but it didn't take him long to realize he still missed his wife. They had much more going for them than he had with his lover. He called his wife and told her. She and he are now in couples therapy, working things out. His message was received loud and clear: "You never have time for me anymore, and you don't seem to care what I do when you are busy." Today both spouses are rearranging their schedules to spend more time with one another.

Restoring the Balance of Power

These days, affairs may start because the previous power balance in the relationship has been upset. That was the case with Brian. He was used to Geraldine catering to him. The house was always clean, his meals were on time, and he made the decisions about how money was to be spent, until Geraldine returned to work at the age of thirty-five. Geraldine found a job as a real-estate saleswoman, and she became successful very quickly. Soon she was earning a great deal of money, almost as much as Brian. Geraldine now had interests of her own, a new sense of pride, and money that she alone controlled.

She started insisting that they eat out more often because she was so busy. She wanted Brian to help out more with the housework.

It was at this juncture in their marriage that Brian started an affair with his secretary, a young woman who looked up to him. The affair, which devastated Geraldine, was his way of taking back some of the power he felt he had lost in the relationship when Geraldine returned to work and became successful. It was no accident that his paramour was a young woman he could still dominate.

Geraldine, frightened by the affair, thought maybe she should quit her job so that she could cater more fully to Brian again, but she didn't have to. In couples therapy, Brian came to realize the motivation for his fling. He loved Geraldine and he was ultimately able to accept the shift of power in the relationship without resorting to an affair in an attempt to reestablish the old order at home.

Affairs based on power plays often take place when a wife returns to work, when she starts to earn as much as or more than her husband does, when a woman suddenly starts to become more famous or successful than her mate, or when she decides she has rights in the relationship that previously have been overlooked.

TRYING MY WINGS: DIVORCED MEN

Within the first two years after a man leaves a marriage, it is unreasonable to expect him to be faithful. It isn't built into the way he is feeling.

Although there are notable exceptions, as a group, newly separated or divorced men are dazed, depressed, unsure of themselves, afraid women will reject them, afraid they won't even know how to meet women. Small, everyday, practical matters may seem like insurmountable problems. "My greatest triumph after I moved out," exclaimed one man, "was learning how to use the washing machine and dryer at the Laundromat."

On top of this, some of them are very angry at their spouses, their fate, their divorce settlements, the fact that their children are no longer part of their everyday lives. Some divorced and separated men nurse anger as a way not to experience an underlying sense of vulnerability, even helplessness. Anger makes a man feel strong. If a man is at the post-divorce stage of anger, he often takes his fury out on the women he meets. He may, for example, use women only for sex, mindlessly or frantically running from bed to bed.

In any case, screwing as many women as possible is what many divorced men want to do, especially if they have been confined in a marriage for many years, or if they feel that during the years of their marriages they missed out on the sexual revolution. They try to make up for lost time.

One man, looking back on the year after his divorce, told me, "At one point I had clean shirts, socks, shorts, and handkerchiefs at three different places around town. My high or low point in this period was when I got out of the bed of a woman with whom I had spent the night, left her to go to a brunch, hopped into the sack with a girl after the brunch, left her, and met a third one with whom I spent the night.

"I would end up sometimes going from one woman's apartment to another's," he continued. "I pulled myself out of one bed and into another. Up to a point it is a great game, being able to keep three, four, or five women balanced . . . very good for the ego. But very soon it stopped being much fun. I was physically tired. I wasn't getting much sleep, I was really dragging around, and I began to think, 'Oh, shit, now I have to go and see her, what the hell am I doing?' It had kind of built up. I'd meet one that I wanted, then I would meet another one, so it was Tuesday, Thursday, Friday with one and Monday, Wednesday, and Saturday with the other. Then another would come along, or there would be an occasional one-shot. I told the most outrageous lies. It got to be a hell of a bore after a while. I just couldn't do it, I had to cut down and I did."

Some newly divorced men do the opposite. They latch on to one woman right away, propelled by intolerable loneliness or insecurity. They may seem nice and sincere, which, given their limited capacity at this time, they may very well be. The problem is, nice or not, they can't maintain a monogamous relationship. Sooner or later another woman will come along and they will want to try their wings with her. They may simply be stronger, thanks to the first woman who helped them through the worst, and may now be ready to experiment more before settling down.

An advertising man told me of this kind of progression as a divorced man. Bruised, depressed, beset by loneliness, after weeks of just staying in his new apartment and crying, he ended up going with one woman steadily after being introduced to her by a friend. "I knew it wouldn't last. She was completely unsuitable for me. But I couldn't stand being alone." This relationship had gone on for about a year when he met another woman at work and started an affair with her. "I was feeling much better by then. And this woman was much more my type." The first woman could not understand his infidelity and found it unforgivable. In her fury she harassed him at the office for weeks, before finally giving up on the relationship.

She, like a great many women in her situation, simply failed to understand that you can rarely win as the first woman in a divorced man's life. You will either be treated to residual anger at the wife, or you will be a nurse or a way station. Even basically nice guys do this. To their credit, this isn't conscious behavior. But, conscious or unconscious, when the divorced man's wounds are more closed up he will move on from a first relationship, often straddling for a while between you and the next woman in his life.

Even more common than the latch-on relationship that can go on for months, or even for a year or more, is a post-divorce pattern of brief relationships when he may seem to you to be more promising than he actually is: the guy is sincere, communicative, and appears to like monogamy. But because he is not yet ready for commitment, he starts backing off rather quickly. Some of these men are afraid to tell the truth, so they plead the demands of work or children in order not to see you as often. The next thing you know, a friend is telling you she saw him playing tennis or holding hands in a restaurant with another woman.

A final kind of divorced man is unfaithful with, of all people, his ex-wife. He runs between the new woman in his life and the ex-spouse. For him, the marriage is not yet really over emotionally. His ex-wife is often just as confused by this as is the new woman. Neither can understand that sex with an ex-wife is either a hard-to-break habit, a convenience, or a reflection of a man's inability to end what is already over.

THE MID-LIFE AFFAIR

By now the mid-life crisis is a familiar fact of life in American culture. The male in middle age, struggling with lost dreams, a stalled career (or one that has peaked and lost its thrill), an emerging pot belly, graying hair, and the inevitable loss of youth may decide that the answer to all his *angst* is an affair, often with a younger woman. Sometimes the feeling of unease and melancholy that can occur at this stage of life gets blamed on the marriage or the wife. And, indeed, some marriages have become all too predictable and stagnant. In addition, studies have shown that communication and companionship decline for each decade of a marriage, so the man and his wife may actually be living congenially in middle age, but without much real zip in the relationship.

All the more reason why a new woman will provide him with a sense of romance that he may yearn for, a feeling of excitement about life that he may have lost as he shouldered the responsibilities of earning a living and raising a family. Particularly if she is younger, a new woman (or several new women) will make him feel that he is still vigorous and "with it"—in other words, young. Some men find it difficult to face the aging of a wife. They may feel that she has lost her attractiveness, but more pertinent may be the fact that her sags and wrinkles remind them that they, too, are aging.

Frequently, men at this stage of life feel they have missed out on sexual experiences, and they have a burning desire to experiment.

Many middle-aged men who have affairs are actually in covert competition with a son. The boy is now an adolescent, and the father, envious of his son's bursting new sexuality, feels the need to prove that the old man is still in the running, too. Even more subterranean a reason for his affair may be the presence of an attractive teenage daughter. It is normal for a man to notice his daughter's new womanly beauty and emerging sexuality, but he doesn't know what to do with the feeling that his daughter has become a sexy young woman. He deflects the whole issue into an affair with a younger woman. On another level, watching their kids in romantic relationships of their own can prompt romantic stirrings in parents. Some men fall in love with their wives again. Others look outside the marriage.

Some men simply feel that they have lost their way in life. Their jobs and lives bore them, although their wives may not. They don't know what to do with the rest of their years. An affair may be part of a larger attempt by a man to create some interest in his life, to explore different parts of his personality in an effort to find himself again.

Affairs at this stage can be dangerous because the sense of rejuvenation and excitement that may accompany illicit romance can seem like love or the way life ought to be, rather than a last sip at the fountain of youth.

For example, one businessman had been happily married until the age of forty-nine, when he began to feel that he was not being fulfilled romantically in his marriage. He still found his wife attractive, but he was yearning for ecstasy, which he felt was absent. He started an extramarital affair. He got very involved with the woman, and in order to be with her he began to tell his wife that he was attending conferences and conventions out of town. He would disappear for days at a time. She became suspicious and eventually discovered his infidelity. The husband begged her forgiveness and told her he would give up the other woman. However, he found he couldn't give up his passionate affair, so he started secretly seeing the woman again.

His wife found out once more and was enraged. They agreed to couples therapy. He insisted that he still loved his wife but he loved the other woman as well. He felt he could not give up the wonderful sense of magical romance that his affair provided. The wife decided to divorce him. He was agitated, couldn't sleep, and finally decided he did not want to lose his wife. He was able to reconcile himself with the thought that he had at least tasted the sweetness of high romance before he died, so he could give it up and go on with his marriage.

Some middle-aged men are bachelors or divorced, and for them the dating game can often be an exercise in proving to themselves that they are still young. For many, this means that as they age, the women they date get younger and younger. Or they may reach forty-five or fifty, but they tell friends who offer to fix them up that their "cut-off age" for women is thirty or thirty-five. They may wear toupees or let whatever hair they have left grow long and then sweep it over a bald spot. A freshly divorced middle-aged man is often treacherous in terms of infidelity. Too many of them have felt sexually confined during their marriages, or that they never had as much sexual experience as they would have liked before marriage. As a result, they covet the freedom to sample whatever wares strike their fancy. They can go wild for a while on the dating scene.

Statistically, the risk of depression increases in middle age. It can be a reaction to the realization that you are never going to become what you dreamed of, that success has not given you the fulfillment you expected, or it can be a response to losses such as youth, teeth, ideals, and parents. Coming to grips with your own mortality, which occurs in middle age, also can be a downer. Interestingly, some men who have been monogamous until this juncture in their lives embark on an affair or a series of affairs in response to depression. It's a misguided effort to cheer themselves up.

HOMOSEXUAL AFFAIRS

Harriet had gone to a meeting of a community organization to which she belonged. She had a headache, and so she decided to return home earlier than she planned. As she entered the house, she heard the sound of low voices in the bedroom. There she found her husband, Henry, and another man hastily dressing. That was the first indication Harriet had that she was married to a bisexual man. After the other man left, Henry asked Harriet if she wanted a divorce. Still stunned, she answered, "No, I love you." Harriet and her husband stayed together for another five years, during which time they had another child, but now that his secret was out, Henry started disappearing more often and finally told Harriet he could no longer stay married—he preferred men to women, and wanted to live with a male lover.

Betty and Lester worked in the same field and had been dating for a year. "We always had such good times together that we finally decided to get married," Betty explained. "After we got an apartment and started entertaining and visiting Lester's friends, I found that all of them were men. Every dinner party we went to was composed of men alone. I felt it was sort of funny, but I didn't specifically identify what was bothering me. Also, as time went on, sex occurred less and less frequently."

Betty continued like this, feeling only dimly bothered, when another incident increased her anxiety. A man who said he used to be Lester's roommate called. Since Lester wasn't home, Betty talked to him. This man announced that he and his new roommate had just split and that he had also lost his job. "Tell Lester I'm coming to stay for a while and that I'll bring my dowry," he said. Betty thought that was a peculiar statement, but again she didn't say anything.

Lester, who had always had a problem with alcohol, started drinking more and more in the company of his ex-roommate, and the two of them began coming home later and later. Betty, disgusted with Lester's drinking and general irresponsibility, decided this marriage wasn't for her. She packed up and left Lester a good-bye letter. Within a short time, Lester ran off to Paris with another man.

"It was only then that I could no longer hide it from myself," says Betty. "I had to admit that Lester was gay."

Secret homosexual affairs are just as apt to happen in single life as in marriage. One of the most heartbreaking stories I know concerns a young woman who was a student at a prominent Ivy League college. She met a fellow student and fell in love with him. They started having sexual relations. She saw a great deal of him and assumed he was not seeing anyone else. What she didn't know was that he was having brief homosexual encounters. How she discovered it is horrifying. After a series of illnesses she found out that she had AIDS. Her boyfriend, a carrier, had infected her.

The exact number of men who have homosexual affairs while in heterosexual relationships is not known. But experts feel that bisexuality is a much more common phenomenon than most people imagine.

Some men, like Lester, have a lifelong history of homosexuality. Some have bisexual inclinations that lead them into relationships with women as well as men. Actor Tyrone Power had two marriages and affairs with other women in addition to an active homosexual life. Many want to marry to have a comfortable family life and children, but intend to carry on their homosexual liaisons secretly. Some marry in order to hide their homosexuality when they are in careers that demand a more conventional life-style. According to biographer Joan Peyser, the conductor-composer Leonard Bernstein's homosexual activities started as a youth, but he saw some of the impediments to his career as a conductor dissipate once he married his wife, Felicia, and became a father, even though he continued his homosexual liaisons through the marriage. Other men are genuinely conflicted. They may have homosexual fantasies but only engage in heterosexual relationships until some time in their lives they are seduced by a man or decide to act out their hidden inclinations.

One man in his fifties was recently arrested for soliciting another man in a bar. He had been married since the age of twenty-five and had fathered three children. Although he was aware of attraction to other men while he was in college, he had completely suppressed his homosexual inclinations. His first attempt at a homosexual relationship, which led to public disgrace, was the only time he had tried to live out his deep-seated, hidden desires.

Many of the women in relationships with these men are genuinely shocked and surprised when the facts come out. Actress Elsa Lancaster admitted that she became psychosomatically deaf for a week as a shock reaction when her husband, the renowned actor Charles Laughton, confessed his homosexuality to her very early in their marriage. Others, if they are honest with themselves, admit that they have had suspicions for a long time, but have denied what they knew. The truth was too threatening to their well-being. For some women, marriage to a basically homosexual man is a perfect solution. These are women who don't have much interest in sex, or who prefer to lead rather distant lives from their husbands. Each leads a separate existence.

One woman in North Carolina, with two children from her marriage to Calvin, a homosexual man, was content with very little sex from the beginning of her relationship. In addition, she and her husband worked out a life-style that they both liked. She lived most of the time in the couple's country house. He lived in their city apartment, where he was free to entertain his male lovers. Neither of them ever openly discussed Calvin's homosexuality, but on some level, both were aware that she knew.

Sometimes a man's homosexuality is out in the open. Marriages like this can be congenial. They may be based on commonality of interests, partnerships in careers, and liking rather than sexual passion. There are well-known theatrical couples like this, whose marriages have lasted a lifetime.

An altogether different category comprises men whose basic orientation is heterosexual, but who have homosexual affairs at certain times of crisis in their lives.

Frequently these crises are connected to their careers. A man whose business is failing, or one who is feeling that he is incompetent at his job, or someone who has been fired, may feel weak and unmasculine. Going after a man sexually is really a symbolic action. It is his attempt to get another man's penis and thus recapture for himself a feeling of masculinity. These are compensatory affairs. There were reports of a spate of homosexual affairs on Wall Street when stock prices plummeted in October of 1987.

Paradoxically, for some men the crisis may be success rather than failure. An example of this is a corporate executive who was promoted into a very important job in his company. He was both elated and frightened. Although he had been working toward this goal for some time, now that he had what he wanted he was overwhelmed. He felt he might not be able to do the job. At this time he started picking up young men at a well-known homosexual haunt in the city where he worked. He didn't know why he did this, since he had been heterosexual all his life. His flings with men didn't solve his problems. Heterosexual affairs that are compensatory in nature never work as solutions to other problems. What did work for this man was time. He began to see that he could do his job and was able to relax. As his anxiety disappeared, so did his homosexual desires.

Some women may not consider a homosexual affair cheating, but rather an act of perversion, a compulsion over which the man has no control, as opposed to a voluntary liaison, which is the way most women think of heterosexual infidelity. For this reason, especially if there are no children involved, there are women who can tolerate homosexual affairs better than heterosexual ones. The infidelity is not experienced as a rejection in favor of a more attractive female. There are cases on record of wives who lived with their husbands' homosexual activities, but insisted on a divorce only when they became involved with other women.

However, because homosexuality is still considered a taboo, other women think it is worse than an affair with a woman, with more shame and humiliation attached to the fact. A good number of women who discover their husbands' homosexual preferences berate themselves for not being enough of a woman. In addition, when there are children, wives worry about the effect on the offspring.

These days, because of AIDS, homosexual affairs are rightfully considered life-threatening if a man continues to sleep with his wife. TV station WCCO in Minneapolis–St. Paul conducted an on-air interview with a former male prostitute who carried the AIDS virus. He claimed that most of his clients were suburban married men. He hoped his appearance on the air would result in some of the men with whom he had sex recognizing him and getting tested for AIDS. There were many frantic calls after the show aired, including one from a woman whose husband had introduced the prostitute to her as a new employee.

If AIDS continues to spread at the predicted rate, it seems likely that more divorces will occur more quickly, once a husband's homosexual affairs are discovered.

NINE

Running from Love

SYDELLE HAS BEEN MARRIED TO PAUL FOR THREE YEARS. Their marriage seemed to be getting better and better. They were making plans to buy a house and have a child. It was shocking and mystifying to Sydelle when she discovered that Paul had begun an affair recently with a co-worker. "We were so happy," she exclaimed over and over again. "Why would he want to get involved with someone else?"

When I asked unfaithful men in interviews why they cheated, they came up with typical reasons such as boredom, unhappiness, sudden opportunity, a chance for romance, sexual variety, fun, drinking, working with an attractive woman. Only one understood and mentioned what experts today consider to be the most important underlying reason of all for infidelity—a problem with intimacy. Infidelity is a strong sign that someone in the relationship is trying to run away emotionally.

When Sydelle and Paul entered couples therapy as a result of his affair, it soon came out that Paul was, indeed, very happy in his relationship with Sydelle, but he was also feeling scared about loving and needing her so much. He felt that there would be no turning back emotionally for him after buying a house and filling it with a child. His affair was a subliminal attempt to create some distance in his relationship with Sydelle, and in that way to soothe his mounting fears as he drew closer and became more and more committed to her.

As in Paul's case, the need to pull back is common in even the happiest of relationships. In fact, the better the relationship, the greater the chance that problems connected with intimacy will crop up. This may seem peculiar unless you understand the dynamics. What's at work here is an odd ratio of anxiety to happiness. For people who can't handle intimacy, the more comfortable, happy, and close the relationship becomes, the more they feel subliminal discomfort, anxiety, or even terror.

Infidelity then becomes a faulty solution. It's a way of relieving anxiety through running; without understanding what is really happening, the single man may find himself overwhelmed by a sudden urge to switch partners or begin another simultaneous relationship. The married man may find another woman irresistible.

Infidelity *always* manipulates distance between partners. In most cases it cools things off; the affair creates more emotional space. However, as I'll show later, infidelity can sometimes do the opposite—it can heat things up between a man and a woman.

DOUBLE TROUBLE

An unconscious fear of intimacy frequently exists side by side with other psychological problems that lead to affairs. When it does, it greatly increases the likelihood of infidelity.

John's case is an example of a dual problem at work. John started an affair soon after his first child was born. His wife, Diane, became all wrapped up in her child, and John resented the fact that she wasn't paying as much attention to him as before. His anger alone could have pushed him into the arms of the attractive co-worker who became his extramarital partner. But that wasn't the only reason for his sudden itch. The birth of his child also made John feel much more committed to the relationship. He felt trapped and overwhelmed by his new responsibilities. So his affair was both a way of expressing his resentment over what he felt to be his wife's neglect, and also an attempt to feel less tied down. Many husbands use affairs as John did—to distance themselves from their responsibilities as family men.

A macho man may have affairs because he assumes the right to screw around to be a male prerogative, but he too may have a hidden agenda. A one-to-one relationship and commitment may also make him feel stifled and trapped. Carousing with other women is acting the way he thinks men should, but, in addition, it helps him deal with an allergy to intimacy, as well.

Men who go compulsively from woman to woman, unable to be faithful to anyone, are often shoring up poor self-images. They reaffirm their desirability by conquest after conquest. However, on top of that, many also have a low tolerance for intimacy, so their sexual escapades, in addition, become an ongoing way to dilute closeness in a primary relationship, or avoid intimacy and commitment altogether.

Women can get very confused by single men who react negatively to intimacy. This is a typical scenario: You find yourself having a great time with a new man. He seems to be responding and sharing in the fun. Perhaps after the best evening together of all, he suddenly stops calling and disappears, or he starts calling and seeing you less often, and you begin to have the sneaky feeling that he is seeing other women. Or he even tells you he is.

This happened to Jane, a computer programmer. She met Arthur through a mutual friend. They hit it off right away. She and Arthur started going out, and each date was wonderful. They joked together and had many interests in common to talk about. When they had sex on their fifth date, it was great, too. Jane was sure that Arthur was having as good a time as she, and she felt the relationship might have a future.

Jane's perceptions were correct. Arthur was enjoying her company. But the more affectionate he felt toward Jane, the more he enjoyed their times together, the more he felt emotionally on edge. As a result, Arthur started backing off. He asked Jane out less often. If she called him, he made excuses for why he couldn't see her. He started dating and sleeping with other women when he was not seeing Jane.

This was part of a pattern for Arthur, but Jane wasn't aware of that. She was bewildered by what was happening. She couldn't figure out what had gone wrong. Was it something she did, she wondered, that offended or turned Arthur off? Was it the fact that her breasts were too small? Had he met someone more attractive to him? Jane didn't realize that the problem was intimacy, and that when closeness causes cabin fever for a man, it creates a no-win situation for a woman. The more he likes her, the more he will have the urge to see other women, create fights to cool things off, or drop her altogether because he finds the relationship too hot to handle emotionally.

One man's story of a love affair illustrates this. "I was really hooked on Ruth, but I was screwing other girls all the time. I would tell her terrible stories. I would go out at· night, telling her I would be back, but sometimes I didn't return. It was a confused situation. Although I said I was in love with her, the screwing around and not showing up sometimes was a way of not getting too involved, because, with her, I would have fallen head over heels, and I couldn't lose that kind of control. I was scared stiff of getting into the thing. At times I felt helpless, I was so sappy, smitten with her."

HOW INFIDELITY CREATES DISTANCE

Affairs also encourage distance because of the tensions they create, certainly when an affair is discovered, but even when the infidelity is hidden. A wife may wonder what the husband does away from home so much and may feel neglected or resentful. She may sense that his attitude toward her has changed, and she is hurt. She may know that sex has become infrequent or that he doesn't talk to her much. She becomes preoccupied and suspicious. She may become aware that he has made passes at neighbors or friends. She feels humiliated by him and enraged.

A girlfriend may notice that the man she has been seeing isn't calling her as much as before. She wonders if there are other women. She may hear that he was seen with someone else. She is devastated.

A woman may have stumbled onto proof of cheating. She is afraid to confront her man. She is withholding her emotions from him.

The man knows he is keeping important things from a woman when he is leading a secret life. He becomes evasive or uncommunicative. A philanderer may come to think of his wife as the enemy. She is keeping him from doing what he wants to do more openly. And he may be afraid of her. What if she finds out?

The doubt, insecurity, anger, fear, or confusion and secrecy implicit in the situation, whether it is held in or expressed openly, can make spouses feel separated from one another.

Even when a partner refuses to recognize the signals of an affair, and instead walls herself off from knowing, it causes emotional distance. The wife or girlfriend is afraid to broach certain subjects for fear of opening doors she wants to keep tightly shut.

SEX WITH THE OTHER WOMAN AND INTIMACY

Fear of intimacy can add to the luster of sex in an outside relationship. When a man cheats, his relationship with his lover is often emotionally shallow or brief through circumstance or by design. Time together with the lover (or lovers) is limited. He may confine his sexual encounters to one-night stands or very short flings. He may monitor his emotions during a longer affair to make sure he doesn't get involved beyond a certain point.

"If I start feeling something for a woman," explained one husband, "I cut the relationship off immediately." When the call upon emotions is thus reduced or avoided altogether, the anxiety that is produced by close or committed relationships does not get invoked. The result? In limited or more casual relationships without much emotional involvement, men frequently feel freer to enjoy sex.

For too many people in our society, closeness and sex are antagonistic. If they are close or committed, they can't be sexy. If they are sexy, they can't be close or committed. It's a developmental issue. The more a person can join love and sex, the more emotionally mature that individual is. When a man (or woman) can't make the two work together, it means he (or she) has failed to get beyond a certain stage of psychological growth.

Men who have a problem in this regard tend to divide their emotional and sexual needs between two or more women in one of the following ways:

He Can Feel Close to a Partner, but Not Sexual, and Sexual but Not Close with a Lover

Typically, a man like this can live with a woman or relate intimately to her, but once he does, he starts to feel turned off. This leads him into sex with other women. He can be turned on in his affairs, but only if he doesn't become emotionally close to the other woman, or have to live with her.

Tom was having an affair with Susan without his wife, Karen, knowing about it. Although Tom felt that Karen was his best friend, someone he could always confide in and count on, he found sex with Susan much more exciting.

Tom told his wife he was going to a four-day convention in Hawaii and would stop for two days in San Francisco on the way back, to conduct some other business. It was a ruse to sneak in a week-long vacation with Susan. He felt guilty toward Karen, but both he and Susan had been looking forward to the first extended time they would have together.

Tom rented a cottage at the beach for the two of them. As the week wore on, he and Susan got to know each other better through long conversations. Susan cooked, since Tom didn't know how. Tom was surprised to find himself feeling less and less turned on. He was relieved when the week was up and he could return home to Karen. Tom couldn't join sex with closeness in his marriage, and he could be sexual with his lover, but only until they spent time together getting closer in a somewhat domestic situation, at which time his sexual feelings dried up.

He Can't Feel Either Close or Sexual in a
Committed Relationship, but Can Feel Both with a Lover

A man like this is clammed up, emotionally inaccessible, and only minimally sexual or completely asexual at home. Unlike the man above, who can share his feelings but not sex with a partner, this man can't give her either. Although he has a sense of commitment to his mate, he can feel closer to a lover. He is able to reveal himself more, and feel sexier, in an affair. This kind of man can open up in situations where there is less sustained contact and where he feels that less emotional demands are placed upon him.

He may mistake what is happening in his affair (keeping intimacy separate from commitment) for love. If, for example, he leaves his wife for the other woman, you can be sure, once they marry, that soon he will stop talking to her and retreat into work or other things that will make him as emotionally inaccessible to wife number two as he was to wife number one. No matter how hot and heavy sex was while they were having their affair, that will gradually fade out of the picture too, leaving the woman confused.

This happened to a stockbroker in San Jose, California, who left his first wife for the woman who became his second wife. He is now living an estranged existence with number two, although they were close and passionate during their illicit affair. He has persuaded her to live in their country home, supposedly because it is a better environment for the children. He sees his wife only on weekends. During the week he lives in their city apartment. He is having an emotional, sexy romance with a third woman.

He Can Be Very Sexual, but
He Has No Feelings for Any Woman

This type of man can't be emotionally close to anyone. He is as inaccessible to a partner as he is to the various lovers who float through his life. He is capable, however, of being a sexy guy in bed. For him, sex is a substitute for any kind of closeness.

Many men like this are workaholics. They like the fact that emotions are not part of the work world, and they don't want to bother with them in their private world, either. Although wives are often part of the package in these men's lives—they make their working operation smoother by providing them with a service station from which to sally forth each day—they are really not much concerned with the wife personally. The same is true of their affairs. They may like sex or feel it is a necessary outlet, but the women they have their affairs with are almost faceless bodies. Men like this are apt to be chronic philanderers because they find they can have sex in brief affairs without emotional entanglements.

THE SEARCH FOR THE PERFECT WOMAN

A phobia about intimacy can be behind the inability of some single men to settle down with one woman. The man is sure he is looking for someone with whom to spend the rest of his life. He goes from woman to woman, searching for an ideal that he can't ever seem to find.

George is like this. He yearns for a woman he can love and marry. A lively, intelligent man, over the course of a year George meets many females to whom he is attracted. He starts dating them and he likes many women at first. But after seeing them for several weeks or months he begins to notice little flaws. This woman is too greedy, that woman has big thighs, another has eyes that are too close together, still another is not passionate enough.

There is always something that bothers George and makes him start looking around again and dating others. He thinks he is searching for the perfect woman, but what is really happening is that as soon as George starts to feel close or attached, he becomes uncomfortable and anxious. He does not recognize this on a conscious level, however. His anxiety, instead, gets translated into nitpicking. He starts to see bad points in the woman that went unnoticed before his phobia about intimacy and commitment came into play.

Frank, a computer expert in Dallas, is also looking for an ideal woman with whom he can settle down. The only trouble is, he spends all his time and energy trying to get woman after woman into bed. Because he really isn't looking beyond immediate sexual goals, he ends up with women who submit to his sexual demands easily, but don't have the other qualities he seeks. Frank is always feeling disappointed in his experiences. He maintains that they are shallow, which, indeed, is the case, since the only basis for his relationships is sex. If, by chance, he occasionally meets a woman he likes or enjoys in other ways, he always finds something wrong with her, or he manages to do something that will drive her away. Frank is bored by all the women in his life, although many of his sexual relationships last for years. No matter how long he sees someone, he always continues to think she is not up to his standards.

Frank is not rude to women. He enjoys pleasant times with his dates, and in relationships that persist there is an attitude of minor friendship. But underneath it all there is no emotional attachment to anyone. He tells the women he sees regularly not to expect commitment or fidelity, but many of them get their signals crossed. Despite his warnings, since they see him consistently over a long period of time, they begin to think there is more to the relationship than really exists. After a while these misguided women get angry that Frank is still seeing other women, that the affair is not developing as they would like, and finally they stop seeing Frank. Their departure does not make much of a dent on him.

There were two women over the years with whom Frank became more interested and involved, a wife and a girlfriend. With the girlfriend he had trouble functioning sexually. With the wife he lost all sexual desire. This is not uncommon among men who fear intimacy. In relationships of any length or depth, they become disinterested in sex or develop other sexual troubles. With women they don't care about, they can be satyrs.

Some single men who are afraid of closeness have a pattern of intercourse with women they don't care about and completely platonic friendships with women they can communicate with on a more intimate level. They wonder why they can't get it together in one woman.

Others may reject all the women who are interested in them, dismissing them as boring or defective. They fall only for women who don't want them or who are unavailable because they are married or live three thousand miles away.

How Couples Avoid Closeness

In a relationship where the fear of intimacy is one-sided, it becomes a game of hide-and-seek. If it is the husband who wants more closeness, he keeps after the wife. He wants to spend time with her, share his feelings, bring up emotional issues. She is always evading him. She's busy with the kids, with the housework, with her job. She has community meetings to go to. She only wants to talk about practical issues, or whether they should go shopping at the mall. She never discusses feelings. Or just when he feels he is getting somewhere and some closeness is developing, she gets angry at something or starts a fight, or she gets hurt and starts sulking. He is always trying to get more from her than she is willing to give. He finally gets tired of the whole thing and feels angry and deprived. In some cases he starts an affair to get the emotions he yearns for from someone else.

More often it's the other way around. It's the man who doesn't want to deal with anything emotional. He resists closeness or tenderness (except perhaps during sex). At home he sits in front of the TV or reads his newspaper or works on papers from the office. She is always trying to get him to speak to her, to be more affectionate or expressive, to spend more time with her. He resists her efforts and begins to feel crowded and pressured by her. Her attempts to reach him are experienced as a threat and an invasion, which may even make him hostile. She feels hurt and rejected. He is puzzled. What does she want from me? Whatever I do, she wants more. A casual affair or some one-night stands can seem to bring relief from the emotional pressure at home for a man like this.

For some couples, it's a mutual problem. If two people have the same need for distance and they can maintain it on a fairly constant level, they can lead relatively calm lives. Rather than communicating, they may watch TV or play golf, tennis, or bridge, or hang out at the country club. They may arrange to spend most of their leisure time with other couples so that they don't have to be alone. They may lead relatively separate lives, each pursuing his or her own interests. For example, one woman goes to the opera and art exhibits with female friends and male business associates. Her husband hates art and opera. He likes to play poker with his cronies and enjoys working late.

The only common meeting ground for couples with distinctly separate interests may be the children whose welfare concerns them both. Or their bond may be based on maintaining a certain life-style, with discussions centering about material acquisitions—what home should they buy, what car should they drive? Nothing really personal gets discussed.

More and more often in our world, distance between two people is maintained by frantic work schedules in two-career marriages. The lack of time alone together is often compounded by the demands of kids, jogging or workouts at the gym, and the need to see relatives or friends and run errands on weekends.

For couples who create little time for interaction or communication, sexual interest often atrophies. The partners either give up on sex, have it only occasionally, or have affairs, often sandwiched in somewhere during their workdays.

Sometimes wide-open space is created through acrimony, bitterness, or hostility. Again, intimacy issues may be a hidden ingredient. People who feel uncomfortable with closeness often unconsciously choose partners with whom they are doomed to be incompatible. Staying in these marriages assures both partners that closeness will never occur.

Most often you see the issue of intimacy played out in a dance of advance-and-retreat by couples who want to be close but can't. They each have a boundary that, when crossed, creates underground anxiety. These partners will start to draw close, but when one of their comfort zones is invaded, something will happen to break the intimacy. A fight will break out, one partner will hurl an accusation at the other or become critical, or one will become busy with work or a hobby. The couple will pull apart and will feel comfortable that way for a while, but then they will start to yearn for more close contact again. They will draw together until once again they reach the invisible point where discomfort and anxiety starts. Then they will pull away again. Their life together is lived in this back-and-forth pattern, and often, as a result, there is a great deal of turmoil in the relationship.

In single life, this game of advance-and-retreat results in turbulent courtships in which one partner is always chasing, the other running away. She wants more closeness and commitment; he resists. At some point he weakens and starts to respond. Now it is the woman's turn to run, which makes him want to pursue. They take turns advancing, then backing off. When fear of intimacy is mutual, courtships can be marked by fights, separations in which each person starts to see other people, and plans to live together or marry that get canceled and then reinstated, time and time again.

TRAPPED BETWEEN TWO WOMEN

When a man finds himself running back and forth between two women—enmeshed in two love affairs that he can't end, or caught between a wife and a lover—it is often a subliminal way of avoiding complete closeness and commitment to either woman. On a conscious level, however, the man may have other excuses that he thinks are valid. The single man says, "I love them both. I can't choose between them." The married man says, "I can't leave my wife because of the kids," "We don't have enough money to get divorced," "I would get excommunicated," or perhaps, "I would lose the election."

What can complicate this is the fact that, because of psychological problems, a man also frequently sandwiches himself between two or more women because he can't integrate all he wants from a woman in one person. He can't be truly close to one partner because he must split his needs between women. This woman has one set of qualities, that woman has another.

In cases like this, women are not seen as whole people, but rather as projections of certain qualities the man either likes or hates. In marriage, the husband may flee from his wife's bad traits to the mistress's good ones. Or maybe he bounces back to the wife from the mistress because she has something the girlfriend doesn't. For men who have an unconscious need to split in this way, dividing themselves between two (or more) women is actually more of a psychological necessity than a choice.

CHOOSING ONE

Staying with the Original Partner

Some men get so pressured by the women in this kind of situation that they ultimately are forced into a choice. They may decide to stay with you. However, unless they have solved the problems that interfere with intimacy, subliminal anxiety will return. They will start to get antsy in the recommitted relationship, and sooner or later they will either call up the old girlfriend or find a new one.

One advertising executive, who entered therapy because he wanted to reaffirm his marriage after years of affairs, was feeling very itchy. He told the therapist, "Maybe it could work out if I could at least phone her [his current lover] every night." Interestingly, it is not so much the sex as knowing they have another woman out there that is important to many men who are unfaithful. The other woman is their emotional escape hatch, no matter how little they actually see her. A married stockbroker has managed to see his girlfriend only once or twice every year for the past five years. He talks to her every six weeks or so. He fantasizes a lot about sex with her. This is really enough of an emotional buffer for him to be able to feel comfortable in his marriage.

In the case of the man who thought he could get by with a nightly telephone call, his therapist pointed out the emotional distancing that would be caused by his actions. His loyalties would still be somewhat divided, and his wife would resent his calls.

Leaving for the Other Woman

Some men finally decide to leave and go with the lover. It is predictable that intimacy problems will start again, with the other woman, once the man starts living with her. For example, Harold and Bettina had been having an affair for eighteen years. They felt they were in love. Harold, certain that Bettina was the perfect woman for him, swore he would leave his wife if only Bettina would leave her husband. Bettina couldn't do that, but in the eighteenth year of their clandestine relationship, Bettina's husband had a heart attack and died. Harold immediately did what he said he would if Bettina was free. He left his wife and moved in with Bettina. Two months of living together undid the fantasy of love that had existed for nearly two decades. They couldn't get along. Harold had to move out. He started wooing his wife again.

If a man actually weds his mistress, he often finds that, once the new marriage is established, the old pattern reasserts itself. He starts feeling dimly claustrophobic in the one-to-one situation, and his response is to start cheating on the new wife. Soon he finds himself involved in another hot and heavy affair that has him shuttling once more between two loves.

How Affairs Can Heat Up Your Relationship

It's odd, but sometimes when a man really cares for a woman, an affair may help him keep the relationship alive. Some men regard the wife as a foe, once an affair is in progress—she is the disciplinarian who would want to clip his wings or cut off another part of his anatomy if she found out what he was up to. Men who regard their wives as their punitive consciences become aloof and distant in their infidelities. However, for another kind of man, an outside relationship allows intimacy to be dispersed so that he is able to be more giving or more sexual with the mate than he would be otherwise. Although I have found that this can happen at any stage in a relationship, one study found this to be particularly true in older marriages. The husbands in these marriages claimed that affairs increased emotional closeness and sexual satisfaction.

Sam, a dentist in Maine, illustrates this kind of paradoxical solution to the fear of intimacy. I asked him when he started having affairs in his marriage. He laughed and confessed that he had had a sexual encounter the night before his wedding—which, incidentally, is when many men with intimacy problems feel intense panic. "My affairs have kept me from feeling trapped," he explained. "I can be more attentive, more loving at home. I don't know what would happen if I couldn't have them. I am always careful not to wear myself out when I'm with another woman so that I can make love to my wife that night. I don't want to deprive her."

Some unfaithful husbands have confessed to purposely not having a climax and emission with their mistresses so they could go home and make love to their wives.

"If I came home and didn't have my wife, I would feel guilty," explained one man.

This kind of solution is more complicated than it appears, however, because at the same time that the affair allows the man to feel happier and more giving to his wife, it is also distancing, since there is an important part of the man's life that is being kept hidden. When something has to be kept secret, whole areas of conversation and the revelation of certain feelings are also assiduously avoided.

INCREASED CLOSENESS AFTER YOU KNOW

Affairs sometimes actually warm up a relationship after the cat is out of the bag, when the man has been caught or confesses. A certain number of men have affairs as an unconscious tactic to pull an aloof wife closer— which is what happens when the wife discovers what he has been up to. But whether that is the case or not, after disclosure, many couples who have not communicated fully in a long time may start talking to each other about their feelings and issues in the relationship that have been neglected. In the midst of the *Sturm und Drang* they begin reaching each other emotionally again.

There is a danger, however, that this end-of-the-affair honeymoon could make things too close for comfort for one or both. As Dr. Frank Pittman, a family therapist in Atlanta, wryly notes, "The danger of bringing an affair into the open is not that the infidel becomes more likely to leave, but that the infidel becomes more likely to stay and try to get close." If the newfound intimacy becomes too close for comfort, one or both may start to back off unless one of them recognizes the intimacy issues at work and intervenes.

WHERE DOES FEAR OF INTIMACY COME FROM?

Causes of fear of intimacy vary, but here are some of the more common ones:

Men who can't get close have often been raised by parents who were never close to each other and/or were very emotionally unresponsive to the child. This became the model for future relationships.

Also, early experiences, such as losing a parent, can create a fear of being abandoned that makes a person afraid of getting too close to one person. In the case of Albert, a North Carolina shopkeeper, fear of abandonment

came from being raised in a series of foster homes that he
always had to leave just as he was beginning to care for
the new family. As an adult he was delighted to get
married and have a family of his own, but he soon felt
compelled to have a number of affairs. Divorced because
of his repeated infidelities, he now lives with the woman
he originally hired as his housekeeper. He has sex with her
once a week. The rest of the week he has affairs with other
women. Albert finds it intolerable to stay with one woman
only. He is afraid of being left all alone.

Sometimes the fear of intimacy is caused by a poor
self-image. The man feels, on some level, that if he lets
someone get too close, his defects will be revealed and he
will be rejected.

Other people have had experiences while growing up
that have made them unable to become truly intimate
because they can't trust anyone. Men who were ignored,
abused, or used only as ornaments by parents, for example, could find trust a problem.

The fear of being overwhelmed or suffocated by a
partner is another common reason behind fear of intimacy. Studies have shown that this is particularly prevalent
among men who have had overinvolved, critical, or
domineering mothers. In these men's psyches, every woman has the potential of overwhelming them as Mother did.
Men who fear suffocation often react to marriage as a
prison in which they are trapped. The wife becomes, in
their eyes, their jailer. Single men who suffer from this
may start to feel stifled or crowded once a relationship
continues past a certain point. This effectively keeps them
from being able to commit themselves.

For many men, truly intimate relationships become
threatening because they entail a certain amount of
dependence on the partner. Dependency is a troubling
issue for men in our culture because independence is
considered a masculine trait and dependence a feminine
one. Some dependency is normal and healthy in a good
relationship, but when men start to feel it they often think
that they are losing their autonomy or, even worse, that
they are placing themselves in the partner's power.

In addition, dependency in a love relationship echoes
the time in infancy when the man relied on his mother for
everything. Dependency, because of this early memory,
may be unconsciously associated with helplessness.

For all of these reasons, when a man feels close to a woman and that he needs her, he also may feel weakened, feminized, and infantilized. Sensing his masculinity in peril, he pulls away and creates distance, perhaps through an affair, to reassert autonomy, strength, and virility.

CHANGING INTIMACY NEEDS

Sometimes the mid-life affairs that I have already described start because a man who has previously wanted to be distant in his marriage finds his needs changing. His life experiences have taught him to overcome innate fears, or he is willing to struggle with painful issues. Or perhaps, like some men at mid-life, he has matured and his needs for affiliation have increased. He finds he is ready for more intimacy. Frequently, however, he has selected a wife who, because of her own problems with closeness, does not want things to change. She resists his attempts to draw closer, to solve the problems that have kept them apart. He ends up having an affair to find increased emotional depth and responsiveness. This kind of affair is dangerous because if a man discovers what he is looking for with someone else, he may find it intolerable to continue living at home without it.

When a problem with intimacy exists, you can help break down barriers between you and your partner by employing the suggestions in the section on "Creating Healing Communications." In Chapter 14 on pages 249–250 you will find another section that will help solve differing intimacy needs between your partner and yourself.

It is essential, too, that you learn how unwitting collusions are formed between partners to prevent intimacy, and how infidelity fits into this. The chapter that follows will help you to see how this occurs.

TEN

Do You Want Him to Be Unfaithful?

DO YOU WANT YOUR MAN TO SLEEP WITH ANOTHER WOMAN? It seems shocking, but, in a hidden way, many women do—even those who are devastated by a man's infidelity.

Take Wendy. When she entered therapy she was a mess—enraged, saddened, frightened. She had just discovered that her husband had been secretly seeing another woman for a year. She had been married only three years.

"What were you getting out of the affair?" her therapist asked her. Wendy was startled. "Me? Don't you have it wrong, don't you mean what was *he* getting out of the affair?"

"No," her therapist persisted. "You. Think about it and tell me your thoughts when you come back next time."

At first, Wendy was angry at the very idea that she had benefited from what she regarded as her husband's treachery. But she continued to mull the idea over, and at her next session she said, "You know, I hate to admit it, but there were advantages to me. I was free to see my mother and sister and friends on the nights he didn't come home—he hates my mother and sister, and I didn't have to cook for him so often. He is a very picky eater, and cooking for him is a real pain. Nothing is ever the way he likes it. I don't like cooking much, anyway. Besides, I didn't have to rush home from work when he told me he was working

142

late. I could wait until the rush hour was over. It was nice coming home on a train that wasn't crowded."

Two sessions later, after exploring the matter more, Wendy went even further. "I guess I did want him to be in an affair," she began. Then her eyes filled with tears. "But I don't want him to be in one anymore. How can I get him to end it?"

Her therapist suggested she tell her husband the same thing that she had just told her.

Wendy followed the suggestion, and after a long conversation the next day, her husband said he was going to tell his lover that it was all over. Wendy suddenly went into a panic. She called her therapist and blurted out, "It's only been a day since I told him. I never expected he would act so fast!"

Wendy's husband lived up to his word. He visited his lover for the last time and ended the affair.

Was Wendy happy? You would think she would be, wouldn't you? The terrible truth is that she went into a depression. She was so depressed, in fact, that she was in a stupor a good deal of the time. Her depression made her muted and emotionally unavailable to her husband. Wendy needed something to maintain the distance between her husband and herself. The affair had previously done it for her; now the depression was acting as a substitute.

Because Wendy couldn't cope with closeness, the affair, on a hidden level, was to her liking. Without the space it provided, Wendy felt threatened, overwhelmed.

This is not an unusual case. Many women, even those who feel agonized by the discovery, are willing partners to their husbands' affairs. Infidelity could be the result of an unconscious collusion between you and your mate.

In subliminal cooperations of this type, there is generally a hidden trade-off. The husband is allowed to be unfaithful, with whatever psychological payoff is involved for him, in return for something that is of advantage to the wife. Although circumstances vary with the marriage, many women end up making trade-offs around similar issues. Here are some of the most common.

COLLUSIONS ABOUT CLOSENESS

Like Wendy, many people find that their relationships with their spouses are more tolerable with outside relationships than without them.

Jessica, for example, was hysterical when the police called her to tell her that her husband, Martin, had been beaten up by the boyfriend of a woman to whom he had been making advances at a downtown bar.

Although they had never discussed it, Jessica knew on some level that Martin had been playing around for some time. Two years before, he had even given her herpes. He and she recognized the existence of the disease, but never discussed where it had come from. Jessica had never confronted Martin about his activities.

When the account of Martin's beating hit the local newspaper, Jessica felt confused and humiliated. It had become public, and she would have to acknowledge Martin's philandering to herself, to her parents, who kept calling, to the lawyer she was considering seeing, to Martin, and, as it turned out, to a therapist.

In a depressed condition she arrived at the therapist's office with her husband. Martin played around, but he did not want to lose Jessica. He came because she was threatening to divorce him. All along, Jessica, on some level, felt that divorce would be her only alternative if she acknowledged Martin's infidelities.

At first Martin refused to own up to his extensive extramarital history, but gradually he came to see the wisdom of revelation in the context of the couple's therapy. Out poured a story of many affairs and occasional orgies. He also included details of his background. His father had been a chronic philanderer. His mother had practically had her face rubbed in it, but had continued to deny the possibility of adultery to herself and her relatives. Martin opened up, for the first time, about his insecurities as a man. He felt he needed his affairs and that he probably was incapable of monogamy.

Martin told Jessica more about himself than he had ever done before in their relationship. Through the therapy they became intimate friends for the first time. After deciding to stay together, Martin began spending more and more time with Jessica. He enjoyed some of their new-found closeness. He stopped taking many of the business trips he had used as occasions to indulge in affairs. Instead of being grateful for this new attention, however, Jessica began to feel crowded. She preferred life the way it had been before the police called her. Then she could be with her children mostly by herself during the week and spend time with Martin on weekends when he stayed home.

Jessica encouraged her husband to start traveling again. She suggested he might be neglecting his business. Martin once more took to the road and soon was having affairs not only while traveling but on home turf, too. They kept him out of the house two or three nights a week. Martin and Jessica never talked about his absences, although both knew what was going on. Martin's escapades suited them both, as long as they didn't become public again. They helped Martin feel more virile, and they provided Jessica with the space she needed to feel emotionally comfortable. Of course, if Martin was not discreet enough and a new affair became public, Jessica would feel as depressed, outraged, betrayed as before.

Patty is a single woman who supports her lover's infidelities, although she would vehemently deny this. She has been having an affair with Gregory for over five years. Although she sees Gregory two nights a week, she is aware that in between he is with other women. She complains to her friends and periodically breaks up with Gregory, but always goes back to him. She can't find anybody she likes as much, she says. During their separations she has gone out with men who are attracted to her. She has found each one to be boring or a wimp.

Patty thinks, on a conscious level, that if she just hangs in there, Gregory will give up the others and marry her. Unconsciously, however, the relationship with Gregory suits her fine, just the way it is. Patty is afraid of a more intimate relationship. By continuing to go with Gregory, she can blame him for the lack of commitment and avoid having to face the truth that she is just as afraid of closeness as he is. Gregory is happy with the arrangement. He likes women. He likes Patty. He likes having someone steady in his life. He has found this to be a problem because women generally get fed up with his lack of constancy and leave. Patty puts up with it and stays, so Gregory can have his cake and eat it too.

THE BOY/MOMMY COLLUSION

Many collusions that encourage affairs have as their basis the desire to keep established roles going in the relationship. This is certainly true of Cynthia and Peter. They met in the late sixties in Chicago. Peter was a hippie and an artist. Cynthia was a flower child and a designer. Peter and Cynthia fell in love and married. As the years passed, Cynthia got a job and became very successful as a designer of furniture. Peter painted a little but played a lot. Cynthia supported them both in increasingly handsome style. She had given up her flower-child image long ago. Now she was an ambitious, responsible, successful businesswoman. Peter, however, continued to be charming, vague, and playful. He played the part of the undependable boy to her role of responsible mother as the relationship evolved.

In recent years, Peter has fallen in love with other women four times. Each time he has confessed the affair to Cynthia, proclaimed his great love for the other woman, and moved out. He lives with his mistresses between three and five months. He then falls out of love and, contrite, comes back to Cynthia and begs forgiveness. He promises to be good in the future. Cynthia is always upset and devastated by Peter's infidelities, but no matter how many times he breaks his promises and is unfaithful again, she always takes him back. She continues to support him and allows him to play his days away.

Cynthia and Peter's collusion is based on maintaining his role as the charming, irresponsible boy and her role as the good, understanding mother who can be counted on to take care of him and forgive him for his vagaries and escapades. Cynthia is collaborating in Peter's affairs. If Cynthia refused to take Peter back, she would lose her little boy. She would be left with no one to whom she could play bountiful mother. If Peter didn't have his affairs, he could not test his wife/mother's love and he couldn't enjoy the bliss of being taken back into his good mommy's arms and forgiven for being such a bad boy. Peter's infidelities work for both of them.

Another variation on the boy/mommy collusion occurs when the man is a defiant rebel boy and his wife is the strict, punishing mother.

Gloria and Herb play this out in their marriage. Gloria is a rather cold, critical woman. If she can find fault with someone, she will. Her barbed remarks do not spare her husband, Herb. In contrast to Gloria, Herb is outgoing, friendly, rather wild.

Herb and Gloria belong to a local country club. Around the pool, on the tennis court, or at the bar, Herb is always trying to seduce women. His attempts often take place within sight of Gloria. He is away from her many evenings, a situation that always provokes a barrage of criticism from Gloria, but her hostile remarks are always about something else—not Herb's affairs. Herb continues to carry on outrageously with other women, but he sticks with Gloria. His seductions are a way of defying his strict mother/wife and provoking the disapproval and punishment he wants from her, owing to a deep psychological need that stems from childhood. Gloria will not confront Herb directly about his dalliances, because she fears he may leave her or she may have to leave him, and she would lose the role she plays in the relationship, which gives her great power over Herb. She and he are locked into an interplay in which she is the critical overseer and he is the willful, insubordinate rebel boy, roles they both want to continue, so no end is in sight for Herb's affairs.

STAYING DEPENDENT

Often the roles that are being maintained are based on dependency and domination. In a case like this, the woman is afraid of raising a rumpus or even of consciously knowing what may be painfully obvious, because it might mean a rupture in the relationship and she is afraid she can't take care of herself. Frequently she is married to a man who is a take-charge type. He likes to feel in control, and so he does nothing throughout the relationship to make her feel more competent, independent, or able to care for herself. On the contrary, many husbands reinforce a woman's sense of helplessness and fear with remarks like "What would you do without me?"

When fear of being unattached keeps you maintaining the illusion that nothing is wrong, it can have a hidden cost. Joan's case illustrates the kind of price that gets paid. Joan and her husband, John, moved to Los Angeles when his company transferred him there. Not long after they settled there, John began mentioning a fellow executive at his company, with whom he had become friendly. The co-worker was a woman. He invited this woman to gatherings at their home and then he started asking her over by herself. Joan felt funny about playing hostess to this woman. For some reason she didn't like her and told John so. John said the woman was really very nice, and that since they worked closely together, he wanted to entertain her. He insisted on inviting her over. Joan, as she always did, complied with John's wishes, even though she still felt uneasy in this woman's presence.

A year and a half after their move to Los Angeles, John was transferred again, to a city in the South. Joan was relieved. She was sure the woman was now out of the picture. One day, not long after arriving at their new locale, Joan went with John to a party given by one of his new co-workers. Joan was startled to find at the party the woman she thought had been left behind. She discovered that the woman had applied for a transfer and was now living in the same city. Joan was so upset that she literally broke down right there and then. She fainted, then started crying uncontrollably, without being able to explain why. Her husband asked her, "What's wrong?" She kept saying, "I don't know." He rushed her home and put her into the care of a psychiatrist within a few days. Neither could understand Joan's episode at the party. Both Joan and John felt she must be going crazy.

Joan was driving herself crazy by trying so hard to deny the obvious: her husband and his female co-worker were having an affair. She could no longer contain her emotions about this, but she also could not allow herself to name the reason for her upset. This inner conflict accounted for the seemingly unexplainable fainting and crying.

Joan insisted on hiding things from herself because

she was frightened of the consequences if the affair was to be acknowledged. Perhaps her husband would leave her, and then she couldn't survive. While in therapy, she was guided toward more independence. Her psychiatrist started her thinking about getting a job. At this point her husband decided that she had had enough therapy and refused to let her continue. John wanted to be able to do essentially whatever he wanted, which included his affair. He could get away with it as long as his wife continued to feel she couldn't survive without him. In her occasional "spells," which continued, she could vent her feelings without accusing him of anything.

Many, many women who are afraid of being on their own collaborate in their husbands' extramarital adventures by (1) refusing to acknowledge what they really know and (2) not confronting him about it. In this way they allow an affair, or many affairs, to go on indefinitely and with impunity.

FEAR OF GOING BACK INTO THE SINGLES SCENE

Charlotte has been going out with Warren for four years. She sees him once or twice every week or two. Charlotte is crazy about Warren, and he makes her crazy because he does not return her love and she is sure he sees other women. They have such good times when they are together that Charlotte forgets the pain she feels between times, wondering when Warren will call, or *if* he will, wondering if he will break his date as he sometimes does, wondering who those other women are whom he seems to prefer. Warren likes Charlotte, but he has no intention of making a commitment to her. He likes to play the field.

Charlotte knows this, but she refuses to believe it fully. She hopes, unrealistically, that if she stays in the relationship long enough, eventually Warren will give up the others and become hers for good. Meanwhile, she continues to see him, never complains when they are together for fear of driving him away, continues to try to impress and please him, spending too much on clothing, makeup, and food for the elaborate meals she cooks for him in an attempt to show him what a terrific wife she would be. Warren gets the best of Charlotte, but Charlotte

does not get what she wants—fidelity and commitment—
no matter how hard she tries. In effect, Charlotte is
cooperating in her own fate—to be tied to an unfaithful
man in a go-nowhere relationship. Her payoff? She doesn't
have to go out and try to find another man. Charlotte
needs to feel attached. Without a man she is lost. She is
sure that if she gives up Warren she will never find anyone
again, at least anyone as attractive as he. She puts up with
Warren's infidelities and lack of commitment because she
is scared stiff of having to go back into the singles scene.

Many women hunting for a mate are involved with
men who won't commit to them, don't love them, and see
other women. Although the relationship makes them
miserable, they stay with it, don't put limits on what they
will accept from the man, and thus become collaborators
in what is going on. Like Charlotte, they would rather be
partially attached in an unhappy relationship than out on
their own.

SEXUAL COLLUSIONS

Lea does not like sex, Jason does. At first, in their
marriage, Jason kept trying to make love to Lea, but Lea
kept refusing him. Jason finally decided to give up. He
went elsewhere for what he needed.

On evenings when he was seeing a lady friend, Jason
would call home and tell Lea he was working late. Jason
has had, for years, a series of short-lived affairs. There is
always another woman in his life. Lea has accepted all of
Jason's absences and excuses over the years without a
murmur. She never questions his whereabouts. The truth
is that on some level Lea knows that her husband plays
around. If it came out in the open, she would be furious,
sad, angry. But as long as it remains hidden, Lea is
relieved. She doesn't have to be bothered for sex. This kind
of collusion, in which a wife covertly encourages a
husband's infidelities to avoid his sexual demands, is very
common.

In Allison's case, her husband Sanford's wild demands
in the bedroom far exceeded her own desires. Her temper-
ament was much cooler, and she was content with a

couple of standard positions and silence. Her husband wanted every conceivable kind of variation, exchange of erotic fantasies, experimentation with kink. He thought he wanted his cool, contained wife to be wilder, and yet he had married her for her ladylike, elegant, aloof manner, which, when combined with her good looks, made him think of her as an ideal wife. When she turned out to be as ladylike in bed as out, Sanford decided he had to find his wildness elsewhere. He started having affairs within the first year of his marriage.

Allison was just as happy not to have to contend with pressure from Sanford for more kinky sex, or variations she didn't like. He was happy to be married to Allison, whom he respected. She was the kind of mother to his children that he wanted—someone refined and cultured. Once, Sanford forgot himself and started telling Allison about his sexual fantasy of a threesome while they were making love. Allison muttered, "Don't tell me your fantasies," and added as an aside, "I guess what I don't know won't hurt me."

Sanford was sure Allison did not know about his affairs. "I was very careful," he told me. Allison blotted out any thought that Sanford was unfaithful, and yet that statement gave her away. She knew, but didn't want to know, because Sanford's extramarital involvements took the heat off her sexually. And the truth for Sanford was that he didn't want Allison to be wild, because then he wouldn't respect her. He needed his wife to be cool and elegant and his girlfriends to be firebrands. His affairs solved problems for both of them.

Some women have been forced into unwilling recognition of their husbands' infidelities because someone has let the cat out of the bag. Sometimes it is a desperate or vengeful other woman as in Frieda and Gilbert's case.

Frieda and Gilbert had never been sexually compatible. He wanted a lot of sex, while she wanted the barest minimum. He liked oral sex, but she found it disgusting. Gilbert started his first affair within the first two years of his marriage. Sometime in the seventh year, Frieda picked up the phone and found herself talking to a woman who said she was having an affair with her husband. The woman hoped that the call would mess things up enough so that Gilbert would leave Frieda for her. It didn't work out that way. Frieda never told Gilbert about the call. She continued to pretend that nothing was wrong. She went on accepting Gilbert's late nights out as work-related.

Now, in the eighteenth year of their marriage, Gilbert is frightened by the possibility of catching AIDS from one of his sexual partners. In an attempt to make his marriage work better, he started pressuring his wife for more sex. She continued to refuse him. He said, "Frieda, I am a sexual man. Do you want me to find sex elsewhere?" She blurted out, "So what else is new?"

Although the discussion never went any further, now they both know that she knows, but they still have not discussed it. Gilbert has conquered his fear of AIDS by using condoms. Frieda continues to ignore the fact that he comes home late two or three times a week. Frieda is not-so-secretly collaborating in Gilbert's affairs because it takes the pressure off her to be sexual.

In another case, a wife quietly encourages her husband's affairs because they give her the excuse she needs to carry on herself. She has been having affairs of her own for ten years. Her conscience doesn't have to bother her if he plays around too.

MONEY, POWER, PRESTIGE

There are many women in this country who are going with or are married to men who make anywhere from a good living to a fantastic one. They are willing to trade their men's infidelities for a comfortable life-style.

The same is true of women hooked up with men in powerful positions: politicians, royalty, movie bigwigs, well-known artists, musicians, authors, and Mafia chieftains. A woman exchanges her man's affairs for the continuation of the status or even the excitement he provides.

Some of these women consciously know that the man is cheating. Recently a woman married to a powerful Hollywood producer became aware that he was having an affair with the leading lady in his latest film. She raised the roof and threatened to divorce him. He calmed her down by saying he wanted to stay married to her but he also couldn't exist without some affairs. "Couldn't you live with this one affair?" he asked. She did. And because she agreed, she will have to live through many more. She is now a cooperator in her husband's extramarital adventures.

Other women married to powerful or rich men continue to deny their husbands' philandering to themselves and others, even though it is no secret to the rest of the world. In therapeutic circles, this is known as the Rose Kennedy syndrome.

There is ample evidence that Gary Hart's wife, Lee, has long known about his philandering. A Denver attorney and friend of the family admits talking to Lee about her husband's many affairs: "A couple of times I was so outraged that I told Lee, 'Get a divorce. You don't have to put up with this.' And I wasn't the only one who told her that."

It is apparent that Lee Hart has accepted her husband's infidelity, and the public humiliation that made women around the country wince, as a tradeoff for her continuing marriage to a man prominent in politics, as well as his economic support. Lee Hart had taken a job as a real estate agent when she and Gary Hart separated temporarily in 1979. She told Gail Sheehy that the only thing tougher than campaigning ten hours a day with her husband was competing eighteen hours a day, seven days a week with the other real estate agents around Washington, D.C. Sheehy describes the relationship between Lee and Gary Hart as "mutually exploitive." I believe it is also privately painful for Mrs. Hart, but hidden anguish and covering up for her husband in public statements are the price she has decided she is willing to pay.

Here is a sampling of other famous women who have put up with their men's philandering: Grace Kelly; Nancy Sinatra; Jacqueline Kennedy Onassis (with both husbands); Joan Kennedy; Mrs. Gary Cooper; Mrs. Bing Crosby; Mrs. Marcello Mastroianni; Queen Elizabeth; Mrs. Gary Hart; Lady Bird Johnson; Mrs. Max Lerner, Federico Fellini's wife, Guilietta Massina; Michael Douglas's wife, Diandra; Lili Palmer; Mrs. Steve McQueen; Eleanore Roosevelt; Norman Lear's wife, Frances; Lee Krasner, the artist, who was Mrs. Jackson Pollock; Simone de Beauvoir, and countless others.

In some upper-echelon circles, infidelity of the rich and powerful man is taken for granted. Jacqueline Kennedy has said, "I don't think there are any faithful men." But among some ethnic groups, there are poorer people who live the same way. Husbands are expected to cheat, and wives are expected to look the other way. These are generally very male-dominated societies in which men consider infidelilty a male privilege. Wives are killed and beaten up for the same thing. There is often a great deal of animosity between the sexes in this kind of setup. In one marriage the husband had betrayed the wife on innumerable occasions, barely taking the trouble to hide it from her. She remained silent for thirty-five years, until her husband fell ill, became crippled, and had to be taken care of by her. She has been verbally hostile to him ever since. Knowing she has him in her power, she now reminds him time and again of his past transgressions.

SAINTS AND SINNERS

Sometimes a woman puts up with her man's affair or affairs to maintain her position as a victim. Women like this are often tied to tyrants, sadists, alcoholics, or men who never work, who verbally abuse them, or who take advantage of them. The infidelity is either just one more cross to bear, or perhaps, in the case of flagrant womanizers, the chief thorn in her crown of them. These women are burnt offerings on the altar of love. They put up with anything in the name of loyalty or because "I can't help it, I love him."

It appears that the man has all the power in these arrangements. After all, he is the one putting her through hell. The woman's martyrdom, however, is often a subtle power play. He may be a rotter, but she is a saint. And that makes her one up. She is superior to him. She likes being on top morally. That is her payoff, and is the reason why she puts up with cheating and everything else.

Another kind of saint is the woman who suffers from a disastrous lack of self-esteem. If a man is unfaithful, she may cry, but she completely understands it. Of course he is attracted to other women. She is so unappealing. The payoff for her of his affair is sad; it is a confirmation of her feeling that she is unworthy of a man's total affection. She will either let him continue because she may not see how she can compete, or she may gracefully offer to step aside because in her heart of hearts she knows he deserves better than what she has to offer.

MISERABLE MATES

Another kind of woman welcomes an affair because it gives her an additional chance to torture her partner. Miserable mates are always at each other's throats, and do whatever they can to spite each other. This includes having affairs and either being found out, or flaunting them. A woman in a warrior relationship like this may have sexual escapades of her own to "show him." But even if she doesn't, if a man is unfaithful she won't order him out of her life, no matter how much he carries on, and no matter how miserable both of them already are. It's her chance to attack and his to counterattack, setting off another round in their everlasting battle. Men and women trapped in these kinds of relationships are happy only when they are unhappy. Affairs and counter-affairs are part of the arsenal for the agreed-upon game of "let's make each other miserable."

To learn what to do about collusions, turn to the sections of Chapter 14 entitled "Try to Discover If a Collusion Exists in Your Relationship" (pages 237–238) and "Breaking Up Existing Collusions" (pages 248–249). But first you'll want to find out what to do when infidelity is staring you in the face.

ELEVEN

When You Know the Awful Truth

YOU HAVE JUST FOUND OUT YOUR MAN IS CHEATING. OH LORD, what do you do now?

The first thing you have to do is realize that you aren't going mad. The intensity and power of the emotions you are feeling at this time are normal, but many women doubt this. They think they must be neurotic or crazy to feel so overwhelmed.

You are shocked. You are devastated. You feel betrayed and any or all of the following: angry, hurt, anxious, insecure, fearful, humiliated, despairing, jealous, shamed. Perhaps you feel confused or disorganized as well. Surprisingly, you may even feel relief along with the pain, if you have long harbored suspicions and at last have had them confirmed.

"I couldn't sleep for weeks after finding out the man I had been going with for over two years had made another woman pregnant," a thirty-four-year-old divorcée told me. "That's all I thought about for months."

"I tried, but I couldn't eat," explained a woman whose boyfriend had become involved with another woman. "I lost fifteen pounds in three weeks."

"I obsessed about the other woman. I kept picturing them together. I couldn't get those pictures out of my mind," a wife told me.

"She was young and sexy. I felt old and ugly," another wife remembered.

A therapist revealed her feelings before colleagues at a

156

recent conference: "When I found out my former husband was having an affair with another woman, what came out of me was a sound I barely even recognized as my own. It was the sound of an animal howling in pain, and it was totally out of my control. I opened my mouth and this sound came out."

Each new batch of letters I receive contains some that reflect the agony:

"I recently found out that my husband tried to have a sexual encounter with a friend of mine. I have spent many sleepless nights over this. My physical and mental health are in jeopardy."

"My boyfriend and I have been dating a year. I contracted a venereal disease from him. I was cured. Then eight months after that I was diagnosed as having genital herpes. I am so confused."

"I have been involved with a young man for the past year and a half. Everything was going fine until I found out he was still involved with his ex-girlfriend."

"Recently I found out that my husband has been having an affair with the same woman off and on for ten years. I can't begin to describe the horrendous fights that have ensued since the revelation. I scream and cry, he begs for forgiveness and pleads with me not to divorce him. I am obsessed with getting revenge. I dream about killing him."

"It has been nine months since my husband told me of a year-long affair. It is now over, but I am still decimated by the whole thing—the lies, cheating, and sneaking around. I've lost all trust and respect for him. I'm moody. I get angry, then melancholy."

"I have just been told by my husband of twelve years that he is planning a two-week vacation and is going with someone else. His plane took off last night."

"I am having problems with my husband cheating on me. I'm hurting inside. I want a shoulder to cry on. I'm trying to be strong for my kids."

The discovery of infidelity by a man she has trusted is probably one of the most shattering experiences a woman can have.

A love-betrayal touches deep chords in most of us. Whatever feelings of undesirability we have been hiding for years come to the surface. Whatever rejection or rivalry we felt in our early lives gets relived.

For example, if, throughout childhood, you had a father who never paid enough attention to you, when you discover your man's infidelity you may experience it as the same kind of profound and hurtful rejection. If, as a child, you were in competition with a sibling for a parent's love, you will feel the same type of desperate rivalry with the other woman.

Remember, although you are facing a crisis in the present, you are bringing to it feelings from the past that may contribute to the depth of your despair or desperation. These emotions may distort your assessment of your man's motivations in the present, often making his affair seem much more of a threat to your relationship with him than he considers it to be.

Before infidelity became a reality in your life, you may have sworn, "If he ever is unfaithful, that's it! I'll kick him out." Most women say something like this ahead of time. But now that he has actually cheated, you may realize that no matter how enraged, hurt, and disappointed in him you may be, you don't want to lose him. Sure, you may feel like pummeling him, but no matter what you shouted at him in the first heat of discovery, you aren't yet ready to say, "It's over." What you basically want is for him to change and love only you. Is it possible? How do you go about doing this?

WHAT TO DO ABOUT HIS INFIDELITY

PART 1: FOR SINGLES

The problem of infidelity and what to do about it is a different one for single women and for wives.

To begin with, the married woman is in a relationship in which there is the expectation of continuity. A married couple looks forward to going on together through life. Of course, we know about divorce—but still, when you are married, you feel you have signed up "till death do us part." Whether it really works out that way or not, the expectation is there since it is built into the marriage contract.

The underpinning of your relationships when you are single is altogether different. The dating game is based on the principle of tentativeness. When single men and women go out, they are really engaged in a trial-and-error process. You start to see a man, but neither of you knows what will come of it. You don't know if you will like him or if he will like you, if you will be compatible, if the relationship will last beyond the night, or for a few dates, or for several weeks or months. You may hope otherwise, but the possibility that it may end is always implicit when you take up with a man.

Indeed, the purpose of dating in the first place is for men and women to learn something about each other, about relationships, and, it is to be hoped, about themselves in the process, so that by the time they settle down with one member of the opposite sex, they will have developed the knowledge and experience needed to have made a wise choice.

Unfortunately, many women either have never learned that dating is a trial-and-error process in which one should expect to go through some bad experiences and some good ones, or they lose track of it once they become interested in someone. If it doesn't work out with a man they like—if, for example, he continues to want to see other women—it turns into a tragedy. The woman has forgotten the tentativeness that is built into dating. Instead of calling a philanderer or a man who has no interest in commitment a mistake and chalking him off with a little bit of mourning, she becomes bogged down in depression, fright, and self-doubt. Instead of knowing when to call it quits and move on, she may develop a desperate desire to change the outcome—to hang in there in the hope of getting his interest back, or making him stay faithful to her. Women who do this are generally very dependent and needy, or they get so lost in romantic daydreaming that they fail to perceive reality.

So the first thing you have to do as a single woman is to keep in mind that some relationships with unfaithful men should be written off, without further ado, as errors; many men are not worth the effort of trying to change them, because they are either basically not able to change, or they are simply not interested in changing *for* you.

And you have to learn to resist the female tendency to blame yourself when you encounter situations like this.

Most women feel as if they have failed when a man is unfaithful. They think they are not attractive enough or that they must have done something wrong that made him look for someone else.

Women feel this way because they are trained to be responsible for the success of relationships in our society. When something goes wrong, if a relationship does not succeed, your feminine identity gets shaken. On a hidden, profound level, you feel as if you have failed at an important task in a woman's life.

This underlying attitude is so ingrained in women by society that self-blame is an almost universal female reaction to male infidelity, whether it is warranted by the circumstances or not.

A man's inability to commit or his desire to see other women is not always your fault and should not be interpreted as a sign that something is wrong with you. Not every relationship with a recalcitrant man has to be "worked" at by you. Some should simply be surrendered.

You have to learn, then, to distinguish between which relationships involving infidelity may be worth working at and which are not. To do this, you have to understand something about relationships in general, and how fidelity fits into them.

THE STAGES OF RELATIONSHIPS

It is important to understand that a relationship is a process; it is something that takes time to develop and goes through stages.

When a woman doesn't understand that a relationship is a process that evolves over a period of time, there is a tendency for her to make hasty, and often mistaken, judgments about men. Instead of saying, soon after meeting a man, "There are things I like or don't like about him, but let's see what happens as I get to know him better," the woman starts to think in more absolute terms: "This one is for me," or "This guy is not for me."

When the woman decides the man is not for her, she often rules him out right away, or she keeps focusing on the man's faults instead of his good points, or she continually wavers about how she feels. A good, committed relationship, under these circumstances, can never develop because of the woman's attitude. But when a woman decides she likes a man, she often makes an even worse mistake. She starts playing for keeps much too early, and as a result she starts applying rules for the relationship in her head that may not be appropriate yet.

For example, Dorothy started going out with Randolph after meeting him on the ski slopes. After their sixth date, Dorothy started thinking about him seriously. He had a lot of the qualities she wanted in a man. He was athletic, successful in his career, and imaginative. After seeing him for a month, she thought she was in love. She had no desire to go out with other men, and she assumed Randolph would play by the same rules. As it turned out, Randolph liked Dorothy a lot, but he was not ready to make any kind of commitment to her yet, and occasionally he would see one of his old girlfriends. Dorothy found out about this when one of her friends reported seeing Randolph having a drink with another woman. Dorothy was irate. Randolph could not understand this, because the relationship was relatively new and he hadn't promised her anything. Dorothy was making assumptions too early in the game.

The second thing women often don't understand about a relationship is that feelings must be mutual as the relationship evolves. It cannot be a situation in which you want to get more involved and he hangs back. A woman who doesn't grasp the principle of mutuality often fails to judge her relationship correctly, or has unrealistic expectations of the man. She expects, because she is interested and wants to see him more and more, that he should want to do the same. The man becomes a rat in her eyes if he doesn't go along with her unilateral desires.

Peggy made this mistake with Patrick. She met him at a local singles dance. They started dating and saw each other once a week for a month and a half. Peggy wanted to go out with Patrick more often because she liked him a lot. After hinting about this to no avail, she finally asked him if they could see each other more often. Patrick said no. He wanted to be free to see other women, as well as Peggy. Peggy was shocked and angry. She had assumed Patrick was as interested in her as she was in him. She had no idea he still dated other women. She was moving into a more involved part of the relationship all by herself. Patrick had no interest in being there.

As a result of both mistakes—(1) failing to grasp that a relationship must take time to evolve and (2) that it must be a mutual process—women frequently expect to get everything all at once from a man, based on their own desires. They want him to fall in love, want him to see them all the time, and want him to be committed from the beginning. Falling in love and devotion and commitment don't come instantly, no matter how movies, TV, and certain novels portray wonderful relationships as instantaneous happenings. Sometimes these things don't occur at all and the relationship doesn't get very far off the ground. But when love (as opposed to infatuation) and commitment do develop, they do so gradually, over time, and these emotions must be shared by both partners, not just you alone.

The following illustration shows how relationships evolve:

Stage 1	Stage 2	Stage 3
0–3 months	*4–6 months*	*7–9 months onward*

Relationships generally go through three phases. As you see in Stage 1, above, when you first start seeing someone, your lives touch only peripherally. However, by the time you enter Stage 2, involvement has increased and personal space has decreased considerably. Note, however, in Stage 2, that there is still plenty of individual space left. By Stage 3, when final commitment to each other occurs, there is still more involvement, but even so, some private space remains. Don't make the mistake that many people do. They think, in good relationships, that two people completely merge their lives. In good relationships there is always room for personal activities and time alone.

How does fidelity fit into all of this? As a relationship develops, there are times when it is appropriate to expect monogamy and other times when it is not.

Stage 1: The First Three Months

From the time you first meet, through the first three months of dating, fidelity should not be expected automatically unless your partner and you *both* agree that this is a rule you will play by. However, in a good relationship, there is an initial spark that catches and slowly ignites, making you want to be with one another more and more. For example, over the course of three months you may go from a date once a week to seeing each other twice a week. Then you slowly start to spend some entire weekends together, then every weekend. Sex will generally occur as you get to know each other more and feel comfortable about it together.

Note that the relationship has *progressively* escalated. It has not taken off all at once. Relationships that take off like rockets are generally fueled by neurosis. When people fall head over heels in love on the first one or two or three dates, they are usually responding to a fantasy they have manufactured, rather than to who this new dating partner (whom they barely know), really is. Or it may happen because you have an overwhelming need to be dependent or to merge with someone in order to feel more complete. Passion may start too soon, as well, when your instincts or early subtle clues tell you that this new person will fulfill some neurotic need of yours—for example, that he will be elusive or abusive.

When emotional deprivation is in your background, you should approach dating relationships with particular caution. In such a case there is the tendency, based on your underlying desperate need to be loved, to picture each new man as the answer to your dreams.

Many women are especially prone to reacting in the wrong way to what Dr. Frank Pittman calls "third date panic." Of course, this does not always occur on the third date. It happens whenever one of you begins to feel an attachment. In our society it is most often the woman who feels a sense of attachment first. When a woman is insecure and/or needy, she will often panic if she feels her affection is not being returned. Her desperation is almost palpable. The man, sensing it, may either cut and run or, driven away by her panic, start to see other women.

Monogamy may actually occur by itself when you start to spend a great deal of time together. However, it is certainly not a given, nor should it be interpreted as a promise at this stage.

Even though he may feel a real pull toward you, he may not yet feel bound by any rules. Or he may not be ready for an emotional commitment. To many men, monogamy is synonymous with commitment.

You may be moving toward monogamy in a good relationship, and you can discuss monogamy, but you can't *expect* it or, realistically, *demand* it in the first three months. This is getting-to-know-you-better time.

Because of the AIDS epidemic, however, when monogamy is not yet an expectation, you must practice safe sex. This means that you have to insist that he wear a condom made of latex and that, at the same time, you use a spermicide containing nonoxynol-9, which has some negative effect on the AIDS virus.

Your other choice in the age of AIDS is an increasingly popular one: you don't sleep together at all in Stage 1. You allow the relationship to grow in nonphysical intimacy, and sex does not occur until you both feel you are ready for an emotional commitment and monogamy, no matter in which stage that occurs.

Stage 2: Four to Six Months

By about the fourth month, if all is going well, a pattern of being together has generally been established. You may expect to spend all of every weekend together, for example, plus a day or two during the week. You expect to talk to each other almost every day on the telephone, as well. When this has happened, monogamy appropriately begins to become an important issue.

But fidelity deserves to become an issue *only* if you have been seeing each other *steadily* and *progressively more often.* You shouldn't even consider monogamy if you have been seeing less of each other than you originally did, if you date only sporadically, or if your relationship stays stuck in the same place—if, for example, you see each other steadily once or twice a week and never go beyond that. This tells you that the relationship has gone as far as it is going to go. You aren't involved in anything that is meaningful enough to justify raising the heat about monogamy.

If, however, all the signs seem to be good—the flame between you is growing and you both want to spend more time together—don't make the mistake of *assuming* he will be monogamous. When you begin to feel it is important, you can raise the issue of fidelity with him, and express your desire for it. However, you have to bear in mind that although many men will be as ready as you are for fidelity in a tightening love relationship, some, at Stage 2, still can't bring themselves to promise it.

If he thinks he isn't ready for monogamy yet, find out if, at least, he has a basic belief in fidelity in a serious relationship. Without that, it is hopeless to think he might become faithful if the relationship endures.

Discussions about monogamy often turn into moments of truth about him.

Some of you may already have encountered the man who can have a wonderful relationship with you just until the subject of monogamy comes up. Once it does, it brings into the open what his actions may have hidden before. Yes, he has not been seeing anyone else, but no, he can't promise monogamy in the future. If he meets another woman who interests him, he wants to be free to pursue her. Soon after you have introduced the subject of monogamy, this kind of man suddenly stops wanting to see you, and disappears. When this happens, you may blame yourself for having brought the subject up, but the truth is you did yourself a favor. You found out how he really felt and that the relationship was not as strong as his actions led you to believe.

There are other men who may be crazy about you, but they are simply too young for any kind of commitment. A young man in his early twenties may simply need more time to sow his wild oats and grow up. No matter how much he wants a relationship with you, he feels an urge to experiment before settling down. Or he may be a man who is still struggling to make a career for himself and he refuses to commit himself to anyone until he feels more secure in his profession. If either is the case, even if he is terrific in other ways, you have to recognize that you have become involved with him at the wrong time in his life.

A similar situation exists for many newly divorced men, if you meet them soon after their marriages have ended (see pages 113–116). They need more time to sample a variety of women before becoming committed again to one relationship, and it is practically hopeless to try to impose fidelity on a man in this position.

The prognosis for the very young man who feels he needs more experience, the man whose priority is his career, and the newly divorced man who needs to experiment for a while is poor in terms of fidelity in the near future. There is still another kind of man, however, with whom there may be a better outcome as the relationship progresses, even though he is not ready to be altogether faithful at the moment. This is a man who has some fear of intimacy or commitment. However, he isn't phobic about it and it doesn't completely cripple him—which would make a close relationship impossible. (The man who is crippled by a phobic fear of intimacy or commitment can't stay close for long, and by this time he generally has shown signs of backing off, or he quits the relationship as pressures for fidelity mount, leaving you with no choice about the outcome of the relationship.)

One part of the battle against intimacy or commitment in a good relationship by a man who is only partially afraid may be an occasional fling with someone else as the relationship with you intensifies.

When they are running scared, some men do this to assure themselves they aren't caught yet. A quick fling that you know about should be confronted and discussed, but it does not necessarily mean the death of the relationship, unless you absolutely cannot tolerate the idea. If you feel this strongly, you have to let him know and see how he reacts. He may, for fear of losing you, promise never to do it again, or he may bolt as he feels the noose tightening around his neck. However, when your feelings are that strong, this is a risk you have to take.

A slip once or twice is far different from a situation in which a man has sex with different women on a regular basis—for example, a man who, once a week, like clockwork, takes another woman or a series of women to bed, even though he is seeing a lot of you. That kind of pattern is the sign of compulsive womanizing. It will continue forever, and it is not a good idea to fight for the kind of man who does this, unless you are willing to accept infidelity as part of your life with him forever.

A stray affair as a relationship begins to intensify is different, too, from a case in which a man is seeing one or more women as much, or almost as much, as he is seeing you. A man who does this is a lost cause as far as emotional commitment is concerned and should be treated as such by you.

If you can be forbearing, give him the benefit of the doubt and assume he may be fighting with his own fears if he has had one brief fling.

Here are some clues that you can apply during any stage of a relationship to spot a secret womanizer:

• He is never where he should be if you call him at night.
• He avoids telling you what he does with his time when he is away from you.
• There are inconsistencies in the stories of his whereabouts, making you think he may have lied on many occasions.
• He has a history of nonmonogamous relationships with women. Don't be afraid to ask him about past relationships. If it turns out that he has never been able to stay with any woman for long, or he has had longer multiple relationships but none with just one woman, or that he was unfaithful the whole time during a marriage or during other committed relationships in his past, this gives you a hint of what you can expect from him, too. Monogamy in at least one relationship of some duration is a sign that at least he is capable of it, while a history of infidelities tells you the opposite.

If, when you bring up the issue of fidelity, he refuses to discuss what he is doing in terms of other women, or he seems evasive about it, this will tell you that he is not being completely honest or open with you—a negative sign about him and your relationship.

Stage 3: Seven to Nine Months Onward

In a good relationship that has been moving steadily forward in terms of time and emotional involvement, a full emotional commitment to each other takes place during this stage. You may decide to move in together, or perhaps you start discussing marriage. If this doesn't take place, pressures from one or the other for commitment generally start to mount. If the issue does not get resolved, the relationship may start to falter and fall apart.

Now is when you may become aware that you are with a man who can do everything right in a relationship except make a final commitment. A man like this often forces you to decide the fate of your relationship. He could let it go on forever the way it is, but he refuses to marry, or, in some cases, even to move in together. If you want more of a commitment from him, this inevitably leads to unhappiness on your part. After pressuring him for a long time without results, you may decide enough is enough and move on.

In a relationship of emotional intensity that has lasted into Stage 3—even when the man is resisting a final commitment—fidelity deserves to be a big issue. You should have discussed it by now, and at this point you can realistically expect monogamy unless you have agreed otherwise.

However, there is one ticklish time in this stage, and if you don't handle what I call "the last gasp syndrome" correctly, you could precipitate flight to another woman. As marriage comes closer, many men suddenly pull back in the relationship. They want to assess things to make sure they aren't making a mistake and, importantly, to reassure themselves that they are still in control of their own lives. Few men share women's enthusiasm for completely losing themselves in love.

If you start to panic at his sudden cooling off and slight withdrawal, and fail to recognize it as a temporary state, you may do just the wrong thing. You may try to rein him in. At this sensitive time, this may convince him that he is, indeed, losing control of himself in the relationship, so, in reaction, he does something to reassert his autonomy, like have a fling with someone else. If you are in love and discussing marriage and he momentarily cools, keep your own cool and, instead of clutching, discuss with him what is going on. Try to reassure him that you expect him to be his own person in your relationship. In that way you can avoid the "last gasp" kind of infidelity that wrecks many good relationships.

INITIAL TACTICS

What do you do when you think you have a good relationship going, and you find out he has been unfaithful? First, double-check the following:

Take Another Look at Your Relationship:
Are You Overestimating It?

If you are hooked up with a man who has shown no intention of becoming committed to you, no matter how long the relationship has gone on, in essence his affairs with other women are not infidelity but simply a sign of his unavailability. The fact that you view his sleeping with other women as a betrayal is a symptom of *your* problem—you are refusing to face facts concerning what this relationship is really all about. You are in an affair in which he doesn't feel about you the way you feel about him. To expect fidelity in such a lopsided situation is folly.

Let me point out, too, that his infidelity may be helping you to overestimate the relationship. His involvements with others may be tuning you into your own hidden fears of loss of love. These feelings started when you were a child, when something made you think you would lose your parent's affection. Infidelity also brings up forgotten emotions connected to rivalry with a sibling in childhood, when you thought that a parent preferred a brother or sister and was giving him or her more love than you received. These powerful early emotions are being replayed in your present relationship. When you get jealous, you clutch even more desperately at the relationship and exalt your need for your lover, because it is based on an earlier need for fuller love from a parent.

Check the Possibility that You May Be Expecting Fidelity Too Soon in the Relationship

If you are within the first weeks and months of your relationship and you are still at the stage where, essentially you are finding out if you like each other enough for a further commitment, you may regard his desire to date other women as infidelity, but he may think of it as his right at this stage. He hasn't promised you anything. Or he may see it as experimentation—an attempt to see how he reacts to other women. He is not ready yet to deepen things between you. I get many letters from women shocked by the infidelity of a man they have known for only weeks or a couple of months. This is a tough problem for women, because there is a natural urge toward monogamy once you start sleeping with a man you like.

The female urge for monogamy worked better in the past, when intercourse took place at much later stages in a relationship, perhaps when the couple became engaged, or at least not until after a long courtship, when men were more ready to commit, too. Today, a woman generally starts sleeping with a man she is interested in by the third to sixth date. The AIDS scare, of course, has slowed things down for certain men and women, but probably not the majority as yet.

In self-defense you have to step back and broaden your view to include the male viewpoint as well as your own. You will get hurt a lot less, and a lot less often, if you realize the differences between the sexes, and do not expect fidelity from the minute intercourse begins. If you can't do this, then it is better to wait for a man who feels the way you do and is willing to let you know that he, too, thinks that once you sleep together it means you stay faithful to one another for as long as the relationship endures. You may have to hunt a bit, but men like this really do exist.

*Did You Expect Him to Remain Faithful to You
Indefinitely, While You Made Up Your Mind About Him?*

Sue made this mistake with Brad. She became involved with him six months after she had broken up with someone else. Sue had not met any other men during that period, and she was hankering to be in a relationship again. She met Brad at a party. Although she found him a little dull, he seemed nice enough, and when he called her the day after the party to ask her out, she went. She started seeing him regularly.

She found Brad to be intelligent and sensitive and kind. But as she got to know him better, he also seemed passive, unambitious, and still somewhat dull. Brad asked her to move in with him about two months into the relationship. Sue resisted; she had too many doubts about him. Nevertheless, she continued to see him on a steady basis for close to three years and she expected him to be monogamous.

During this time, she could never make up her mind about him. On the one hand she thought he was very nice, but on the other she became irritated at his lack of personal assertiveness and professional ambition. Neither of them ever discussed where the relationship was really going. In the privacy of her thoughts, Sue was trying to make her own mind up about whether she should marry Brad or not. He and she were going steady, and it seemed to her to be a choice she had to make sooner or later. But Sue continued to waver. One day she decided she would marry Brad, and the next day she felt he was lacking too much to suit her.

Sue was both shocked and devastated when Brad told her on the telephone one day that he had become involved with another woman. She called him a cheat and a liar. However, the problem was mostly hers. She had assumed Brad would wait forever until she made up her mind. She didn't account for the fact that Brad had a mind of his own, and that he might grow tired of a relationship that was going nowhere with her and decide *he* wanted something different. Granted, he might have told her about his desire to see other women before the fact. One of their problems was lack of communication. But Sue also was making a big mistake in falsely assuming that Brad would always be waiting there for her until she decided whether she wanted him or not. Don't make the same mistake.

Don't Decide All Men Are Like That

Many women blame it on the whole male sex if they find themselves involved with one unfaithful man after another. Infidelity probably goes along with the unwillingness of these men to commit to you in other ways, or even to love you. If you consistently choose elusive, womanizing partners because they seem the most attractive and exciting, and you reject as boring other men who are more commitment-minded, you may have a problem with intimacy.

- A womanizing man is unavailable emotionally, which may suit some women's hidden agendas more than they realize. You can blame him when the relationship goes nowhere, instead of having to face the fact that you can't really be close to a man, which is why you are always attracted to men who can't be completely yours. The origin of your problem may be with your father, who never gave you the kind of love you wanted as a young child. You are reliving this same old drama with the men you keep picking in your adult life. The intensity of the relationships with them is based on your trying to make these men do what your father never did—love you fully.

If the unfaithful men you always hook up with are married men cheating on their wives and perhaps on you as well—the same thing applies. You may claim that married men are the only good men around, but their real appeal lies in the fact that they are unavailable.

Don't Cling to Him or Chase After Him

Some women, when they think a man is straying, start to call him continually and pressure him to see them. They frantically search for compliments or seek other reassurances from him. This is liable to make him feel smothered and create the desire to run from you—producing just the opposite kind of behavior from what you want.

Don't Try to Make Him Jealous

It is common for women involved with unfaithful men to flirt with other men, and to try to attract different men's attentions in other ways in the hope that this will bring him into line. It won't. In fact, it generally worsens the situation, so don't do it.

Don't Become His Slave

Some women think that the way to make a man monogamous is to turn themselves inside out trying to please him, and to do everything they can think of for him. This tactic almost never wins a man back and often lets him know that with you he can get away with everything.

Don't Use Sneaky Tactics

I have known women to look through their boyfriends' drawers and closets, read their mail, or pore over their address books in secret, searching for clues. Some women have trailed their men, called them in the middle of the night to find out if they were home, asked their men's friends. They rarely have done what they should, which is the following:

Talk to Him About It

Some women are afraid to ask the men they are seriously connected to if they are seeing other women. They just stew around with their suspicions, living in silent agony. You must be open and direct. I have never believed in silence—it harms more than it helps. However, given the menace of AIDS, I don't think it is even a choice anymore. His sexual habits have become a threat to your health.

So you have to bring it up. If you want to be diplomatic or nonthreatening, use the subject of AIDS. Tell him you are worried about AIDS and need to know if he is sleeping with anyone else. Almost any man can understand this approach these days. This will give you an opening to find out other things about his infidelity.

Ask Him What His Involvement Consists Of

Is he seeing only one other woman? Is he seeing her occasionally or on a regular basis? What does she mean to him? The more serious the involvement, the more you have to question what your own relationship with him really means. Maybe there is less to it than you or he or both of you think.

Ask Him Where He Thinks Your Relationship Is Going

I am always surprised that this is a question rarely discussed between two lovers. And yet lovers sometimes have different agendas even in a seemingly good relationship.

This was the case with Brenda and Mort. They were both students at the same law school. They met at a party and began seeing each other regularly. By the end of ten months they were seeing each other almost every night. At this point, Mort, by chance, met a married woman with whom he began an affair. Simultaneously, Brenda began pressuring Mort about commitment. She assumed, because they were seeing each other so much, that that was where she and he were headed. But when the question of commitment came up, Mort let her know that he regarded their relationship as very nice, and quite helpful to him in weathering the rigors of law school, but he had no desire to settle down permanently with Brenda. He also told her about his other involvement. Brenda was livid. She had harbored false expectations about their relationship because she and Mort had never discussed exactly where they might be going together.

Clarifying discussions along the line could reveal to you that the man in your life may like you a lot but regard the affair as a temporary one, and that he mentally reserves the right to transfer his affections, should the need arise. His infidelity may arise out of his belief that this affair is limited by his intentions. An honest discussion about where he thinks the two of you are heading may not give you the answer you want, but if this is the case, at least you will know that there is no future for the two of you, so it is best to move on. If, however, he reveals that he deeply loves you and thinks in terms of a possible future with you, but he has strayed, he is worth fighting for. Go on to the next suggestion.

Tell Him to Cut It Out

You have to let him know your basic ground rules. It isn't really an order, but simply an explanation of what *you* need in a serious relationship. If fidelity is very important to you, you have the right to say, "If you value what we have together, you have to give up other women. I can't tolerate your sleeping with anyone else." Of course there is a risk involved in this. But self-respect and maintaining your own integrity require that you take this kind of risk. Setting limits on what you will tolerate may lose you a lover, but should that happen, remember that you have lost someone who can't give you what *you* need. Sometimes, though, setting clear limits gains for you what you want—monogamy, from a man you care about. Here is an example:

Beth, a nurse, had been going with Norman, a chiropractor, for eleven months. They saw each other several nights a week. The friend at whose party Beth met Norman told her that Norman had had brief flings with other women several times over the past four months. Beth was angry and she confronted Norman about his actions. Norman was devastated when Beth said she would not see him if he continued to sleep with other women, but he valued his freedom and refused to promise her fidelity. They separated and both started going out with other people. After two months of being apart, Norman found he missed Beth a lot. He called her and told her so. She confessed that she missed him too. He said he wanted to get back together and he was willing to stop seeing other women if she would have him back. Beth, now that Norman was willing to be faithful, agreed with a joyous heart. They are currently living together, and Norman is monogamous.

Stick to Your Own Values

Don't let him talk you out of your desire for a commitment of monogamy from him. He may say things like, "You're ruining things. Everything is great the way it is. Why are you screwing us up?" or "You are being possessive. I can't stand possessive women." Don't let him make you compromise your beliefs with statements intended to scare you or make you feel guilty or defensive.

Examine Your Own Background to See If an Unfaithful Man May Be Something You Really Want

Because of experiences while growing up, you may need someone who will hurt you, or whom you have to share or fight over with another woman. This was the case for Gina. Gina grew up in Washington, D.C., with a father who was a politician and a mother who drank too much. Gina adored her father, but she rarely saw him. He worked late and traveled a lot. When she was a teenager, Gina began to realize that a major reason why her mother drank was that her father was always having extramarital affairs.

Today Gina is involved with Hank, a well-to-do stockbroker in New York. Hank often has to entertain clients at night, and he works late many evenings, too. Gina felt she could put up with his work habits—she works hard at her job, too. She was content with her arrangement with Hank until she found out that he was having affairs with other women on some of the nights he was pleading he had to work. Gina ranted and raved, but continued to see Hank, who continued to see other women. In fact, Hank does so more and more openly now. Gina is miserable. She says she loves Hank and can't give him up. Recently she became so frustrated and unhappy that she consulted a therapist. What has started to come out in her sessions is that Gina is glued to Hank and puts up with his infidelities because this is what she is used to in men. Hank is like her glamorous, elusive, womanizing father.

Lucy grew up with a father who was a dapper ladies' man. He had several affairs that the whole town knew about. Lucy's mother looked the other way when these liaisons were taking place. Lucy, in her current relationship with Franklin, has chosen a man very much like her father. He is tall, handsome, and a flirt. Recently, Lucy found out that Franklin had carried a couple of his flirtations to the point of physical intimacy. Although she is upset, Lucy is also oddly comfortable in this situation. She is, in essence, reenacting in her love affair the roles she saw her mother and father play out as she was growing up.

Laura had a rather cruel father who hurt her and her mother with his frequent angry remarks, criticisms, and put-downs. She is now hurting because of her lover Robert's infidelities. Robert makes fun of her feelings—calling her a jealous, possessive woman. She accepts Robert's criticisms, and although she doesn't like it, she accepts his affairs by remaining with him. Her life with her father accustomed her to cruel and unfair treatment from men.

Are You Trying to Save Him?

Very often, infidelities are part of other ongoing problems—drinking, drug addiction, inability to hold down a job, mental illness that sends a man in and out of psychiatric hospitals. The woman excuses his affairs as part of the larger trouble with alcohol, drugs, and so on. She feels she is there to take care of this poor, crippled man no matter what he does, and she hopes to rescue and reform him. When a woman assumes this kind of caretaker role, in which she accepts his infidelities because they are part of a larger sickness that she hopes to cure (or they are *the* sickness), she is generally part of the problem. She may complain about her burdens in the relationship, but in truth she loves being his caretaker and would-be rescuer—it makes her feel powerful and needed. She has a vested interest, therefore, in keeping the man drinking, taking drugs, or womanizing—it protects her role. In relationships like this, if the man joins AA, stops taking drugs, gives up the womanizing, the woman almost always tries to sabotage the cure in one way or another. If the man, despite her best efforts, remains cured, the woman will sooner or later give him up and find another poor sick man to take care of. Make sure you aren't in a caretaker relationship with him.

Don't Put Up with His Infidelities Because You Are Afraid You Will Never Find Another Man

Some single women hang on to relationships with men who are sleeping with other women because they believe that half a man is better than none at all. They are sure that if they refuse to put up with their men's infidelities, their relationships will end, and then no man will ever want them again. They continue to be miserable, but are too afraid of venturing back on the singles scene. Fears like this are almost always unrealistic. If you are truly determined to find another relationship, you will find one. You should not settle for pain as the alternative to trying again with someone else.

Don't Accept His Cheating Because You Are Convinced He Is the Only One for You

The view that there is only one person in the world who is right for you is based on feelings you had very early in life. As an infant, you believed your mother was the one and only person in the world—the powerful person upon whom your survival depended. You now feel that your partner is the powerful person upon whom your survival as a woman depends. There never is just one person who is right. Try hard to believe that there are many people in the world with whom you can have a good relationship.

Don't Believe He Will Stop Being Unfaithful Once He Is Married

Marriage doesn't work miracles, although some women believe it does. They think a man will give up his wicked ways once he settles down. If he has had a pattern of infidelity throughout much of your courtship, he will almost certainly continue to womanize after the wedding, so if you can't put up with this, think twice before accepting him or even thinking about him as your husband.

Try to Reassure Him

If you think he is having stray sexual adventures because he is fighting fears about intimacy and commitment with you, gently bring the matter up. Men are generally afraid of intimacy because they are afraid of being overwhelmed by someone they are close to and losing their own identity; they are afraid of being abandoned by an intimate partner; they are afraid of losing their autonomy and being controlled by a woman they love; or they are afraid of being rejected if a woman knows them too well and sees all their faults. One man in Baltimore confessed, "I remember I used to cheat or leave women altogether all the time. I wanted to be one step ahead. I felt they were going to leave me anyway."

Here, using the fear of losing autonomy as an example, is how you can bring the matter into the open and try to reassure him about his fears: "You know, sometimes I'm scared when I feel close to you. It can be very frightening when you think that someone else may have the power to tell you what to do. I would never try to run your life. I want to be an independent woman, and I want you to be an independent person too."

Don't Keep Reminding Him of Past Transgressions

Your man may have slept with other women at the beginning, before he fell in love with you. Or he may have continued to see someone he had been going with for a while after he met you. Although this may have been painful back then, if he has given up other women and is now firmly monogamous with you, there is no point in hitting him over the head with what he did to you in the past. You have to put it into perspective, realize it was part of a period that is over, and give up your old resentment. Not forgetting past sins will only make him resentful, keep your old wounds from healing, and get in the way of your present relationship.

Don't Keep Nursing Anger or Hurt

If he says he will stop seeing her or them, and he sticks with it, don't keep secretly obsessing about his former betrayal, and don't, for heaven's sake, turn into an inquisitor, always checking up on him. Regard his infidelity as something that happened in the past and get on with your life together.

Tell Him It's Over

If he says he will stop playing around, but you find he has lied, it is time to end the relationship. Don't back down and put up with being lied to time and time again. You don't want to be stuck with a lying womanizer, do you?

Don't Go Back to Him

It is natural after a breakup to be lonely, to miss the guy, and, when you are feeling low, to want to call him. You are mourning him, which is healthy if you have had a relationship of some length and depth. You will have some painful moments, but don't give in to the urge to take him back on any terms—meaning you will put up with his infidelities. Call a friend instead, when your hand is on the phone and you are starting to dial his number. Or, if you must hear his voice one last time, call his home answering machine during the day when you know he is at work, listen to his recorded message, and then hang up without saying a word. Allow yourself to do this just once. Any more would be masochism or harassment.

Refrain from Calling His Friends, Bosses, Co-workers, Mother, or New Girlfriends

Don't contact your ex-partner's friends, relatives, and associates to tell them what a cheating liar he turned out to be. Don't send poison-pen notes about him, either. Bess Myerson cast herself in a bad light when she made anonymous phone calls and sent letters to the women friends of a man she had been involved with. You will appear to be a little off center if you do things like this, too.

If You Find You Can't Stop Seeing Him Even If He Continues to Cheat, Remember You Are Then Part of the Problem

You should stop complaining about him and turn your attention to yourself. You may need to suffer, to feel humiliated, like a victim, or simply feel unfulfilled. I would recommend professional help from a licensed therapist to help you figure out what is going on to keep you so glued to a painful situation. In the meantime, I suggest you stop clinging to monogamy for yourself while he plays around. Try to meet other men and go out with them. Try to not live your life around him. Take courses, go out with friends, do anything except sit around waiting for him to call and wondering who he is with now. And stop believing that if you only love him long enough and hard enough, you will win, and he will see how wonderful you are and give up other women. He won't.

See Chapters 13 and 14

If he says he wants to change, Chapter 13 will tell you if he can. Chapter 14 will show you how to work together to effect change.

Read the next section for married women if you have been living with him. Live-in relationships are similar to marriages in many ways, and you will pick up additional pointers.

TWELVE

What to Do About His Infidelity

PART 2: FOR WIVES

HOW DOES HIS AFFAIR FIT INTO THE LIFE CYCLE OF YOUR MARRIAGE?

AS A GENERAL RULE, ADULTERY EARLY IN A MARRIAGE HAS A different meaning from infidelity after many years. According to sociological studies, men who play around early in a marriage are doing it because of dissatisfaction with the marriage. This isn't the whole story, however. We must add to this what we know about the psychological motivations for affairs, and the life events that trigger them in the early years.

We know that men who are compulsive about sex start having affairs very early in their marriages. If a man has little confidence in himself, no matter how he hides it from the rest of the world, he may need to prove his desirability through sexual conquests that often start soon after the honeymoon. We know, too, that many men who have a problem with intimacy also start having affairs in the early years to create some distance and counteract the anxiety they are feeling in their committed relationships.

Other personality disorders propel a man into early infidelity, too. For example, if a man suffers from narcissism (see pages 80–85), which is characterized by self-centered behavior, magnetism, self-assurance, energy, and grandiosity—he gets involved in affairs early in the game because the spouse loses value in his eyes almost immediately.

The arrival of children in the early years of a marriage often kicks off intimacy fears or resentment in a man who feels the wife is neglecting him in favor of the children.

The coming of children can also be the start of sexual problems. One or both partners may become much less interested in sex, thereby causing a man to look for it elsewhere. The wife may become identified as a mother in the man's eyes, which makes her a forbidden sexual object, and so he turns his libido toward others.

Both Morton Hunt's book *The Affair*, and a study conducted by *Psychology Today* found that two-thirds of unfaithful men began their affairs within the first five years of their marriages, so if this has happened to you, you are in good company.

Affairs that occur later in the game, during the middle years, for example, may have different meanings. Looking once more at sociological studies, we see that in older marriages dissatisfaction declines markedly as a reason given by men for their affairs. Indeed, many of them rate themselves quite happy and content with their wives. If this is so, what leads them to other women? When men in older marriages stray, they are often searching for the kind of passion that only comes with a new partner, or, according to Morton Hunt, for romance.

Once more, to understand affairs better, we have to go beyond the sociological studies and add what we know about pyschological motivations and stress points in the life cycle during the middle years and beyond. If a man has been able to be monogamous for many years, and then starts playing around, intimacy, compulsive sexuality, and narcissism are probably not his issues. More likely he is feeling some anxiety about losing his youth, or the possibility of declining sexual powers. Or he may find himself trapped in predictable, dull routiness: he may be bored with his job, or the marriage itself may have lost a lot of its vitality and he feels a lack of zip at home, even though he has few other real complaints about his wife.

It is possible, too, that a man's needs may have changed over the years. If he has been sensible and rational in everything previously, he may now yearn for more emotion, excitement, or spontaneity if these qualities have been lacking in his practical, utilitarian marriage. If he has previously concentrated on making a good career for himself, he may be ready to relax and kick up his heels—something he didn't allow himself to do when he was younger. If his wife is not willing or able to change along with him, he may feel a distance growing between them and a dissatisfaction that did not exist before, or if it did previously, it now becomes magnified. In some marriages, the man over the years has become more successful and grown more confident and magnetic due to his soaring career, while the wife, if she has been stuck at home, raising the kids, may have a more limited set of interests and capabilities. He may still respect or like her, he may retain a sense of obligation toward her, but he finds her rather limited, and sometimes boring. Enter the exciting affair.

As I have pointed out previously, stress points like the death of a parent, children leaving home, or the shake-up when a wife returns to work after years as a homemaker can sometimes give rise to infidelity too.

Based on this, you have to look at what part of your marriage and life cycle you are in, as well as who your husband is psychologically (reread Chapters 5 through 9), to give you some background clues as to why your husband is having an affair.

Next, you have to start dealing directly with him. Before you do, be wary of any assumptions you may have made about his affair.

Women often jump to the wrong conclusions about a husband's philandering. Here are some of the more common ones:

He prefers the other woman to me. Most frequently, this is not the case at all. The other woman (or women) may mean very little to him. He may have few if any real emotional feelings for her, and in some cases he may even not respect her very much. If he does have feelings for her, they may be minor compared with his feelings for you and the kids.

She must have more on the ball than I do. Often, the most important thing the other woman has to offer is the fact that she is a fresh face and body. Sometimes, however, the man does think he is getting something from the other woman that he is not getting from you. Most often, this means that what he gets from her is different from what he gets from you—and not that you are totally lacking in qualities that are attractive to your husband. Or it may mean that he is getting something from her that he wishes he could get from you. In other words, he would *prefer* to get it from you—something you should remember.

He wants a divorce. It is only a very small minority of husbands who either have affairs because they want out of a marriage, or whose affairs have become so intense that they want to leave the wife for the other woman. Most husbands, even those who screw around a lot, absolutely do not want a divorce. Remember this; it is your strongest card. Even when there is an emotional involvement with the other woman, most men still don't scream for a separation. They are simply mixed up and don't know what they really want. This, too, tips the balance in your favor.

As you start to address your husband directly about his infidelity, remember, your goal is not to harangue and be self-righteous, but to find out what the affair is all about. How serious is it? What does it mean in terms of your relationship in the past, and what are the implications for its future?

Here is how to go about doing this best:

IMMEDIATE TACTICS

*Don't Keep Yourself from Confronting Him Because
You Hope It Will Blow Over or You're Afraid He Will Leave*

Some affairs do go away on their own—often to be replaced by another, if you don't raise a fuss. Keeping quiet raises the probability of a repetition. As for leaving, a man never cuts out because of talking; he takes off because he is intent on leaving and will do so whether you keep quiet or not.

Ask any of the many women whose husbands came to them one day and, seemingly out of the blue, announced that they wanted a divorce. Some of these men came clean at that point and confessed there was someone else. More (because they were cowards or had a canny eye on the divorce settlement) manufactured other reasons for why they wanted to split—e.g., incompatability or the need to have more space—or they dredged up some minor or long-forgotten incident in the marriage. In cases like this, the woman often reluctantly acceded to the divorce because the man remained adamant. To their dismay, the day after the divorce became final, the man moved in with another woman.

If the woman was smart, she immediately realized that his new roommate had been her husband's lover all along and had been waiting on the sidelines throughout the divorce proceedings. If she has been hiding her head in the sand—and the letters I receive each month reveal that an incredible number of women are such ostriches—she will wonder how he could have found someone else so soon. Either way, she is terribly hurt. Men like this were intent on leaving, and it didn't matter to them how they did it, or what the wife did or didn't do beforehand.

The rule is, if you keep quiet you may really lose him. If you confront him now with the fact that you know he is having an affair, you have more than a fighting chance of getting him to give up the other woman.

Gather Information Only After You Have Calmed Down

Never hysterically insist, in the initial aftermath of discovery, that he tell you everything about the affair this minute, even if it takes all night. The first part of your strategy is to try to maintain as businesslike and goal-oriented an attitude as possible while you are trying to understand what went on. This doesn't mean you have to suppress your first reactions of shock, horror, hurt, and anger. What it does mean is that you don't attempt serious fact-finding until you have gotten over the worst of the initial shock and, having more fully digested the matter, decided you want to hold on to him if possible. A hint: It may help you to maintain your calm and dignity if you arrange to have your initial talks about the affair in a quiet but public location—someplace where you don't have to shout or strain to hear each other, and where there is plenty of room between you and others, so you won't be overheard. The presence of strangers reduces chances that you will go out of control. If you find yourself falling apart or getting gripped by wild fury despite your best efforts, adjourn the discussion and start again another day.

Avoid Devious Maneuvers

Some women try to snoop around, attempting to discover from others the details of the affair. Others try to trick the man into confessing. He will feel manipulated and resentful if he is trapped into confessing what he then finds out you knew about all along. Your fact-finding mission is really the opening up of better communications between the two of you. It is better to go to him directly to find out what transpired.

Find Out How Long the Affair Has Gone On

Affairs generally fall into one of the following patterns. It is up to you to discover, from him, into which of these three categories his affair fits:

1. The one-night stand or brief encounter in which there is no emotional involvement and no plans exist for future contact on the part of the man.
2. The short affair. Therapists generally consider this to be under six months.
3. The long affair, from six to eight months and longer. As a general rule, the shorter the involvement, the less serious it is.

Find Out How Often He Sees Her

A one-night stand is self-explanatory. It is over as soon as it has begun, but in either short or long affairs, the frequency of contact can vary. Some men see an outside partner frequently, say, once or twice a week. There are even men who manage to see their lovers almost every day. Others, even in long affairs that can go on for years, see the partner only sporadically—every couple of months or perhaps once or twice a year, only when they come to town on business. Again, the general rule is that the more often the man sees a woman, the more serious the affair.

If He Sees Her a Lot, Find Out If It
Is Basically a Convenience Affair

Don't panic altogether if it turns out that he sees her very frequently. It may still be a "convenience" affair, in his mind. A good number of men just like to have something steady on the side. They see the other woman frequently, but the affair, in their eyes, is basically for sexual variety rather than deep emotional involvement. The unconscious motivation, however, may be to feel less hemmed in by their marriages. (See Chapter 9.) A visit to a lover once a day or so can be akin to a pit stop. Men engaged in "convenience" affairs are generally quite committed to continuing their marriages, which drives both women crazy. The mistress figures he must be serious with her because he sees her so often, and the wife goes nuts because she can't understand why he is with his mistress so much if it isn't really serious.

Find Out If He Has Had Other Affairs in the Past

A one- or two-night stand can be a one-time event— something that happened because of a chance encounter. Thank your lucky stars if this is the case. It generally is not a very serious matter. But for many men, brief encounters are part of a larger pattern. Some have a quickie every now and then. Generally, when it is sporadic, it is a search for sexual variety. Others limit these occurrences to occasions when they are out of town. Again, they feel safe to experiment when far away from home. For others, one-night stands are very frequent occurrences—they are always searching for likely sexual partners, and they go from one brief encounter to another. These men are generally involved in an addictive sexual pattern, and it is difficult to get them to stop unless they realize that they are "hooked." They must understand that sex, for them, is the equivalent of drugs to an addict, and they have to be ready to deal with it on this level.

Find Out If He Is Involved with Only One Woman

Some men have ongoing involvements with more than one woman. They see one, two, or three lovers on a regular basis.

You have to ask him, as calmly and kindly as possible under the circumstances, whether he sees only one woman or others as well.

If a man is involved with more than one woman at a time, even if he sees each one of his lovers fairly often, it is a less serious threat to the existing relationship than devotion to one woman. However, the kind of man who has a stable of women is generally a womanizer, which means that he, too, is in the grip of compulsive behavior as far as sex is concerned—behavior that is hard to break, even when he wants to.

Womanizing is generally a sign of a psychological problem within the man. (See Chapter 5.) The fact that he has a problem doesn't let you off altogether, however. Many women are in collusions to keep their partners' womanizing going. (Reread Chapter 10.)

Find Out If His Partner Is a Man

Although no reliable statistics exist, it is the general consensus among experts that homosexual affairs by men in heterosexual relationships constitute a far more common phenomenon than is commonly supposed. An example comes from a recent letter I received:

"I could write a book about my twenty-three years of marriage. I have two children. About two years ago I found out that all through my married life my husband has been having brief relationships. He has even bought them presents. On so-called business trips he has been sleeping with someone else. My husband is gay. It is other *men* I am trying to deal with."

Ask Him What He Feels He Is Getting Out of the Affair

Try to keep your manner, if not friendly, at least neutral. What the man puts into the affair and what he thinks he is getting out of it is important information for you to have. You need to ask him how he personally regards the affair. Was it a "fling"—sowing wild oats? This is generally easy to deal with.

Was his infidelity an expression of discontent in the relationship? Did he feel he wasn't getting enough attention or affection? Did he feel you had drifted apart from one another? Did he feel you had become too dull or too busy or too preoccupied with the children or your career? This will help you define what needs to be done.

Was it a transient episode in response to a temporary pressing circumstance, e.g., business reversals?

Is the affair a sign of an internal crisis—fear of aging, perhaps? Has he been blue? Can it be a flight from depression? Or is it part of a sudden manic phase, when he seems uncharacteristically euphoric, overstimulated, grandiose?

Was he trying to be part of the crowd? Are multiple relationships an accepted way of life among all the men he knows in the business world or in his social life?

Try to Understand Genuinely His Point of View

Explain calmly, as you attempt to discover the emotional needs his affair served, that you are trying to understand him. This statement has to be genuine, not just a ploy to gather ammunition. Women who succeed at putting their relationships back together again are those who have enlarged their viewpoints to consider not only their own feelings, but what is going on inside their men, as well.

Remember, there are two parts to understanding the man's point of view. First, there is his external assessment of the affair: "It was only for sex," "I like her, but I don't love her," "She doesn't mean a thing to me," "I thought I was in love with her, but now I don't know," "It was a passing attraction," "I can't live without her."

Second, if he can understand it himself, you also need to know what he felt she gave him: "She made me feel alive again," "It was so exciting—I felt like a kid again," "She knew how to listen to me," "She paid attention to me," "She made me feel more confident than I have felt in a long time."

Attempt to Understand What Role You Played in the Affair

When he tells you what he felt she gave him emotionally, you should try to find out if this was compensation for something that was lacking either in you or in the marriage, or in his life in general.

If he says he felt a renewed confidence, ask him if something was making him feel powerless either in his work or at home. Or think about whether you have undermined him with criticisms and belittlement. If he says she made him feel alive, ask if he thought your life together, or his job, or both had become boring to him. Or review your present relationship and figure out yourself whether it has become routinized and dull.

To a statement like "She knew how to listen to me," you might ask, calmly and undefensively, "Was it because I seemed too busy to listen to you, or that I seemed not to care to listen to you anymore?" Or ask yourself if you never made time to listen to him. And if he says, "She paid attention to me," you might ask him and yourself if you have been neglecting him or taking him so much for granted that you looked at him as another piece of furniture at home. Experts agree that most affairs are messages, and often they are about what is missing in the marriage, lacks in which you played a part.

Try Not to Be Defensive, Judgmental, or Attacking

Believe me, what you are doing—listening to him with an open mind, even if it entails criticism of you—is the beginning of a constructive dialogue between you. Part of establishing good communications is to resist the feeling that you always have to defend yourself. An example of defensiveness: If he says he felt neglected, you feel compelled to tell him you were busy taking care of the kids, and he should be grown up enough to understand that. Listen, instead, with sympathy to what he is really saying. He is hurting because you didn't pay enough attention to him.

Some women become judgmental when a man tries to explain himself. For example, if he says, "She made me feel young," a woman, being judgmental, might respond, "So you were acting like an old fool!" Judgmental statements are inflammatory, hinder good communications, and tend to alienate.

Other women attack the man. For example, if he says, "You were always criticizing me," she might attack by saying, "If you weren't such a bungling idiot, I wouldn't have to criticize you." This, of course, confirms the man's opinion that you are never going to change. If you refrain from making statements like this, and consider instead whether indeed you may have been too critical of him in the past, you can begin to try to change and perhaps patch things up between you.

You should listen to what he says with an eye toward what can be fixed, rather than feeling you have to defend, judge, or attack.

Consider the Possibility that Your Husband
May Really Have Wanted to Be Found Out

If he carelessly left clues that led to his discovery, or was indiscreet enough so that he was found out, chances are that he really wanted you to know. Occasionally it is because he wants to end the marriage; much more often, it is a hopeful sign. It means he wanted you to receive the message that some need of his in the marriage was not being met—and that he is giving you both the chance to address the problem. The same is true for men who voluntarily confess their infidelities.

Now that you know some things about his affair, here are immediate reactions you should avoid:

Refrain from Making Hasty Decisions

Packing up and leaving or telling him to get out may be the first thing you want to do when faced with the reality and the facts of his affair, but with time to reconsider, it may be really the last thing you want. You want to see if he is willing to work with you and give up his affair before taking definitive action. He needs time to reconsider, too. He may feel, at first, that he wants to leave you, but then may realize what he is giving up and change his mind.

Don't Give Him Ultimatums

Statements such as "You have to choose—either her or me!" uttered without forethought, could force him to choose her. A considered campaign to right things between you could make him choose you.

Don't Call Parents, Other Relatives, or Friends

I know that the temptation is to try to gather up as many allies as you can who will work on your behalf, pushing him to give up the other woman and get back into your arms. Don't do it. Keep it between you and him (and, alas, the other woman, who is an intrinsic part of the situation). Getting relatives and friends into the act only confuses things and can really backfire. Your husband can feel as if he is being ganged up on, which may produce the desire to rebel and drive him to continue the affair. He may feel that his parents or yours are too involved in your marriage anyway, and that this is one more proof of what he has been complaining about all along. He may feel infantilized by parents who are still trying to tell him what to do, which may also make him want to do the opposite. It may sound farfetched, but many experts feel that an affair is sometimes, in part, either an attempt to create distance from parents who are overinvolved (because it is rebellion against their standards), or to draw back into the picture parents who have become too aloof.

Don't Call the Other Woman

It is common to want to call the other woman to revile her or to tell her to get out of your husband's life. Don't do it. If you call her names, it makes you look bad not only in her eyes, but in your husband's. If you order her out of your life, it will do you no good. You are not someone she wants to take orders from. If you plead with her, it strips you of your dignity. If you can manage to think of her rationally, try to remember that she is a human being too. In truth, the other woman and the wife have much more in common than either one realizes. Both women want more from the man than he is presently giving, they both are hurting, and, believe it or not, your husband may have lied to her as much as he has lied to you. A married man may tell the other woman he is not sleeping with his wife, when in fact he is. This fiction is often exploded when the wife becomes pregnant again. He may tell the other woman that he is unhappy at home when in fact he isn't. He may have told her he is going to divorce his wife when he has no intention of doing so. Some men also cheat on the other woman as much as they cheat on you.

Don't Heap Abuse on the Other Woman to Your Husband

Even if they don't call the other woman to tell her off, many wounded wives tell their husbands what they think of her. They call the woman "scheming," they brand her a slut, amoral, a husband-stealer, and so on. This is sure to further alienate your husband and will often drive him to defend her.

Don't Believe You Are the Only One Hurting

"Oh sure," you think, "I am a wreck and he is having a grand time with that woman." Not always so. Your

husband, even if you presently think of him as an untrustworthy rat, may be having unhappy felings too. He may
feel confused; he may be embarrassed or ashamed; he may
be hurt by all the accusations you are hurling at him; he
may feel extremely guilty; he may be mourning the end of
his other relationship if he has decided he has to give it up;
he may be angry at things in the marriage that precipitated his affair; he may be contending with anger and
pressure similar to yours, from the other woman; he may
be afraid, just as you are, that the marriage is in peril
because of the crisis. He may not even understand why he
had the affair in the first place. One man explained how
depressed he became because of his affair. "I knew I was
doing wrong. I felt guilty about what I was doing to my
wife and children, but I kept rationalizing it. Finally, I
started feeling depressed. Then I started drinking to feel
better." A lot of men in the midst of affairs start drinking
too much because of the guilt they are feeling. At least give
him credit for having feelings, even if you have no
sympathy for them at the moment.

Don't Sleep with Another Man

Many women think the punishment should fit the
crime. Having an affair in return for his is one of the most
destructive things you can do in the long run, although it
may make you feel momentarily triumphant. Sure, it will
prove you are still attractive and help you cope with the
battering your ego has taken, but it also could start a
never-ending game of tit-for-tat and make him feel much
easier about carrying on in the future. Your goal should
not be revenge, but, instead, to do everything not to have
it happen again.

Don't Feel You Have to Rescue Him One More Time

Is his infidelity part of his drinking or drugging, or
other self-destructive patterns? Have you always been
trying to reform him, to save him so he won't go down the
tubes? You may be trapped in an attitude that keeps you
playing Good Woman to his Bad Man. On some level you

want to continue to be his rescuer. Unless you realize that one part of you wants him to remain a wreck, a reprobate, a "bad boy," nothing you do now will be effective in terms of dealing with his infidelity.

Don't Turn Yourself into a Doormat

After the discovery of an affair, many women think the way to win a man back is to do his bidding and to try to please him all the time, forgetting about their own needs in the process. No relationship is worth saving if the price is slavery, even if it self-imposed servitude. Your goal should be to get the needs of *both* of you fulfilled in your relationship.

Don't Threaten to Commit Suicide

This may make a husband stay, but only out of fear, not because of an emotional recommitment. Most often, suicide threats keep husbands on the fence. They feel they can't leave you because they are afraid of what you will do, but they also feel so controlled and alienated by the threat that it keeps them glued to the other woman, who, by contrast, may seem like a model of sanity. If you feel so depressed that suicide seems more a possibility than a threat, see a psychiatrist, who can give you medication and therapy that will help. Think of getting rid of a deep depression as part of your strategy of dealing wisely with his affair.

Don't Drink Too Much

Many women turn to alcohol to ease the pain of a man's infidelity. In a subtle sense it is also a punishment of the man. You are showing him what he has done to you. Drinking will ruin your looks and your figure, and will also make him feel disgust rather than pity for you. It is a very self-destructive way of dealing with his cheating. So is overdoing sleeping pills, tranquilizers, or other drugs like pot or cocaine.

Don't Underestimate the Danger to Your Health of His Infidelity

Now not only can he bring home syphilis, gonorrhea, and other curable venereal diseases, but he can also give you herpes, which is epidemic and incurable, or AIDS, the most important reason to worry about infidelity these days. You don't know if his partner (or partners) has slept with a bisexual man or an intravenous drug user, and neither does he. The possibility of catching AIDS and passing it on has made playing around a potentially lethal game.

Don't Keep Clobbering Him

You have every right to feel angry and to let it out, but don't let the tirades continue beyond a week or two, because your goal is to put things back together again. Continued, unbridled fury, coupled with hateful accusations, will interfere with the process.

Don't Keep Punishing Him

There are many ways women do this. Some of the favorites: being cold toward him; refusing to initiate conversation and responding only in monosyllables—the "silent treatment"; taking a "don't touch me" attitude, or refusing to have sex with him; withholding praise for anything, no matter what he does; responding negatively to any of his attempts at reconciliation. An ongoing punishing attitude will only make your man withdraw further from you and will ultimately be self-defeating.

Don't Keep Reminding Him of His
Infidelity Whenever You Argue or Want Something

No matter what causes the disagreement, whether it is his messiness or your own habit of leaving hairs on the sink, some women feel they hold the trump card in any argument by being able to remind the husband of his affair. Others bring up the affair every time they want something. "You owe me, after what you did," is their basic attitude. Don't bring in his infidelity where it doesn't belong. Don't use it as part of power politics—as a tactic you rely on to be one up on him, to bring him into line, or to manipulate him into giving you whatever you desire.

Don't Assume the Children Won't Know
If You Don't Tell Them

Children always know, even when you do your best to shield them from the truth. If the affair or the crisis caused by it is ongoing, you can't make believe that nothing is wrong when they can tell something is. Acknowledge that you and their father are having problems right now, but that you are trying to work things out. If your children are teenagers, don't try to make them your allies against their father. It will do them great emotional harm that may last a lifetime.

Don't Crowd Him

Many women begin to move in on their men; they start to cling after the discovery of an affair, or they decide, "I'm going to make love to him every night," or "I'll make all of our dinners romantic now." And yet, many therapists feel that it is best, at least in the initial stage after the discovery of a husband's affair, *not* to pursue him emotionally. Often, in relationships in which an affair has taken place, before the occurrence of infidelity the couple was involved in a continuous pattern in which the faithful partner was the one who pursued and was more interested in emotional connection, while the spouse who took a lover was the one who generally created some distance in the relationship. Think about it, and if this scenario fits your marriage, at this juncture you need to keep your husband from feeling smothered. The more you run after him by clinging or sudden efforts to become the best wife in the world, the more discomfort he will feel, and the more likely it becomes that he will either continue his present affair or start a new one to create some breathing space for himself. If, instead, you try to establish a more comfortable level of space for him at this point by either standing still or even distancing yourself a bit, he will be able to relax and not feel he has to run away.

Don't Suspend All Other Activities

You may not feel like it, but it is best for your mental health if you continue with your regular individual routines throughout the crisis. If you work out at the gym twice a week, continue to do so. If you do volunteer work, don't give it up. If you meet with friends for lunch or for a drink after work, keep meeting them. Try to include or add to your activities things that you genuinely enjoy—tennis, bowling, golf, movies, plays, bridge. You need all the joy you can get from outside sources to counteract any depressed feelings that threaten to overtake you. You also need to strengthen your sense of yourself apart from him, something that individual activities will provide.

Don't Lose Your Dignity

Don't grovel, beg, or become hysterical. Generally an air of self-respect and independence will be much more attractive to your husband than will whimpering, whining, going into uncontrolled rage, or "falling apart" and becoming a pitiful rag, which can make him want to pull away further. Staying planted on your own two feet throughout your marital crisis will also help you to put your life back together more successfully, whether or not he reaffirms his commitment to your marriage.

Don't Fall into Defeatist Attitudes

You must not allow yourself to think or act like a helpless victim. Decide you are going to take charge and do something about the situation instead.

Stop looking at his affair as only doom and gloom. Start thinking of it as an opportunity to make your marriage better, to set things right that might have gone wrong, to air problems that have not been dealt with.

Stop viewing him only as a lying cheat. Try to shift your thinking to see him as a man in search of a solution to a problem he had—even if the solution he chose was a bad and hurtful one.

Instead of concentrating on what might have gone on between him and her, try from here on to keep your thinking in the present. How do you go on from here? How can you make things better?

There are also two things that you should not allow *him* to do to *you* at this time:

Don't Allow Him to Use His Affair or
the Threat of Future Ones to Control You

I received the following letter recently. It will give you an example of what I mean:

> Three years after my marriage to a man I desperately loved, I found out that he was fooling around. We separated temporarily, but eventually rebuilt our relationship.
>
> Recently I found out he was up to his old tricks. To make matters worse, he was unfaithful while I was hospitalized during a miscarriage. He explained his actions by saying he had a strong sex drive and figured I wouldn't be able to have sex for a while. He went on to say our sex life wasn't enough, and that if I lived up to his sexual expectations he wouldn't mess around anymore. His expectations: we must have sex at least once a

day, with me wearing makeup and sexy clothes; we have to make home porno movies for him to watch; and I must stay very thin. At first I agreed because I love him. But now I resent it. I don't like having to perform for him in order to keep him faithful. He's also a very selfish lover. He hates kissing me and other things I enjoy, he ejaculates prematurely, and he falls asleep immediately afterward. I want to please him, but I want sex to be mutual, not a stipulation of his fidelity. I feel hurt and belittled, and my self-esteem is next to nothing. I need help.

She certainly does, and so will you, if you allow your man to use the threat of infidelity as a means of control, as a way to coerce you into doing what he wants without any consideration for you.

Other kinds of coercion that have been tried by men caught having affairs:

A ménage à trois. The man persuades you that the only way the marriage will stick is if you consent to allowing the other woman to become part of your household. One woman who gave in and tried this came close to a nervous breakdown before deciding that it was better to pack up and leave than to put up with a situation that was against her beliefs and totally distasteful to her.

An open marriage. Some men, after the discovery of an affair, say that the only way you will survive as a couple is for both of you to have the freedom to have affairs. Interestingly, it has been a learning experience for some men whose wives have taken them up on it and had liaisons with other men. The men discovered, to their own surprise, that they were horribly jealous. Since the woman in these situations is being coerced into it, she generally does not enjoy the experience much, either, so the marriage soon becomes a "closed" one again. However, I do not advocate trying an open marriage in the hope that this will happen in your case. If you don't believe spouses should sleep with other people, stick to your guns and refuse to do it.

Don't Allow Him to Drive You Crazy

The way some men do this is to deny everything in the face of absolute proof. They make a woman doubt her sanity by telling her she didn't see what she knows she saw with her own eyes, or that she is nuts to believe what is obvious. Crazy-making denials can occur whether you are married to him or not.

One woman wrote to me telling me she had gone to her boyfriend's home to wait for him after he had told her he had to work late. She found no lights on. After she entered the darkened house with her key, her boyfriend emerged from the bedroom and pretended he had fallen asleep. When she went into his bedroom, she found a woman hiding in his closet. He vigorously denied that anything had occurred and claimed the woman had gone into the closet because she was scared.

Another woman's husband went out every night by himself all dressed up and came home in the wee hours, or not at all on some nights. He told her she was crazy to be suspicious.

In his book *Turning Points*, Dr. Frank Pittman tells of several spouses "brought in and labeled paranoid by their adulterous spouses. Some have even been hospitalized for their jealous delusions. . . . One wife became suspicious that her husband was not jogging each evening when his running clothes never got sweaty. She went to his secretary's apartment and found him naked in the secretary's closet. He told her she had gone crazy and was hallucinating the entire episode; then he brought her in for therapy."

It is a female problem. Only a woman would doubt her own sanity. Faced with the obvious, men would blame the woman and scoff at ridiculous denials. Don't let your man prey on the female tendency to blame yourself and drive you close to madness.

The only time that I approve of undercover tactics is when everything points to an affair, even if you have no positive proof, and he keeps denying it, calling you crazy. Nail him by hiring a detective, or, as one woman did, put a hidden tape recorder near a phone you suspect he is using for clandestine calls. He deserves it for trying to drive you mad by his denials.

The next important thing to consider is whether he is willing to change and work with you to overcome your crisis and build a better life together. Is he a man who is capable of change, no matter what he says?

THIRTEEN

Can Your Man Change and Become Faithful?

KATHY HAS BEEN SEEING PETER FOR EIGHT MONTHS. DURING that time they have spent every weekend together, and one or two nights during the week as well. They get along very well, share the same taste in movies and books, like each other's friends, and have a similar sense of adventure. There is only one problem—and it is a big one. Recently, Kathy found out that Peter has been cheating on her. She confronted him and was almost as upset by his response as by his infidelity. Peter admitted sleeping with other women, but protested they didn't mean anything to him. He saw them once or twice and that was it. Kathy, on the other hand, meant a great deal to him, he stated.

"I just can't help it, Kathy," he explained. "I love you, but I can't be sexually faithful. I have always needed a lot of sexual partners in my life, and I don't see myself as a monogamous type. I like having a good relationship with you, and someday I want to get married and have kids, but the woman I end up with has to accept me the way I am. I guess I'm like my father. My mother learned not to hassle him about his flings. She had a good life with my father. It *is* possible to live like that, Kathy. Why can't you try?" Kathy loves Peter, but she cannot accept him the way he is. She cannot tolerate the idea of him sleeping with others. She doesn't want to be the way his mother was with his father. She wants Peter to change and be faithful to her.

* * *

205

Maureen has been married to Steve for fifteen years. Two months ago she started receiving harassing phone calls from a woman who would say, "Your husband is in love with me, and you are an ugly bitch." Then she would hang up. When Maureen told her husband about the calls, he admitted he had been having an affair with this woman for several years, but had recently broken it off. He added that she had been harassing him at the office since then, alternately threatening him and pleading with him to come back. Maureen was shocked, but she wasn't surprised. She had suspected the truth for some time, but had been afraid to talk about her suspicions with her husband. Although Steve says he is through with the woman and has asked Maureen's forgiveness, she is not convinced that Steve has really changed. She wants him to be faithful to her, but she is afraid he will have other affairs in the future.

Peter is a man who would have a great deal of trouble changing and becoming faithful to Kathy, while Steve, under the right circumstances, could remain true to Maureen for the rest of his married life.

How can you tell if your man can change or not? Here are seventeen ways to estimate the chances.

CHARACTERISTICS HE MUST HAVE TO CHANGE

In Addition to Placing Value on the Relationship He Has With You, Is He Really Committed to It?

Even though Steve had a long affair with another woman, he thought of it as more of a sexual involvement than an emotional one. In his own mind he felt married forever. He liked his domestic life with Maureen and their three children. In fact, it was when his lover started pressuring him more and more about leaving his wife for her that Steve decided to end the affair. He knew he would never leave Maureen for anyone. In fact, he was relieved after he broke off his other relationship; he had never liked lying to Maureen. Despite his escapade, Steve is deeply emotionally committed to his marriage. Peter, by contrast, values his relationship with Kathy, but is not really committed to it. Steve will change to save his marriage and restore harmony at home, but Peter won't change for the sake of Kathy, because of his lack of commitment. He would regret having to do so, but he figures he could always find another relationship if she left him as she is threatening to do.

Does He Feel that There Are Things You Share
that Bond You Together as People,
Apart from Legal or Financial Ties or a Sense of Obligation?

Three years ago, Jennifer discovered that Walter had been having an affair for a year with a woman in his office. He admitted that he had fallen in love with this woman. After a period of much turmoil, Walter told Jennifer that he had decided to stop seeing his lover. Jennifer was relieved. However, she has become increasingly agitated as time has gone by.

On the surface, Walter seems changed. He acts like the perfect husband. He comes home early every night. He is kind and polite. However, Jennifer feels strongly that something is missing. Walter never talks to her much— and didn't for a long time before his affair started. He encourages her to stay for the winter at their home in the South. Like a good wife, Jennifer goes, and like a good husband, when she is there Walter calls her on the telephone every night. Despite this, Jennifer still senses that something is wrong, and she has repeatedly asked Walter if he sees the other woman. Walter assures her the relationship with his lover is over.

Indeed, the affair *is* over, but Walter is, in effect, still missing from the relationship. He is operating out of a sense of obligation to Jennifer; they have been married twenty-six years and have raised two children together. Although he acts out all his obligations to her as he sees them, there is no personal bond, no chemistry or communication between Walter and Jennifer anymore. There is no hope of closing the chasm that exists between them, because Walter remains so emotionally aloof and uncommunicative. Walter is staying in his marriage because he feels it to be his duty, but basically he hasn't been willing to change. He remains emotionally estranged—polite but distant—although he is physically present. There is nothing holding Jennifer and Walter together at this point except Walter's sense of obligation to her, and Jennifer's belief that she can't live without a man to take care of her. Their marriage is really a shell.

Your man has to feel you share something together—a sense of humor, a deeply held religious belief, a way of looking at the world, a joy in the family life you have together—something that is still very attractive to him and that is a real tie between you. You, of course, must feel this too. Habit or duty by itself is not enough of a motivation to create real change.

Is He Willing to Change?

You can never *make* a person change; something has to make him want to do it himself. It may be that although he has been unfaithful, he has never really been comfortable in that kind of deceptive life-style. Perhaps, as the years piled up, he has grown up, and although he didn't in the past, he now wants to put all his emotional eggs into one basket and deepen his relationship with you. Maybe he realizes that all of his relationships have fallen apart, that he has not been able to remain close to anyone over the long haul, and he is feeling very unhappy with himself because of this. It may be something as simple as fear— he knows he may lose you and he realizes that he must change to prevent that from happening. Maybe he realizes, after one or two or more affairs, how much more he has going with you than with his other women, or that you are far superior as a human being to anyone else he has been involved with. Whatever it is that serves as the force, inside himself he wants to end the cheating and deceit and stay true to you, and change himself in ways that will make that possible.

*Does He Value Monogamy
Even If He Hasn't Always Practiced It?*

Some men feel that monogamy is for the birds, or at least for other people, not for them. The majority think of it as an ideal that they would like to attain but haven't been able to, for one reason or another. Unless your man thinks that monogamy has some merit, there is no way you can get him to change and remain faithful to you.

*Is He Willing to See Things from Your Perspective
as Well as His Own?*

A man who steadfastly refuses to put himself in your shoes, who is concerned only about what he wants and how he is feeling, has little chance of changing. It is a positive indication that he can change if, in addition to considering your viewpoint intellectually, he is able to *feel* for you. In other words, he has emotional empathy for what you need and are going through.

Is He Capable of Admitting that He Is Sometimes Wrong?

Change requires that a person be able to see that he is not infallible, and know that there are times when he will have to tell you he has been wrong. A person who always insists that he is right is incapable of compromising, negotiating, or doing any of the bending necessary to reshape himself and the relationship.

Is He Willing to Listen to You?

To understand where you are coming from, he has to be able to sit still, allow you to talk, and listen attentively when you do. He can't be wedded to behavior that makes him constantly interrupt you, tune you out, rebut what you are saying, or put you down for what you are trying to tell him.

Is He Willing to Look Inside Himself?

In dealing with the issues that are involved in his infidelity, he is going to have to go beneath the surface, to delve into what goes on inside himself in terms of what he is feeling and thinking. He has to be willing to recognize that both of you have a hidden inner life that often dictates how you act.

Is He Able to Communicate with You, or Is He Willing to Learn How To?

A person who will not reveal himself cannot change. He hides emotionally, not only from you, but from himself. The only way to root out the cause of his infidelity is for him to try to be open and honest and in this way help you both to understand him more. Communication, in the sense in which I am using it, means that he is willing to talk about personal things: his emotions, his hopes, his triumphs and disappointments, his expectations, fears, and vulnerabilities. It means being willing to talk about painful issues. It also means exploring with you how he may, as a man, have feelings that are different from yours as a woman, so that gender differences and attitudes don't continue to polarize you and can be better understood by both of you within the context of your relationship.

Is He a Chronic Liar?

If a man habitually deceives others in order to protect or aggrandize himself, so much so that it is an entrenched part of his character, there is very little chance that he can do the things that are necessary for him to change. Honesty from your man will be a very important ingredient in restoring your ability to trust him again.

Is He Willing to See that His Infidelity
May Be the Result of a Mutual Problem?

He may have thought of his affair as all his fault, as a
sexual fling, or as an irresistible attraction to one special
person. Or perhaps he refuses to admit to, or complain
about, things he has been struggling with about you. On
the other hand, perhaps he feels it was all your fault—his
reaction to your lack of interest in sex, your lack of
support, your weight gain, your pressuring him for marriage, or some other flaw in you. If he can enlarge his view
to see that his infidelity is a symptom of a problem that
exists in the relationship, and that perhaps both he and
you are to blame in certain respects, it improves his
chances for change.

Take Barry. He had been going out with Dawn for ten
months. From the fifth week of their relationship, Dawn
had been pressuring him for commitment. Barry was very
attracted to Dawn, but he was unsure how much she
really cared for him as a person. "I think she sees me only
as suitable husband material," he complained to a friend.
Barry admitted he was afraid of commitment, but he was
trying to overcome his resistance. He had cautioned Dawn
to take it easy and not pressure him. When she pressured
him, he felt invaded.

Barry had grown up with an intrusive mother, so he
reacted to pressure as being smothered. Despite his early
warnings, Dawn persisted in trying to get him to commit
to her. This made Barry withdraw, which in turn made
Dawn pursue him even more and berate him for trying to
run away from her. Her recriminations made Barry feel
guilty, so that he became moody when he was with her,
which drove her crazy. "You don't love me," she would
complain. "I only don't love you when you keep after me,"
Barry would retort, which made Dawn angry enough to
say, "This relationship is going nowhere, I can't afford to
waste any more time with you." This made Barry feel even
more that all she was interested in was getting a husband.

Soon their relationship, which had been so promising,

became a series of skirmishes in which Dawn felt deprived and frustrated and Barry felt guilty and unloved for himself. This led to his becoming attracted to other women "who won't hassle me." When Dawn found out about Barry's subsequent affairs, she was furious. She was sure it was all his fault, that he was a man who couldn't be trusted. He was sure it was all her fault because she kept after him all the time. In this state they came into therapy, because, despite their problems, they still felt they loved each other. Barry learned (as did Dawn) that they *both* were at fault. Each had been insensitive to the other's sore spots and each had become expert at doing things that pushed the other away.

In Hank's case, he was certain that his affairs with other women started because his wife, Cindy, didn't enjoy sex as he did. He felt justified in his philandering because Cindy, in refusing him so many times, was frustrating him sexually. When Cindy discovered his infidelities, he and she started talking in an attempt to save their marriage. What came out as they talked was that their battles over sex were really a symptom of a larger power struggle going on between them. Hank was a rather controlling, domineering husband, and Cindy felt angry at him for this, and the only way she felt she could fight back was to refuse sex. It was not a sexual issue that was all Cindy's fault, as Hank had firmly believed. It was, instead, an issue of who controlled whom, and both were involved in this battle.

Is He Willing to Give Up His Lover?

There is no way your man can continue indefinitely with his infidelity and still be willing or able to make the kinds of moves necessary to improve things between the two of you. If he does break it off, remember that he may have some grieving to do over the lost lover. Even though he is sincere in his recommitment to you, he may still feel a little depressed and may think of her sometimes, or even occasionally yearn for her, even though he does not see her. Try to be understanding of what he is feeling, and realize that it is a phase that will pass. Some men continue to have phone conversations with the departed lover, even though physical contact is cut off. Since this acts as a distancer in the relationship between the two of you (she is still there for him as an emotional buffer between you), he has to be willing to end even this kind of contact, which he may define as "innocent" since it precludes sexual involvement.

Does He Have Enough Control Over His Impulses to Be Able to Pass Up Immediate Gratification in Favor of Long-term Goals?

The man who habitually gives in to his urges will find himself embroiled in an affair again, no matter how much he loves you or how much he swears he is through with infidelity forever. Temptation is all around, and he won't have what it takes to resist. In addition, the work of fixing your relationship is not an overnight matter, and he must be able to understand that, despite some immediate discomfort, there will be gratification at the end of the road. He must feel that the quick fix of a pleasure-giving new romance is not worth sabotaging the long-term objective of a better relationship with you.

Is He Willing to Work at the Relationship?

A lot of people think that change comes about magically, or simply through the desire to change. True change, in matters of infidelity, comes about when both partners are willing to put time and hard labor into changing the relationship. A man must be willing to give priority to working at changes in his life. This means that no matter how busy and demanding his career is, he must create time and put effort into working with you to heal the rift, and make your life together better now and in the future.

Some couples assume that all that is necessary for change has occurred when the man gives up the other woman. Both partners breathe a sigh of relief and consider the crisis over. This is really a false solution, because they have neither addressed the problems that led up to the affair nor worked at what needed to be changed in each other or the relationship. They have, in effect, swept the underlying problem that led to the affair under the rug, which increases the chances of another affair occurring in the future.

Can He Give Up Control?

A man who always has to be in charge is a poor prospect; he feels he always has to give orders, be obeyed, and have things his way—a rigidity that prevents the fluidity of change.

Is He Willing to Allow You to Change?

Probably the most important factor in his changing is your ability to do so, and he has to be willing to let that happen. Generally, couples get locked into roles in their relationships. For example, he may be the capable, strong partner while you are the submissive, helpless one; perhaps you are always clamoring for more closeness and he is always running away; or you may be the competent one who keeps things running, while he is passive and lets you run the show. Part of fixing a relationship that has run into trouble is to change roles so that, for example, the partner who has assumed the role of the helpless one learns to become more competent, and the one who was the strong caretaker learns to let go of that role. He has to be able to let you act differently with him.

Is He Willing to Give Up Liquor or Drugs, If These Contributed to His Infidelity?

If he loses control when he takes drugs or drinks, and claims that this is what made him have the affair, or if he is the kind of man who always starts making passes at women when he has had one too many, the only way he will be able to remain faithful is if he stays away from the substances that lead to his playing around.

All of the prerequisites for change (except giving up his lover) apply to you as well, so reread this section to see if *you* are willing to do the things that you expect from him. Neither of you should make the mistake of wanting to remain the same while demanding that the other change.

What If He Can't or Won't Change?

What if you are stuck with a man who doesn't fit the bill for change? What if he refuses to communicate? What if he lies, or needs to maintain control in the relationship? What if he refuses to believe any problem exists in him, in you, or in the relationship? What if he has a psychological problem, such as narcissism, that makes it extremely difficult to effect change? What if he simply doesn't want to work at changing with you?

Your choices are very limited when these or other factors make you aware that there is no hope of cooperation, no way of working together to get through the crisis precipitated by his affair. You should first attempt to see if he will at least try some couples therapy with you. (Or individual therapy for serious psychological disorders such as narcissism.) If he agrees and stays with it (some men quit after one, two, or three sessions), with the aid of a professional you may get him to start working with you for change, after all.

Barring this, or if he drops out of therapy, you may decide to leave him—a choice some women make. Or you may decide to adjust—to learn to live with his infidelity or other shortcomings in him or in the relationship. There is a whole hidden population of women in this country who stay with men they know are cheating. The question you have to ask yourself is, are you willing to settle for this kind of arrangement? Is whatever payoff you think compensates for it really enough? There is a legion of women who have decided that the man's wealth and the comfortable life-style he provides, his exciting personality, the status he confers on his partner, his charm, his good looks, his talent or genius or whatever is worth it, or that it is important, for the children's sake, not to break up the home.

There are positive and negative ways to make this kind of adjustment.

Bad adjustments are being made by women who constantly complain and moan about a man's infidelities and other faults. Both parties stay stuck. Neither of them does anything to make their lives better. These women often nurse a corrosive inner life of resentment and bitterness.

A better form of adjustment is to concentrate on making a fuller life for yourself as an individual, to find the fulfillment you can't have with your man in other ways. Some women lead a happy second life with friends in whom they can confide, and with whom they can enjoy pursuits they can't with their partners. They don't sit at home feeling bitter and abandoned when they know their men are out with other women. They keep themselves busy instead. They know the bargain they have struck, and they no longer complain to whoever will listen. If they are married, they don't make alliances with their children against their husbands as a form of hidden retaliation. They learn to enjoy and make the most of whatever they can share with their men, and not to expect miracles. They know what is never going to change.

Another tactic—one that works best in the long run—is to work at changing yourself alone. A good way to do this is to go into individual therapy to explore further why you are putting up with him the way he is. Often a hidden reason is plain old fear—you are afraid of having to take care of yourself or of never being able to attract another man, or of the economic or emotional burden of raising children by yourself. You may be afraid of never finding anyone better.

Frequently, in therapy, a woman sorts out the rationalizations from true motivations. She learns to strengthen herself—to improve her confidence and self-esteem, to prepare better to earn a decent living—all things that, in the end, help her to decide from a position of strength rather than weakness what she really wants for herself, and if this relationship is really worth it to her.

Even without therapy, you can work at changing yourself. Often this has the happy result of also changing the man.

If, unilaterally, you stop playing your expected part in

the relationship, he will have to alter his role in reaction and change will occur in him whether or not he intended it to. For example, if you have always been after him to spend more time with you, you can start doing the opposite—begin to get more involved in activities of your own, so that sometimes you are not there waiting for him when he arrives home late, or when he finally decides to call or come over. He will be puzzled and perhaps upset; he will wonder what you are up to, and you may find that he now wants to know why you can't get home earlier and where you have been, and that he feels you should spend more of your time with him.

Change may mean that you decide to stop acting like his helpless victim and take charge of your life. You may decide to confront him more about his actions, rather than passively accepting them. You may decide to go to law school or get other training that will let you achieve status in your own right rather than depending on him for it. You may decide to master skiing or other things you have been afraid to try, which will help raise your self-esteem. Changes in your behavior and manner have to make him look at you and react to you in new ways. He could respect you more, or decide he can't take it and leave. He could try to sabotage your changes, to get you back to wherever you were as a person originally. Don't let him do it.

Change always entails risk. It breaks up the status quo. But the upside of risk is that through change you may achieve a better life with or without him. Changing yourself in positive ways will help you to be able to adjust well to a split, if that becomes necessary. It may even make you decide you don't need him, after all, to survive.

FOURTEEN

Improving and Healing the Relationship: Can You Work Together?

BILL CAN HARDLY EXPLAIN WHY HIS AFFAIR HAPPENED. "IT WAS just so easy," he says. "There she was, this attractive woman, and she let me know that she was available." Bill is speaking of Sandy, a nurse he met in the hospital where he works as an administrator. Originally he thought of it as a quick fling. He would sleep with Sandy once, since she was practically asking for it, and then forget about her. But he liked the sex with Sandy. He had been living with Tina for three years, and some of the original excitement with her had worn off. With Sandy it was new territory, and there were fireworks.

Besides, Sandy pursued him. She called him at his office. She spoke suggestively and invitingly. Soon Bill was more embroiled than he ever intended to be. He snuck in "matinees" with Sandy on lunch hours so that Tina wouldn't know. Occasionally he would plead he had to work late to squeeze in a nighttime tryst.

One evening when he said he had to work late, Tina came to the hospital to surprise him with some cookies she had baked. She figured she would pop in and leave them for him to nibble on while he worked. That was when she found out he wasn't where he was supposed to be. When she confronted Bill on his return home, he admitted everything and the whole story came out.

The full impact of what he had done finally hit Bill. Tina was furious. She told him to pack his things and

218

move out. Bill was distraught at the idea of losing Tina. He begged and pleaded. She refused to listen to him. Finally, because she was adamant, he went to stay with his brother. But he kept calling Tina, pleading that he had made a horrible mistake. "I love you, Tina," he said, his voice shaking. "I want to come back. I'll never do it again, I promise. I want to marry you, Tina. I never want to lose you. Please let me come home."

Gary has been married for twelve years. He and his wife, Martha, have two children, a boy of eight and a girl of six. Recently, through an acquaintance who works in the same field, Martha found out that Gary had picked up women and slept with them sometimes when he was out of town at conventions. Sobbing, Martha asked Gary if what she had heard was true. At first he denied it, but this made him feel bad, so he finally admitted his guilt. He never liked lying to Martha, which was why he kept his flings confined to an occasional out-of-town "quickie." He didn't have to account for his whereabouts to her, and he felt he harmed no one in that way. Gary never wanted to do anything to hurt his wife or endanger his marriage. And yet here he found himself having done both. He swore on his children's heads that if only Martha would forgive him, he would never be so dumb again.

Bill and Gary are examples of men who make working together to heal a relationship relatively easy. Like Bill, such men have had just one isolated affair, or, like Gary, they have succumbed to only a few random one-nighters. The affairs are over, and these men are through with such experiences forever. They are eager to recommit themselves and to do whatever is necessary to create a better relationship so that the infidelity can be considered a mistake and put in the past.

With other men, of course, joint efforts are more difficult. The man in love, for example, is a tough case.

WHAT IF HE LOVES HER?

If your man is in love with the other woman, he may not want to give up his affair. What do you do then? Some men leave you little room to maneuver. They are quite clear they want to leave and they do—they move in with their lovers. Others are ambivalent; they are torn between you and the new love. They don't want to break up your relationship, but they don't want to give up their other involvement either.

If a man is sure he wants to leave, the best thing you can do is to let him. Pleading, bargaining, threatening, or groveling won't help if a man is determined, and such demeaning efforts are bad for your self-esteem.

If he isn't sure, go slowly, and don't issue an immediate ultimatum. Use the time thus gained to try to talk to him (see how in the section that follows) and, if he has specific complaints, to try to work to correct them. However, I should warn you, your anger and his indecision will probably get in the way of your efforts if his liaison persists.

If you are tempted to try cosmetic touches in an attempt to compete with the other woman, you shouldn't count on them too much at this time. The fact that you have gotten a snazzy new hairdo or have gone on a diet will probably be largely lost on him. His affair is likely to have blinded him temporarily to you. When a man imagines himself to be in love, most of his emotional energy is being funneled into his affair. However, making yourself feel more attractive can boost your own battered self-esteem.

It is important for you to place restrictions on how long you will let a "limbo" situation, in which he is still with you but continuing his second relationship, go on. If he is still seeing the other woman after several weeks, insist that you separate for as long as he continues to see her, unless you feel you are such a frail personality that you will have a nervous breakdown or commit suicide if he departs.

Separation—whether it comes about because of him

or you—often has a miraculous effect all by itself. For one thing, if he is using an affair to feel more independent and less controlled by you or trapped by your relationship, it may lose its allure once he no longer has to carry on in secret. Even without this, a dose of reality can work in your favor. Once he moves in with her or is free to see her as often as he likes, he will begin to relate to her less in fantasy and more on a day-to-day level. On closer contact, he may see things about her that he doesn't like. Or he may find that he misses you or his home or family more than he ever imagined he would. Men for whom secrecy is sexy often find the zip gradually disappearing once the relationship is out in the open. Any or all of these factors make many men sour on their illicit romances once they are completely free to pursue them. When this happens, many—but not all—want to return to their original partners.

During a separation, some men visit their old homes, particularly if children are involved. If the hour grows late, they may expect to stay over. Even if he doesn't try to share your bed and offers to go into the guest room, don't let him. He really cannot have his old creature comforts on call.

What if you tumble into bed together? Don't kill yourself for it. It happens often enough in these circumstances, and it can be quite a steamy experience, but don't make the mistake of taking this as a sure sign of reconciliation or a signal that he is ready to give up the other woman. More likely it is merely indicative of just how mixed up he really is, or an attempt on his part to keep you on hold.

A separation may have a surprising salutory effect on you. You may feel intense relief. After all, it is stressful, infuriating, and humiliating to stay with a man you know is in love with someone else. You may find, too, once he isn't around, that it is easier for you to concentrate on pulling your own life together as an individual, which is what you should be doing under any circumstances.

Don't launch a guilt-producing campaign. A torn, ambivalent man is almost always already tortured by his conscience and sense of responsibility to you—and your efforts to compound his guilt will not help you. Attempts to wreak vengeance, to punish, or to use the kids against him will work against you as well. In some ways he sees you as the enemy—the person who stands between him and what he wants. Maneuvers like this will reinforce that view and maybe even intensify it, so that he may start to think, "I never knew she could be such a bitch," and thus feel more justified in having his affair.

What *will* help you is sympathy. It will disarm him and present you in the best possible light in his eyes. *Phony* sympathy won't help—he'll see through it. It has to be genuine. To summon it up, remember, if you can, that he really is feeling pretty miserable—he is caught in warring emotions, he is probably under a lot of pressure from the other woman at this time, he doesn't sleep well because he doesn't know what he wants to do. Like many men in these circumstances, he may be drinking because he feels he is coming apart at the seams. If you have had a reasonably good relationship in the past with him, beneath your anger there probably is the capacity for sympathy if you let it emerge—and if he doesn't lie to you. Dishonesty will dissipate any sympathy you feel and you might let him know this.

If he is willing to be honest, and he admits he is confused, caught between his feelings for you and the other woman, ask him if he would at least be willing to suspend his other relationship for a defined period of time—let's say two months—while you try to work things out together. If he says he will do this, or has already told you he isn't seeing her, but then you find out that he has lied, give him the benefit of the doubt—but once only. Perhaps it wasn't deliberate—he meant what he said, but then he couldn't help himself. He had to contact her again. If he has lied two or more times, tell him it's over, but only if you are convinced that you are not part of the problem, because some part of you may want him to continue in the affair. (Reread Chapter 10, on collusions.)

Gail met her lover, Jim, while he was involved with someone else. Soon after starting to see her on the sly, Jim fell in love with Gail and decided to end his original relationship and move in with her. They had lived together for six months when Jim started fooling around with another woman. Gail found out about it, packed all of her things, and left. Jim was contrite and inconsolable. He really loved Gail and wanted her back. He apologized and promised he would be faithful from then on. She forgave him and they started to live together again. Six months after that, Jim met someone else at work with whom he started an affair. Gail found out about this escapade too. Once more she packed her things and left. Once again Jim was contrite and unhappy. He wrote Gail long, passionate letters. He called her on the telephone. He tried to get friends to intercede. This time the campaign didn't help. It saddened her, but Gail felt that although to forgive him once was sanity, to forgive him twice for exactly the same thing would be bad for her. She was right. If she had forgiven him a second time, Jim, after six months, would have started up with still another woman.

The one thing you should *not* do is let him keep running back and forth between you and her—leaving you for her, then returning to you, or telling you it is over, then seeing her again, time after time. Men have been known to keep this up for years. He can't have it both ways indefinitely. You have to set limits on what you will endure.

I must point out that a good number of women, particularly those who have been married for many years, are mistaken when they adopt the tactic of keeping quiet and looking the other way, year after year, because they feel they have no other choice. My interviews with unfaithful husbands reveal that many of them value their family lives enough that if their wives got tough instead, putting their foot firmly down and insisting they give up other women, these men would do it. Never underestimate the strength of men's attachments to their homes and families, no matter where their libidos lead them. This is as true of the chronic philanderer as it is of the occasional cheat.

Of course, there are single women who put up with philandering, too. For example, one woman involved with a very rich man has known for a long time that he fools around. Although this makes her miserable, she feels she can't issue an ultimatum. She is too afraid of losing the status and luxurious life-style that come with the relationship.

Another woman has put up for years with the man she calls "the love of my life," because at age forty-two she says she hasn't been able to find anyone better. "I don't want to go back to going out with creeps, losers, boring men. He is exciting, fun, attractive," she told me. His repeated infidelities, however, keep her unfulfilled in the relationship, and wanting more than she is getting. She has put herself in limbo—neither getting what she wants from him nor giving herself a chance to find it with someone else.

Of course, if you issue an ultimatum, you are more likely to lose a single man than a married one. There isn't the same strong cement of the family to hold him. Issuing an ultimatum can end the agony and restore your dignity, however. It is a rare single woman, connected to a man whom she knows is playing around, who doesn't feel humiliated staying with him.

DEALING WITH A WOMANIZER

Working with a chronic philanderer is difficult, but not always impossible. Chances are you have suspected his sexual treacheries for some time, but were afraid to bring the matter to a head until you were forced to. You have three choices: to leave him, to let his affairs continue openly, or to see if he is willing to work at change. The key to whether you can work with him or not lies in the answer to this question: Does he want to stop womanizing, even if he feels it is something out of his control?

If he does, you have a shot at changing him through cooperative efforts. First you must find out if he will agree to give up other women for a limited period of time—let us say, four months—to give your efforts to work together a chance to really take. This is a prerequisite. Turn his agreement into a written contract. One of the important points of what you will be doing together is to replace the thrill of self-destructive behavior with the rewards of genuine intimacy with you. He must commit himself to keeping no more secrets from you. This means he must try to talk to you about his sexual impulses toward other women, his erotic fantasies, and his history with women. You must listen sympathetically rather than judgmentally. This will break down the chain of rationalizations and denials that many womanizers use to cope with their own behavior.

His ability to open up to you is also a signal that he is

ready to give up his past pattern of cheating and lying and is ready to accept a more honest relationship with you (and you with him). Talking to him about your own emotions—how you have felt as a result of his womanizing—may also help break down any rationalizations and denials he has used to minimize how his behavior may have hurt others. He now has to face squarely the full extent of his problem.

Men who think their sexual impulses are out of control, and who have felt secretly helpless and ashamed because of this, generally endure a certain sense of isolation. Sharing his feelings, secrets, and experiences with you will be an important step in ending the isolation or loneliness he may have felt in his hidden life-style.

Since many men act out their sexual impulses in response to anxiety and stress, alternative means of coping should be supplied. Talking to you about his emotions when he feels anxious or weak or helpless or annoyed with you is one way; exercising and relaxation techniques such as meditation are others.

Working on self-esteem is also important. He should share his self-doubts, and the background that created them, with you. You and he can make a list of his good qualities and keep reminding him of them.

He must agree, also, to give up blaming his womanizing on others—you, for example. It is important that a man like this learn to take responsibility for his own actions.

Follow the steps for working together outlined in the section that follows to facilitate his self-disclosure and to increase in intimacy and gratification his relationship with you. One thing you must bear in mind, however: it is easy to blame everything on a chronic philanderer. If you have been together for any length of time, there is a good chance that a collusion is in operation. Very few women in long-standing intimate relationships with womanizers are completely unaware of their mates' activities. There is some payoff for you if you have let his affairs continue. Of course he has to change, but the relationship between the two of you, and your part in what has been going on, has to be reexamined as well.

If his sexualizing is really addictive behavior, he may find it helpful to join a local group of Sex Addicts Anonymous or Sexaholics Anonymous. These are self-help groups around the country made up of people who want to gain freedom from compulsive sexual behavior. He can locate local chapters by writing to Sexaholics Anonymous, P.O. Box 300, Simi Valley, California 93062; or to Sex Addicts Anonymous, P.O. Box 3038, Minneapolis, Minnesota 55403.

If your efforts don't seem to be succeeding, he will need the help of a professional therapist to break his sexual patterns.

WORKING TOGETHER

Clearly, you cannot work with certain men at all. Almost impossible cases are completely self-centered, unempathic, narcissistic men (see pages 80–85); those who are very chauvinistic and believe infidelity to be a male privilege that women must put up with (see pages 85–88); unrepentent womanizers who have no desire to change; and, of course, chronic liars. Most other kinds of men, even those whose fear of intimacy and/or commitment is so great that their anxiety propels them into affairs (see Chapter 9); very insecure men who use affairs to shore up their egos; men who can see women only as all good or all bad (see pages 77–79); Princes who never feel appreciated enough by the women in their lives (see pages 93–94); or men who come from family backgrounds with adulterous parents, which makes infidelity almost inevitable, can change if they are willing to (1) face up to the fact that they have a problem and that it is having a negative impact on their lives and (2) work on it, which means they are willing to give time and effort and endure some discomfort to create change.

A few men need medication as an adjunct to change. If a man has been propelled into infidelity because he is trying to outrun depression, or if he gets involved with other women during giddy, hyperactive, manic phases of behavior, he needs to be under a psychiatrist's care.

You Both Must Commit Yourselves
to Change

If he is amenable to change, and agrees to work with you to get your relationship straightened out, you must remember that you both will be experiencing some discomfort along the way. Most people are afraid of change because it entails the unknown. What is familiar is more comfortable, even when it involves misery. Because of this, it is often easier to hold on to old patterns, no matter how unfulfilling your life is, than to shift gears.

However, if your relationship is to survive successfully after his affair, you must commit yourself to doing things in new ways. As you embark on this program to redo your relationship, expect some setbacks based on fear and resistance along the way. And don't expect overnight miracles. Change takes time.

The most important part of getting a couple back together in a meaningful way is talk. Enhancement of intimacy and understanding through personal revelations can be learned. Here is how you do it.

Creating Healing Communications

Learn to Talk Effectively with Each Other

This means giving up patterns based on silence, such as never bringing up issues that are bothering you, withdrawing and becoming mute when you are hurt or angry, hoping that if you don't say anything a problem will go away, or assuming that without communication your partner can read your mind and know what you need. For example, Kevin started an affair because he was feeling very frustrated and angry at his longtime girlfriend, Sylvia. He felt she didn't understand him and was not aware of his feelings. But he never talked to Sylvia about himself or what he felt; he thought she should know these things automatically. Kevin had to learn to open up to Sylvia so that she was able to understand what was going on inside him. Sylvia had to learn how to ask Kevin about what he was feeling.

In one way, a hidden affair is always the product of silence: he kept quiet and had an affair instead of coming to you and telling you what he needed, perhaps from you. Silence is the way couples unknowingly retain the status quo in their relationship—things remain the same when you don't confront problems and try to solve them.

Effective communicating also means cutting out repetitive criticism or whining that has become so routine it is tuned out by the other partner. You are complaining, but in an ineffective way that isn't being heard.

You have to talk to each other openly and clearly, and not just about the affair. An affair does not occur in a vacuum. It is most often the product of the entire relationship, so self-therapy after an affair always entails dealing with the entire relationship and the problems in it.

Create a Schedule for Your Joint Talks

Set aside time on a regular basis, for example, two hours once or twice a week. This time must be considered inviolable—there can be no excuses why you can't make it, or why it must be cut short. Make enough time to discuss things fully. Talks should be held in complete privacy, and you should make sure there are no interruptions. Turn on your answering machine if you have one. If you don't, take the telephone off the hook. Choose a time of the day when you both feel relatively fresh. Bedtime talks, when you are both tired, should be avoided. You can start things off in a positive atmosphere by having your first conversation outside your own home, in a setting that has pleasant memories—for example, where you picnicked or hiked during courtship.

Discharge Hostility

If you are feeling full of anger because of his affair, or he is, you have to do something about this before your discussions. Here is how to get fury under control: Admit that you are angry rather than trying to squash or deny it. Go into a room where you can be alone. Lock the door. Sit there and say out loud all the most horrible things about your partner you can think of. You can also take something like a tennis racket or a towel and whack it with all your strength against a pillow, pretending that the pillow is your partner. Both of these techniques will let you release your hostility so that you can then go on to to your discussions and act reasonably together.

Remember These Rules

At each session, before you start talking to each other, repeat the following rules, or write them down and tack them up on the wall: We agree that for the time of this discussion we will not argue, humiliate each other, judge, or blame. We also will not use knowledge gained here to attack or harm the other person.

Don't Have Hidden Agendas

Martha wanted to hear all about Tim's affair because she was gathering evidence to leave him. She said to Tim, "We have been married a long time, let's talk about it. We can work it out." Tim opened up and Martha called her lawyer. That's a hidden agenda. So is the idea on his part that if he pretends to cooperate with you it will throw up enough of a smoke screen so that he can continue his affair.

Agree to Be Honest

It is important that you tell the truth to each other. Often people are afraid to open up because they fear hurting or angering the other person or because they think they will lose the other's love or respect. As a result, all kinds of misunderstandings occur, and problems don't get resolved, to the detriment of the relationship. Honesty is an important prerequisite in setting things straight between you.

Define the Problems in Your Relationship

Tell each other what you feel is wrong or lacking. Does one always put the other down? Does he feel unappreciated by you? Do you feel needy and deprived because he isn't affectionate? Do you have too little leisure or private time together? Has it become a parent-child relationship—with you acting like a helpless child while he acts like Big Daddy, or with him acting passive and letting you be Mother and make all the decisions? Do you have sexual incompatibilities? Have you become too wrapped up in the kids? Does he spend too much time at work? Have you stopped having fun together? Is one of you sloppy about personal hygiene? If you find you have trouble opening up communications about your problems face to face, try writing down your thoughts individually, then exchanging papers. Or try the telephone—you can talk but don't have to look each other in the eye. Writing or telephoning will break the ice and lead to one-on-one discussions.

Use Language that Defuses

In discussing problems, you should avoid directly criticizing the other person. Putdowns, insults, threats, and sarcastic remarks are forbidden. The least inflammatory way to discuss what you think is wrong is for each of you to begin your sentences with "I," for example, "I feel unloved without hugs," "I don't feel supported in my efforts to make a good living," "I need some romancing before I can feel sexy." Sentences beginning with "you" should be avoided: "You are always so insensitive," "You never care about me." Sentences beginning with "you" tend to turn into accusations. They will make the other person feel attacked and therefore called upon to defend himself—opening guns to a heated argument. Stick to explaining how *you* are feeling.

Be Specific About What Could Make Things Better

Complaints aren't enough. They have to be followed up with positive suggestions. You have to define what each wants from the other in order to improve your life together. You can each think about this ahead of time and mentally rehearse what you want your partner to know. A good way of clarifying what each of you would like is to take turns imagining out loud your dream of a perfect day or evening after work together. Explain the behavior you would like to see.

For example, Dave was annoyed and hurt every evening. When he and his wife, Betsy, both returned home after a hard day's work, she would always immediately turn her attention to the children. When Dave imagined out loud how he would like it, he described an evening when, after coming home from work, his wife turned to him and gave him a big kiss before getting busy with the kids. Betsy got the message. She suddenly understood that Dave felt slighted. She had made him feel unimportant to her. She saw how this had resulted in his affair. His mistress's actions were the opposite of Betsy's. She lavished attention on him. In reality, as in many cases of infidelity, the lift to his ego was more important to Dave than the sex in his affair. Betsy now makes sure she shows affection to her husband after work, before turning her attention to the children, no matter how rushed she feels.

Learn to Listen Well

Part of good communication is listening, and part of good listening is to keep yourself from interrupting or making comments while your partner is talking. The perfect way to put this into practice is to agree to take turns: while he is talking, you listen silently; while you are talking, he listens silently. You must listen with genuine attention, signaling to your partner that you are interested, that you care about what is being said, and that you are sincerely trying to understand. The only way one person will really open up to the other is if there is the sense that true attention is being paid (as opposed to just waiting until it's your time to talk).

Clarify and Verify

When one is completely through talking, the other should ask questions if something needs to be clarified. At the end of your allotted time, before adjourning, each should repeat back to the other his or her understanding of what has been said. This will verify that you have heard each other correctly and give you a final chance to correct any misunderstandings.

Talk About Your Expectations

Often what leads to trouble in relationships are hidden expectations that the other partner does not know about and that are not being met. For example, when Joe married Beverly, he expected her to be the kind of wife his mother had been to his dad. His mother believed that a man should be the boss in the family and she let Joe's father make all of the decisions. Beverly, however, believed that women should have an equal role in marriage. She got angry when Joe made decisions without taking her opinions into consideration. Joe felt undercut as a man by Beverly's insistence on being consulted. When Joe had an affair, it was to make him feel more masculine. By talking about his hidden expectations to Beverly, and listening to her point of view, Joe was ultimately able to understand that his masculinity was not at stake— Beverly simply was a more modern woman than his mother. Once he stopped feeling less virile because of Beverly's need for participation in decision-making, Joe's needs for his affair lessened and finally went away altogether.

Chuck, who had been going with Deborah for two and a half years, finally moved in with her. In his mind he expected that if a man and woman were truly in love, they never had arguments. As in every relationship, annoyances arose once the couple shared living quarters. Deborah was able to express her anger when necessary, but Chuck ducked issues and stewed about them silently. Because he suppressed his feelings, anger about small things collected and grew to the point where he began to feel that Deborah was not the right woman for him. Adding to this feeling were his reactions to the occasional outbursts from Deborah. He was sure she didn't love him enough, because she became angry at him. Chuck started a secret affair with a co-worker. Deborah found out about it. They were smart enough to go into couples therapy at this point, where Chuck's unrealistic expectation that anger should never intrude in a relationship was aired. During the therapy he was able to learn that some anger and arguments could be expected to occur in even the best of love relationships, and that Deborah was, indeed, the right woman for him after all. He stopped his affair.

Sometimes expectations have changed. For example, originally he may have wanted you to be submissive, but now, through contact with more assertive women in the work world, he realizes these kind of women can be more exciting as people. He wants you to change and be more assertive, but he hasn't told you so. Instead, he has had an affair with one of the women he finds exciting. Or you may originally have been looking for a man who made a good living. You chose him because he was solid, sober, and hardworking, but now you yearn for him to be more expressive and romantic. Make sure you discuss how your expectations may have changed over time.

Discuss Your Individual Family Histories

Sometimes adultery is something that is built into people because of their backgrounds. Your husband may have come from a home in which one or both parents played around. The theme may go back even further, with grandfathers and great-grandfathers who were ladies' men. If your father cheated on your mother, you may have chosen a man who would not be faithful because that is what you expect from men. Either you or he (or both of you) may have grown up with experiences that made you feel you didn't deserve happiness, and so you have let the relationship persist with serious defects and major lacks.

Discussions about backgrounds could uncover religious or family teachings that lead him to think of you as a "good" woman, and therefore not as sexually exciting as the "bad" women he has his affairs with.

Talking about family histories may help you to understand and sympathize with him more, because you learn of experiences while growing up that made him feel extremely insecure. You suddenly understand why he needs woman after woman—he has to keep assuring himself that he is desirable. Or you may realize that your backgrounds make it very difficult for one or both of you to be intimate consistently, and that affairs serve the function of keeping you sufficiently apart to feel comfortable.

Sometimes in relationships one sees traits in a partner that, in reality, belonged to a parent. You can often trace this in discussions about your families. Generally you assign negative characteristics to your partner, which leads to discontent and then, in some cases, an affair. For example, you may see your husband or boyfriend as an overpowering man because your father was one and react negatively to him because of this. As a result, he feels you don't love him anymore and so he has an affair. Or he sees you as being very critical because his mother was like that. His distorted view of you makes him feel justified in playing around. Each of you may even do things to elicit the kind of behavior associated with a parent. For example, the man who sees you as being like his critical mother may bungle, botch, and forget to do things in order to get you to criticize him.

Once you can establish that there is an overlay from the past in how you view each other, you can begin to relate to each other more as the individuals you really are than as echoes of a person in your childhood.

Many couples have found discussions about family backgrounds extremely valuable, not only because of the important revelations that occur, but because such sharing makes partners feel much closer to one another.

Look for Patterns in Your Life Together

One way to do this is to scrutinize your arguments. Is there a pattern or theme that keeps surfacing time and again? Do all your disagreements turn into a power struggle—is each always vying to be dominant or superior to the other? Are they one-sided—one partner always criticizing, the other always remaining silent or giving in? Are they characterized by a lack of respect or trust on both of your parts, or by one partner? Is there, perhaps, a history of *no* arguments, in which both of you have swept disagreements under the rug and repeatedly denied negative feelings, with the result that the relationship has become lifeless and boring—all form and no content? Hunting for patterns together can reveal destructive interactions that produce discontent and the need for an affair.

Talk About Differences in What You Need to Feel Loved

You may need physical demonstrations like hugs and hand-holding to feel loved. He may not. He may need overtly seductive behavior from you to feel loved. You may not. You have to listen attentively to each other's needs, and then accept, remember, respect, and try to fulfill them, rather than brushing them off, forgetting them, or belittling them. Many affairs are an attempt to get from a lover what you don't get from your mate, or to find someone who won't keep pestering you for things you don't want to give.

Open Up About Your Individual Needs for Space as Well as Closeness

There are often differing needs for closeness and distance between partners in relationships. In our society there is more shame attached to wanting more space than to wanting more intimacy, which is why it doesn't get discussed, although it often gets played out; the need to create distance is implicit in *every* affair. You must talk about how much closeness and how much separateness you each desire. It is important to know if an incompatibility exists, and to work to remedy it, so that the partner who needs more distance does not have to resort to an affair as an unconscious solution to feeling crowded in your relationship.

Change Places with Each Other

Therapists have found it very helpful for couples to switch roles. You have to pretend to be him, and he has to pretend to be you. Try to get into his mind, based on what you know and what he has told you. Present his arguments convincingly. Talking for him, explain how you feel about the affair, sex, loving, your life together. He must do the same, playacting you. This exercise helps couples feel on a gut level the other person's positions, feelings, hurts. It can create a lot of empathy between you.

Address Differing Sexual Needs

Countless affairs start because there are sexual problems in the relationship. You can't pretend, if there is an incompatibility, that it doesn't exist, or hope that it will go away if it never gets mentioned anymore. So if one of you needs a lot of sex and the other doesn't, if one wants sex in the morning and the other at night, or if one likes oral sex and the other hates it, you have to bring it out in the open and discuss it. You have to define the differences, so that you can start doing something about them.

Try to Discover If a Collusion Exists in Your Relationship

One way of doing this is to attempt to figure out what kind of equilibrium in the relationship the affair maintains. Perhaps it keeps two people who have been going seriously together from having to commit themselves to one another. Or maybe you have been acting like the weak little sparrow while he has been the protector and the super-responsible one in your relationship. Maybe he has grown tired of that role and wishes you were more competent and able to take care of things by yourself. Rather than tell you of his discontent and work toward changing things, he has an affair (with a competent woman, of course). Perhaps he even reinforced your role mentally by deciding you were so frail you couldn't handle any criticism, which is why he couldn't tell you of his unhappiness. You, on the other hand, may have had your suspicions that hanky-panky was going on, but you felt so frightened about the possibility of losing him and having to look after yourself that you said nothing until you could no longer ignore it. The affair thus allows you both to maintain your same old roles, instead of changing things.

Another example of how an affair can maintain equilibrium: You originally created a marriage in which neither of you could get too close. You both kept busy with jobs and community and social activities. Your time together was limited. Then the company you worked for offered you early retirement and you took it. You could now take care of your community activities and see friends in the afternoons instead of in the evenings. This gave you more time to spend with him at night. Neither of you could tolerate the increased intimacy. He had an affair that kept the distance between you at a manageable level, and you looked the other way because it gave you breathing space when he was out for the evening.

A third example: Celeste stayed home with the children and was very dependent emotionally and financially on her husband, Grant, a successful contractor. When her two eldest children were in college and her youngest was in high school, Celeste decided to return to work. She found a job in a department store and soon worked her way into a responsible position as a buyer of women's sports clothing. She started earning a good salary and took occasional trips out of town as part of her job. At home she was less available and more financially and emotionally independent. Grant started an affair with his secretary, a younger woman who idolized him. When Celeste found out about his affair, she panicked and started catering and clinging to Grant. His affair returned the power relationship in the marriage to its former status, with Grant as the big man, the wife as his subordinate.

Think about your own situation. Is there something that his affair helps keep the same between you?

With time, the things I have suggested should help you learn to talk meaningfully and locate hidden motivations and rough spots in your relationship. Now you are ready to go on and do something about them, healing the breach caused by the affair and improving your relationship in the process. Many therapists feel that an affair occurs when a person is feeling lost or somehow weakened in the relationship. Taking an outside lover is an attempt to gain an ally to help one feel stronger. Through systematic cooperation you become the ally, lessening his need for another partner.

The next steps will help change a charged, acrimonious atmosphere in the wake of an affair into a more harmonious mood between you.

CREATING AN UPBEAT FRAMEWORK

Find a More Positive Way to Focus on His Affair

Therapists call this *reframing*. Instead of dwelling on the hurt and the deceit, shift to alternative views. For example, the affair is an indication that he is alive. It is good to be a human being who is alive. Or the affair shows that he can be an attractive person. It is nice to be attractive. Don't scoff. If you sincerely want to help yourself, you can train yourself to shift your point of view in this way. Discuss the new outlook together.

Talk About the Good Things in the Relationship

In this negative time, when you are faced with a crisis that threatens the very existence of your relationship, it is important to think about what is right and to tell each other about it. If you admire your partner's intelligence, his way of making others feel at ease, his sweetness, his quick humor, let him know. If he thinks you are a warm, caring human being, someone who can always be counted on, a wonderful organizer, a terrific mother, he should tell you so. If you enjoy traveling, analyzing movies, spending quiet times in front of a fire together, tell each other about it.

Make a List of the Things
You Still Have in Common

In case either one or both of you have forgotten, this will remind you both of what you still share. Compare your list with the one your partner drew up, and see where you agree.

Remember the Good Times

Pull out old photographs if this will help. Wax nostalgic together about your honeymoon, vacations, any incidents or period of time when you both felt happy together. Visit places that evoke happy memories.

Pretend that You Will Never See Him Again

Write a letter to him as if he will be gone forever. Tell him the things you want him to know. Have him write you a letter doing the same. Exchange your letters. Wonderful, warm things are written in this way.

Each of You Do a Chore that You Know the Other Dislikes

If he likes to cook but hates to clean up, do the dishes for him. If you hate to use the vacuum, let him go over the carpets for you. A simple exchange of odious chores shows goodwill and sets the stage for cooperation on more important issues.

Adopt a Take-charge Attitude

Think of yourselves as people who are going to do something about your situation, rather than feeling like injured or guilty parties. (Guilt breeds resentment.) Giving up blame and vindictiveness goes along with this new attitude. Everlasting resentment and a persistent desire for revenge will destroy the guts of your relationship, even if its outward shell is maintained. Is this price worth it to you? If you genuinely believe it isn't, and that it is more important to preserve and improve your relationship, agree to wipe the slate clean and begin again. Anytime you feel yourself slipping back into the need to blame or seek revenge, remember the price attached—the ultimate destruction of the core of your relationship.

Compliment Each Other

Partners are often quick to complain, but develop amnesia about the need to compliment. Compliments help to accentuate the positive in a relationship, something that is important at all times, but particularly necessary in this time of healing. When you admire something the other has done or does well, even if it is a small thing, let your partner know. Watch out for phony praise. It will ring hollow. Your compliments should be based on genuine appreciation.

Start Doing Things You Enjoy Together

Each of you should write down as many things as you can think of that you like to do now, or have always wanted to do. Compare the lists. Pick out mutually enjoyable activities and begin to do them.

Reassure Each Other

Every day, in some way, he has to let you know he cares about his relationship with you—something you have to be told again and again in this post-affair period. You have to let him know that putting your pieces together again as a couple is more important to you than what he has done.

Have Him Do Something As Reparation

Some couples have found that this works wonders toward healing. One husband bought his wife a whole new set of furniture for the bedroom because he had entertained his girlfriend there. Another man took his live-in partner on a long-desired trip to China as reparation for a fling. New coats, new pets, new cars, even new houses have served as reparation. Vacations are particularly effective because they are an occasion for shared pleasure and being alone together. It has to be a gesture coming from him, rather than him giving in to a demand of yours. Reparations like this help both partners feel as if the score is somewhat evened.

SOLVING PROBLEMS

Deal with the Pain

When pain caused by the affair takes over, sometimes something as elementary as flinging yourself on your bed and sobbing it out helps it subside. Even more effective is to banish it, when it strikes, by being productive. Clean up the mess in the basement, volunteer for a project at your place of worship, have lunch with a friend who makes you laugh. I assure you that, unless you are determined to hang on to it, the pain will lessen all by itself with time.

Work at Trusting Him Again

"How can I do this?" you ask. "After what he did, how can I ever trust him again?" It may not be easy, and it won't happen overnight, but it is possible if you really want to. It isn't that he can't be trusted in all ways. You can learn to focus on the ways in which he can still be trusted. You know, for example, that if you were ill, he could be trusted to look after you. Or that if you lost your job, he would support you. Or that if your parent died, you could lean on him. Or that, in case of an accident, he would come to your aid. Think of all the ways he *can* be counted on every time you feel that you will never be able to trust him again.

Another factor that is important in restoring your trust is his ability to be honest with you. If he can sincerely promise to be open from now on, to avoid evasions and lies, you will gradually learn to trust him again. He must also learn to *volunteer* information to help you over the sore spots created by his affair. If he has to work late, he must remember to call you and tell you why, and give you the number where he can be reached, so that you don't have to wonder suspiciously what he is up to.

And, of course, he cannot flirt with other women, even if he intends to go no further. It can also be helpful to see trust as a two-way street. For example, if you fail to do something he counted on, your partner can point out that he can't always trust you, either. Trust then becomes something you *both* have to work on.

Deal with Jealousy

If you find yourself consumed by jealousy that doesn't let up after his affair, even though he is now monogamous, here are some techniques that therapists use to counter this. Try them because, sooner or later, he will get turned off by unrelenting, unjustified jealousy, and it will erode the relationship. He may even feel that he might as well do what he is constantly being accused of anyway.

The first thing to do is to create a "jealousy stool." Keep a special chair in a room you can go into, close the door, and be by yourself. Sit on this "stool" when you are feeling jealous, and stay put until the emotion subsides.

You can also try the "pretend" technique. When you feel consumed by the green-eyed monster, you must pretend indifference even though you feel anything but indifferent. You can't question him about his whereabouts, accuse him of looking at other women, and check up on him every time he leaves the house. Therapists find that pretending helps break the jealousy cycle. By acting more reasonably and normally with your mate, even when you don't feel that way, you gradually see its benefits—a smoother, healthier interchange. This payoff reinforces non-jealous behavior on your part.

The third technique breaks repetitive jealous habits and allows you to give up the preoccupation and vigilance that have become an ongoing state of mind. Become unpredictable. If you are used to questioning him regularly when he comes home, you must stop doing this by occupying yourself with other matters. If you call him like clockwork, four times a day at work, switch to random, irregular phone calls. Instead of indulging your habit of devoting all your energies to watching him like a bloodhound, you must start to pursue your own interests. You have to make yourself do this, even if you don't feel like it.

Therapists find that this reverses the dependent and clinging behavior that characterizes unremitting jealousy.

The final technique should be used only after the affair is well over. When you are out with your partner, point out attractive women to him. In therapeutic circles this is called using a symptom to destroy it.

Finally, you must consider whether your partner is deliberately provoking your jealousy. Some men do this to assert control over a woman; it reassures them of their power over you. Think about it carefully. If this is the case, your partner must be confronted about his deliberately provocative behavior. Explain that it is arresting the healing process.

One last word on jealousy: if you are single, it may be a symptom of a huge investment in the relationship by you that is not being reciprocated by him. You are constantly jealous because he isn't giving you the love and commitment you want, but he doesn't. You can't work with a man in this kind of setup. The relationship isn't mutual and he lacks motivation to change.

Rid Yourself of Your Obsession with the Details of His Affair

Many women become overwhelmed by the desire to know every tiny thing about what went on. The best thing you can do is to shift your focus from her to your own relationship with your partner. It is healing to let him know that your relationship is more important than anything that took place with his lover. If, however, you find it difficult to let go of your need to know everything, you and your partner can use the following technique, employed successfully by some therapists. It is called "crime and punishment." Sit down together for the express purpose of discussing the specifics of his affair. He has to describe in as much detail as possible every intimate and minute thing about his relationship with the other woman. You are allowed to ask as many questions for as long as you want, and he has to answer them. You can repeat these "inquisitions" as often as you want. You will discover, as others haunted by your kind of curiosity have, that sooner or later this ordeal will become odious to you. You will get sick of hearing about all the details of his involvement and stop obsessing about what went on.

Stop Feeling Like a Failure

"I wasn't enough of a woman," or "I guess I'm just not good enough," is the way many wives and girlfriends feel when they learn of their men's infidelities. Sometimes they feel as if they have failed at life itself. Often they are quite specific: they feel as if they have failed in a competition with the other woman.

Feeling like a failure, as if somehow you are inferior, is such a common female reaction to infidelity that I would call it normal; the majority of women, even when they are career-oriented, fall prey to it to some degree. It is a reaction that is imposed on women by our culture.

Traditionally, women are taught to be responsible for the success of relationships, while men are trained to be successful at earning a living. When something major goes wrong in a relationship, women feel they have failed at their mission in life. It attacks the very core of their feminine identity.

Talk with him about your feelings and the gender issues connected to it. It is easier for a man to feel immediate sympathy for you when you tell him you feel like a failure than when you express your anger. He may tell you about the male equivalent—his feeling of failure as a man when his business life is not going well—a time, incidentally, when many men start affairs.

You can also look at your reaction as having a positive side; at least you are in touch with your feelings, which many men are not.

A good way to deal with negative feelings is to take a piece of paper and write down every good thing you can think of about yourself, for example, I am a warm and caring person, I am a good friend, I am a good mother, I am intelligent, I am imaginative. Keep this list in a drawer. Pull it out and repeat what is on it every morning, before starting the day, as well as anytime you start to feel as if you are a failure.

The next and very best antidote to feeling like a failure is to remind yourself that you are doing something about your situation. This will give you a sense of mastery that replaces the feeling of defeat.

Be Willing to Negotiate

The essence of negotiation is compromise: you have to give some of what he wants to get some of what you want. Neither of you should expect to get something without having to budge an inch yourself. For example, if you want him to come home earlier every night from work, and he wants to be able to stay as late as he wants, you can reach an agreement in the middle. He will come home early two nights and stay later the rest of the week. In the same way, if he wants you to pay more attention to the way you look, and you hate to fuss with yourself, you can agree to dress up a couple of nights, and stay in your blue jeans or sweatpants on the rest of your evenings at home.

Start Changing

From your discussions you should know some specifics about what each of you wants changed, how each of you wishes the other would act. Tell one another what you are now willing to change about yourselves. For example, if you have learned he wants you to pay more attention to him when the kids are around, tell him you will try to. He, in turn, should reveal how he will try to fulfill you—for example, by giving you more hugs and other displays of affection, or by talking more about his feelings. You can make your commitment to change even more concrete by writing it down in a contract. The essence of change is to do it on your own instead of complying with a request. For example, he volunteers to help you with cleaning up after meals, instead of waiting to be asked. You tell him to go unwind by himself after returning from work, instead of waiting for him to tell you he needs some time to simmer down.

Let Your Partner Know You Appreciate the Changes

Favorable comments when the other person is doing something to fulfill your needs will show that you notice what is happening, and you like it. Positive reactions will reinforce the desire to continue improvements.

Create Surprises

Total predictability is the enemy of romance and the breeding ground of boredom in a relationship. Boredom sets the stage for an affair. Agree to create a surprise a week for each other. It can be anything. You can get a new hairdo if you have been wearing your hair the same old way for years. It can be surprise airplane tickets for a weekend trip to some romantic or enjoyable place for the two of you. It can be enclosing a note saying "I love you" in his suitcase when he takes off for a business trip. It can be an invitation to a cocktail-hour tryst with you at a hotel near his office. It can be a single rose as a present. Surprises not only break up routines, they make you more interesting to one another, and make each of you think of and react to the other in new ways. Unpredictability, because it creates a certain amount of tension, is also sexy. You will be revitalizing your relationship with your surprises.

Rearrange Your Schedules to Create More Quality Time Together

This is a particular problem today, when most of us lead over-busy lives. We get so bogged down in our work schedules, our exercise routines, and the demands of children, parents, and other relatives, as well as finding time to see friends, that we forget to make time to be alone together. You have to make and jealously guard at least two evenings a week when you can be by yourselves to enjoy and make contact with one another emotionally. Agree to keep the TV set off so that you can interact.

Everything important needs nurturing: plants have to be watered, children have to be attended to and fed, relationships have to be nourished—enough time together is essential food for good, healthy relationships.

Breaking Up Existing Collusions

One sign of a collusion between partners is that some major unhappiness has been present in the relationship for some time. Another is that repeated disagreements occur over the same issue, without a resolution. A third is that your relationship seems stale and without zest. Since collusions keep partners locked into rather rigid roles, they often make spontaneity and fun disappear. A final sign is that your relationship echoes a role you assumed early in life—it seems your partner treats you in a similar way to the way a parent or other family member treated you while growing up. The basis of many collusions is each partner's attempts to mold the other into someone from the past.

If some of these signs are present, if you think you see a pattern in your relationship, a way of interacting that is keeping you both locked into strict roles, and this pattern is helping create stress and unhappiness, here is what to do:

Have discussions with your partner about how you deal with one another, including what each of you does that makes the other react in a certain way—for example, perhaps one keeps repeating behavior that is known to drive the partner up the wall.

If you have a sense of what part you are playing in your interaction, start to act differently. For example, passive partners should begin to try to assert themselves; critical partners should start complimenting instead of carping; partners who are too dependent should consciously plan more activities on their own; partners who have been too independent should let a mate know how much he or she is needed. Even if just one of you changes, the other has to react differently and the collusion will start to unravel. Since the psychological underpinnings of collusions often run deep, you may find it too hard to do this on your own. If this is the case, find an experienced,

licensed couples therapist to help you and your partner
see how you both are contributing to unhappy patterns of
interaction in your relationship.

Work at Solving Different Intimacy Needs

As I have pointed out previously, one of the most
common hidden reasons for infidelity is the need to create
more distance in the relationship. An affair can make a
man feel less hemmed in, trapped, dependent, stifled, and
anxious.

Because of this, it is important to create a more comfortable level of closeness for him. That way he won't have
to resort to an affair to find more space.

The first thing you must do is to work on your own
attitude. You probably are hurt by your mate's need for
separateness. You may experience it as a personal rejection, a threat, or a signal that he doesn't need or love you
enough. It is possible for a man to both need and love you
and still feel that he needs space. Indeed, it is often
because he needs or loves you that he feels so threatened.
He is afraid he will merge into you and lose his own
identity, or, if he thinks of masculinity as being independent, he may interpret his need of you as unmanly.

Understanding that his desire for space is not necessarily a rejection of you is important. You will find it
easier to respect what he needs, and to work toward a
level of intimacy that each of you can live with.

You can pave the way, too, by developing more of an
awareness of your own privacy needs. Women often feel
guilty when they secretly wish they could get away from
the family or a partner for a while. Instead of realizing
that the desire for some solitude is healthy, they think of it
as disloyal. Ashamed, they may deny to themselves that
they sometimes need to be alone. Often without realizing
that this is what they are doing, women take care of their
underground need for space in sneaky ways. When you
dawdle in the tub for a long time, or lose yourself in a good
book for hours, it can be a hidden way to acquire time for
yourself. Learn to recognize and respect your need for
time alone. Start to think of activities that you can enjoy
by yourself, and then do them. In that way you can accept

the fact that you don't always have to be with your partner to have a good time. And he won't feel that you depend on him to join you in everything you do.

A good way to negotiate differing needs for space and closeness in your relationship is to figure out ways in which you can be both alone and together. There are compromises that will satisfy you both. For example, you can be in the same room, each quietly reading. He can listen to music on his Walkman or with stereo headphones while you silently knit, quilt, or exercise. You can go to the movies together but see different films in a theater that shows more than one feature, then meet in the lobby afterwards. You can go to art galleries and walk around the rooms in opposite directions. You can go to museums together but head off to see different exhibits, setting up a time and place to rejoin.

In addition to such measures, in your talks together you can start to delve into what makes intimacy so scary. Family backgrounds often do it. For example, a smothering, intrusive mother can make a person shy of closeness as an adult. The opposite can also be the case—a person who grows up in a household with distant, emotionally aloof parents is not used to closeness, so it makes him feel uncomfortable. Sometimes, illumination as to what created an allergy to closeness helps to remedy it. The person gradually becomes less frightened and starts to tolerate intimacy better.

As a final step, you have to look long and hard at the central, smoldering issue of infidelity—sex, and how to fix it. It is much less likely that a man will be tempted if everything is great in bed with you.

FIFTEEN

Making Sex Work for You Again

TOM HAS BEEN SEEING MOLLY FOR THREE YEARS. HE STAYS AT her house three to five nights a week. He has seriously played with the idea of marrying Molly. "She is the most terrific woman in the world," he explains. "I really love her as a person." He then follows this up with a big "but": "There's only one trouble—sex. Molly isn't loose enough. She's kind of uptight about sex. She never wants to try new things. She only wants to make love with the lights out. I am much freer. Sex is okay with Molly, but something is missing for me."

Recently, Tom met a woman through work. "She was really very sexy," he explained. They had a business lunch, and one thing led to another. Tom and this woman fell into bed one evening. "I guess I was hungry for more spontaneity, more fire," he explained. "Molly is just such a wonderful, wonderful woman, I would be heartbroken if she left. But she has found out and all hell has broken loose."

Saul's wife, Nancy, never was as interested in sex as he was, and now, at age fifty, she has decided she is through with it forever. She keeps refusing Saul in bed. "I can't help it, I'm just not interested," she tells him. "What am I going to do?" Saul asked one day recently. "I'm sorry," Nancy answered. "I just don't know." Saul has been a faithful husband for twenty-five years, but recently he has been eyeing other women. He hates the idea of

251

cheating on Nancy, but he sometimes seriously thinks about having an affair.

Tom and Saul are two men who are struggling with sexual differences with women they really care about—incompatibilities that can and do lead to infidelity.

Although I have spent a good many pages explaining the origins of infidelity that go beyond sex alone, this doesn't mean that sex by itself is not a very important issue. It is. It lies at the heart of infidelity, which, after all, is about intercourse with someone else. A woman can generally handle a man's mere friendship with another woman. It is when sex has taken place that she goes up the wall. And, often unaware that there may be larger issues at work, most men give sex as their reason for infidelity: "I need more variety," "My wife doesn't like sex," "I forgot sex could be so exciting," "I don't feel interested in sex with her anymore, so I had to go elsewhere," "I need things that she finds disgusting." Research shows that men place a greater importance on the sexual aspects of marriage than wives do.

Because sex is so central to men and to infidelity, you have to give it a high priority in your relationship. To prevent affairs in the first place, to counteract them, and to fix up your life together after infidelity has taken place, it is important to look closely at what has gone on in the past and what is taking place now sexually with him.

NEGOTIATING SEXUAL TRUCES

In an incredible number of marriages, sexual incompatibilities, which show up early in the relationship, are allowed to go untended for years. Some men and women feel, "That's just the way I am, I can't help it if we're different from one another." Sexual compatibility need not be only something that happens naturally between a man and a woman with the right "chemistry." It can be created—even if differences have been allowed to stand between the two of you for a very long time. It is essential to do this to overcome his infidelity, and to prevent any future slips.

Talk About It

As in most matters involving couples, the first thing you have to do is talk about it. Dr. Helen Singer Kaplan, the noted sex therapist, has compared attempting to create sexual satisfaction without communication to trying to learn target shooting blindfolded.

To begin with, you have to acknowledge that a problem exists. Some people have simply kept it to themselves. Because they haven't discussed it, their partners remain unaware of any dissatisfaction. For example, Tom never told Molly that he felt something was missing in their love life. He finally opened up to her in the aftermath of his affair, when their relationship was nearly at the breaking point. "Why didn't you let me know before?" she cried. Molly and Tom are now working together to make things better. Tom is gently trying to help her experiment with more positions. Molly is now willing to have sex with the lights on, and, to help matters along, Molly has gone to a sex therapist to help loosen up her inhibitions, inherited from a strict, antisexual upbringing.

Define the Problem Correctly

You have to be sure you really know what's wrong. For example, a husband may complain that his wife has lost interest in sex, or is not an exciting sex partner, because she can't climax. He blames her and she accepts his blame. They both have defined the problem as hers. The truth may be, however, that he is the one at fault. He doesn't engage in foreplay and expects her to reach orgasm through penile thrusting alone when, in reality, what she needs to have an orgasm is direct clitoral stimulation.

Some women know what would turn them on, but don't tell out of embarrassment or fear of a partner's reaction. Others don't have a clue. If you know, you have to tell him.

If you don't know what would excite you, then you have to take responsibility for finding out. Dr. Joshua Golden, director of the Human Sexuality Program at UCLA, makes the point that many people "are not exactly sure what they want. They know they aren't satisfied, but they have no idea how to improve their sex lives."

When this is the case, sex therapists often recommend masturbation to teach you, in unpressured privacy, about how your body responds and what kind of stimulation excites you. You can pass on to your partner the information you have learned during masturbation, and put it into play during intercourse. If a man has had an affair because he was turned off by your lack of response, and he genuinely wants to return to monogamy, he will generally cooperate once he knows that change is necessary in his own technique for you to achieve full sexual satisfaction.

Therapists also recommend joint exercises in which partners learn about their responses by taking turns touching each other all over while telling each other what they enjoy and what they don't. A bonus is that exercises like this lead to discussions of sexual matters avoided by the couple previously.

Sometimes what is needed is nonsexual. A lot of women who got plenty of romancing before sex during courtship find that any kind of buildup disappears once the relationship is firmly established. Resenting sex without warmups, they eventually either stop being responsive or refuse their partners altogether. You have to convince him that it isn't a crazy whim—it is something you must have to feel sexy with him. Most men won't resist taking time out for buildups—hand-holding, hugging, kissing—once they understand it as a sexual *need*, rather than a whim.

Tune In to Changing Sexual Requirements

Sometimes dissatisfactions arise because sexual needs have changed over the years. For a man this may mean that lovemaking techniques that worked fine while he was younger no longer do the trick.

Bart, a forty-eight-year-old owner of a retail store in Missouri, became impotent with Iris, the woman he had been living with for thirteen years. He was convinced it was because she had aged a little and no longer turned him on. He decided an affair with a younger woman was his answer. He had never been unfaithful before. To his chagrin, he was impotent with the younger woman as well.

Bart didn't realize his problem stemmed from not getting what he needed to achieve an erection. Although he was able to get hard quickly without much direct stimulation of his penis when he was younger, Bart now needed more foreplay, more stroking and fondling. He discovered this easy cure when he went to a doctor to discuss his impotence. His love life with Iris has improved dramatically. Both Bart and Iris have changed their lovemaking to accommodate his new needs.

In long-lasting relationships, you have to understand that sex is not static. Stay sensitive to the possibility of changes, discuss them when they occur, and then do something about them.

Another common example of how sexual needs can alter with time is the man who has been in a monogamous relationship for several years. He may need more fantasy or variety to feel excited and remain interested in sex than he did originally. If he doesn't understand this, he may simply tell himself that sex has become boring with you. Or, if he does understand, and you react to his new requests with indignation, refusals, and the accusation that he has suddenly become kinky, you may find yourself with a partner who becomes increasingly dissatisfied in bed with you. This is a perfect setup for an affair.

Take Blame Out of Your Sex Life

Henry blames Carla for his rotten sex life and consequent philandering. "She never wants to make love, and when she lets me every couple of weeks or so, it is as if she is doing it only to keep our marriage together." Carla blames Henry. "He turned me off to sex the first time we made love on our honeymoon," she remembers. "We used to pet before that, and I enjoyed it. The first time we had intercourse, Henry jumped on the bed and wanted intercourse without any preliminaries. I didn't like it at all. I guess I just don't like intercourse." Sex has become a loaded issue in their household. Discussions about it turn into a round of blaming and recriminations.

Often, sexually incompatible partners start accusing one another of having abnormal preferences or making unreasonable demands.

Blaming, nagging, and accusations actually make matters worse. Instead you should resolve to try to do something about it together.

Redo Your Body Image

Some partners resist sex and, unconsciously, even squelch their own sexual feelings because they are ashamed of their bodies. This is often the hidden factor behind wanting to make love only in the dark, when your partner prefers to have the lights on, or covering up, even though he enjoys nudity. Darkness and covers can be more of a problem for him than you realize, because they cut off a great source of pleasure and excitement; visual stimulation is an intrinsic part of male sexuality.

If you are a woman in hiding, you may have to figure out why you have become fat. Have you done it to avoid sex? In response to problems in your relationship? Of course, some women have to work on the psychological reasons behind overweight, but the answer to sexual differences for many women is simply a shape-up program. You will feel more comfortable exposing yourself once you feel better about your body. Trimming down can be helpful in restoring your husband's sexual interest in you, as well. He may have turned off because he prefers a slim body.

Many unfaithful men complain about overweight wives. You can't, as so many women do, refuse to take his feelings about this into consideration or take refuge in the feeling: "He should love me for myself." There are men who don't care what you look like; their sexuality is not linked to an aesthetic preference. But just as many men can't function when their sensibilities are offended. It is the smart woman who respects rather than denigrates her partner's aesthetic predilections, particularly when a love life or even the entire relationship is at stake.

Motivation for shaping up has to come from you—he can't demand it. You will resent it if you are only giving in to threats or demands. A man's affair often turns out to be a miraculous motivator. It scares you into finally getting into shape. But it can't be a temporary measure. You can't allow the pounds to slip back on as soon as you feel that the crisis is over—not unless you want to tempt him into infidelity again.

Sometimes redoing your body image is simply learning to accept yourself the way you are. He doesn't mind a couple of extra pounds, but you think he does, or you are ashamed of an extra roll or a slightly protruding stomach or bulging thighs, so you avoid sex, nudity, and bright lights. Ask him about his feelings and tell him to be completely honest. If it turns out, for example, that your little pudge doesn't bother him although real fat would, then start to look at your body through his eyes—as still being capable of attracting and delighting. Get in the habit of looking in the mirror and concentrating on your good parts—nice big breasts, a firm fanny, great legs— whatever looks good when you scrutinize yourself without prejudice or shame.

Be Flexible

Too many partners just say no to a sexual practice, or "That's disgusting," and leave it at that. You have to try to bend more. You can't create compatibility if you only want to have it your way.

An important part of mediating a sexual difference is to explore what lies behind resistance to a partner's wishes. Once your understand what the objection is, you can both come up with suggestions to help overcome it. For example, if you (or he) resists oral sex because you think the genitals are unhygienic, you can talk to a gynecologist, a urologist, or a sex therapist, or read a book about it to dispel this fallacy.

Sometimes a woman hates the smell of a man's genitals if he doesn't shower before lovemaking, and that is why she refuses to perform oral sex. Explaining this could get him to wash before intercourse and thus overcome your objections.

Therapists also find that a "try it—you might like it" attitude can work. Agree to what your partner wants just once, keeping an open mind to the experience. The thought of something new often turns out to be much worse than actually doing it.

Were You Ever Turned On to Each Other?

Sometimes sex is incompatible because partners married for reasons that had nothing to do with sex. People marry for security, status, or companionship, because they think their partners would be good parents, or simply because they think it is expected of them, but they never had a strong sexual desire for the partner. The excitement of courtship and marriage may have kept them from realizing the lack of sexual zip that was always there, but once they settle into domesticity the truth begins to dawn. They think, "I am not turned on." Many of these couples like each other in other ways, which is why they want the marriage to endure.

An affair may bring into the open this important issue, neither addressed nor admitted before. It is not the end of the world if this is the case. With a lot of goodwill you can improve your sex life even in these circumstances, by trying things that create more excitement and interest—new positions, variety in technique, making love during the day instead of always at night, using private or shared fantasies to turn yourselves on, even if they include other people (this is really okay in fantasy, if not in real life).

Are You Blaming Sex for Other Problems?

Couples sometimes have an easier time saying their problem is sexual than admitting that their whole relationship is in trouble. One way to identify what the real problem is is to think long, hard, and honestly about when your sexual trouble started. For example, you may have started refusing sex as a way of gaining your own power in a relationship in which your husband dominated you, or in looking back, you may recall that two years ago your husband got a new job and began to work late every night.

This left you alone with two young children in the house. You felt abandoned. Even as you think about his behavior now, you feel a surge of anger—anger that has made you lose all desire to this day for your husband. You started acting cold toward him, which made him turn off to you. These turn-offs to each other were blamed on sex—"The chemistry is gone." But the truth is that desire disappeared because you were both unconsciously very angry at each other.

Hidden anger is often behind loss of desire in relationships. Talking about what you are mad at and resolving it is frequently a successful way to keep him interested and to bring sexual vitality back.

Learn the Art of Sexual Negotiation

You have to grasp the principle of giving to get. Taking turns is an example of this kind of trading. Suppose one partner wants sex with the lights on, the other with the lights off. You compromise by keeping the lights on one night and keeping them off the next. Or suppose he likes sex in the morning and you like it better at night. You can break the deadlock by making love sometimes in the morning and sometimes at night. Or if one of you wants sex five times a week and the other wants it once, you can find a solution by each giving a little and meeting in the middle—you have sex two or three times a week.

Looking for acceptable alternatives is another part of negotiation. When a man, for example, pressures a woman for oral sex, he may really be simply looking for more variety and excitement. You can see if exploring different positions, watching erotic movies together, or exchanging fantasies would be acceptable alternatives to oral sex for you both. Of, if he wants you to watch porn movies, which you hate, maybe dressing up in seductive costumes or talking about—or acting out—sexual fantasies would be a mutually acceptable solution.

Sometimes couples can unlock horns about sex by realizing that intercourse is not the only answer. For example, if a man wants sex more frequently than you do, you can sometimes bring him to orgasm manually, without either of you expecting that you climax too. Of course, a man can do the same thing for a woman who wants sex when he doesn't. Another alternative to different frequency needs is self-pleasuring, with the full knowledge and consent of the partner, and even, if you like, in full view of your mate.

RETRAINING YOURSELF FOR PLEASURE

In addition to resolving any sexual differences that may have contributed to his infidelity, you have to make sure your love life with him in the future contains some of the things that may have made his affair so sexually alluring.

Bring Back Seduction and Temptation

Dressing and talking sexy may have been part of your courtship, but did you stop trying to seduce or tempt each other once you became an established couple? This is what happens to most people. Seduction and temptation are staples of affairs. They make the blood boil. Here are samples of ways to bring to your relationship some of the heady flavor of an affair: Buy yourself some filmy nightgowns; ask him to come along to help you select them, based on their ability to excite. Perfume yourself before coming to bed, or, better yet, ask him to apply perfume to you. Buy him some sexy colored bikini briefs instead of his baggy boxer shorts or hospital white jockeys. Tell him he has to let you put them on him the first time (and take them off).

Create Anticipation

Part of the fun of a love affair is wondering when you can get to see your lover again, or looking forward to a secret rendezvous. Anticipation can be a real turn-on. You can create sexual anticipation in your relationship with him, too. For example, call him at his office and ask him to call you back when he has a moment. (This won't work if he has to talk to you when he is in the middle of an important meeting, or is being hassled by a thousand details.) When he frees himself up and returns your call, launch into a description of what you are going to do to him in bed that night, and what you want him to do to you. Or drop a note into his briefcase with a picture (or pictures) cut out of a book like *The Joy of Sex,* and tell him you would like to try this with him when he gets home. Or call him and tell him that you have reserved a room for the two of you at a motel known for catering to illicit lovers, or a place that features hot tubs or Jacuzzis, and that you will meet him there after work.

Bring Back Romance

Romance, even more than sex, is what makes affairs so attractive for many people. The enticement of romance with someone else would not exist if romance was still alive and well in your relationship. So you have to coax it back. At least once a week, go back to a courtship habit— have a well-planned, dress-up date. Places you choose to go to have to be romantic—featuring candlelight, a roaring fire in a big fireplace in the middle of winter, music with dreamy, slow rhythms so that you can crush your bodies together as you dance. A little innuendo in your body rhythm as you dance will heat things up and be a prelude to sex when you return home.

It is very romantic to go away to cozy country inns for the weekend, bringing a bottle of champagne with you.

Little surprise presents that say "I was thinking of you" also foster a sense of romance.

Romance will stay alive, as well, if you remember to say "I love you" often. Whisper it in his ear as you drive somewhere in the car, call him on the telephone and tell him.

It also flourishes when people learn to really look at each other again instead of taking each other for granted. Notice when he looks terrific in his new suit, or make sure he notices you in that sensational dress that shows off the best of your figure.

It is also important to show affection at nonsexual times—the way lovers do—by holding hands or squeezing your arms against each other's bodies as you walk, by pecks on the cheek or pats on the fanny when you pass one another at home.

Be Childish with One Another

Sometimes affairs are a welcome relief from having to act like a responsible grownup at a job and with the mate or family. Men often allow themselves to be more playful in relationships when there are no strings attached. They also allow their sex lives to be richer with lovers than with their regular partners because they don't restrict the flow of childishness in themselves the way they do in their estblished relationships.

One of the world's most eminent psychiatrists, Dr. Otto Kernberg, medical director of the Westchester Division of New York Hospital–Cornell Medical Center, told me that a rich sex life depends, in part, on accepting childish as well as mature aspects of yourself and your partner. He explains: "Everybody has polymorphous infantile trends—which means exhibitionistic, voyeuristic, sadistic, masochistic, and homosexual tendencies. The acceptance of these partial drives means that one can tolerate having sadistic fantasies, for example, and tolerate acting on them in a playful way. What books like *The Joy of Sex* have done is to reeducate everybody to those aspects of one's own needs that may go underground. These aspects should normally be integrated into the sex relationship. It creates intensity and adds variety to sexuality."

For a more exciting sex life, you both have to learn to allow the child in you to surface more often together. Horse around, have mock pillow fights, throw snowballs at each other sometimes. And, as he may have done in his affair, try together to bring into your sex relationship playacting or fantasizing about some of the things Dr. Kernberg mentions that may sound kinky but are really ways of tuning into the uninhibited, sensuous baby that normally resides in all of us. A well-known marriage therapist, Dr. Clifford Sager, has commented on the practice by couples of "playing out romantic or sex-in-danger-of-being-caught situations, mild sadomasochistic play, master-slave fantasies, call-girl fantasies, Don Juan, gay or troilism [threesome] fantasies. . . ." By trying some of these things as a couple, you can add to your love life together still another aspect of what men often get out of their affairs.

Make Yourselves New to Each Other

Of course, newness is a real turn-on and is one of the strongest erotic lures in affairs. You can't become complete strangers to one another, but you can create a fresh aura by taking some of the predictability out of your relationship and putting surprises in. Like many couples, you probably have fallen into some sexual ruts. You may make love always in the same one or two positions, always in bed in your bedroom, always at night, always using the same techniques. You must try some new things. If you have trouble dreaming up novelty by yourselves, buy a book that explains sexual variations and, on a regular basis, pick some to experiment with. Make love in new places, too—in the backseat of your car or on the living room couch, or tumble onto a carpet on the floor. Make a date for matinees on weekend afternoons instead of waiting for the sun to go down.

Introduce some enhancements to lovemaking. Try a vibrator if you haven't before. Use a feather instead of your hands to go all over each other's bodies. Perfume some oil and give each other a sensuous, all-over rub. Rent a sexually explicit home video and watch it together on your VCR. Take sexy nude pictures of each other with your instant camera.

The weekly nonsexual surprise that I recommended before will help you view each other in new ways. To this you should add one or two strictly sexual surprises a week for each other. For example, take him on a surprise tour of a shop that sells sex toys and have him pick out whatever he likes. He can buy you, as a surprise, a sexy teddy, or a fancy garter or garter belt. You can promise him a night devoted only to him, in which you will do anything he wants in bed, and vice versa. An act he or you always wanted, a position you have never tried together—anything your imaginations come up with can serve as your sex surprises.

None of this is silly. It really will create interest and excitement (at any age) if you both put the necessary effort into becoming fresh lovemaking partners by becoming less predictable in what you do.

Make Sex a Priority Again

I assure you, in his love affair, sex got top priority. In your life together you probably let it slip down low on your list. Sex became something that occurred after everything else was taken care of—work, jogging, sports, television viewing, kids, laundry. You have to put sex at the top again. This means you have to set aside prime time for it—when you are still fresh, not at the very end of the day, when you are exhausted. You should also allot sufficient time for it, so that it isn't a hurried, uninspired act. You can bet that lots of time went into lovemaking with her.

Create the Privacy You Need

There is nothing that works against a sense of freedom and spontaneity (two things that generally operate at a high level in an affair) as much as the fear of being overheard or intruded upon.

If you have children, buy a lock for your bedroom door. Explain that there are times when Mom and Dad need to be alone. Send the kids off to spend the day with a relative, and devote that time to making love. Leave them at home with someone you trust, and go away for a sex-filled weekend.

If the walls of your apartment are paper-thin and you are concerned that the neighbors will hear what is going on between you and your lover, move your bed to the other side of the room, put carpeting on the wall that adjoins as a sound barrier, or play a radio with loud music when you are making love.

Train Yourself to Become a More Sexual Person

A good many women have never tried to explore their own individual sensuality. One way to do this is to keep tabs on erotic responses that may occur as you go about your daily life. Do you hear a piece of music that makes you feel sexy or sets you dreaming of romance? Do you think a man who passes you on the street looks sexy? Does your silky underwear, or the softness of the fabric of your blouse, feel yummy against your skin? Is running your hand over the fur on your coat a sensuous experience? Does a passage in a book you are reading turn you on? Do you daydream of making love in some particular place?

Some sex therapists recommend that you keep a daily diary of sexual thoughts, feelings, fantasies. By starting to be more aware of erotic responses you may have shut out before, you will be cultivating your sexual self. In addition, by finding out more about things that turn you on, you can bring them into play in your love life. Let him know that hugging and lots of foreplay turn you on. Put on music you have found sexy while you are making love. Or use this music or a passage you find sexy in a novel to get yourself in the mood. Think of sexual fantasies that have turned you on to excite you more while making love to him. Share your fantasies with him. Bring out the sexiest part of yourself. Believe me, if you learn to look for it, it is there.

Make Your Bodies a Thrilling Voyage of New Discovery

Not only will you find out little things you never knew before about each other's bodies, but this will also banish tension that may have intruded into your sex life, because of past problems or because you now feel anxious together in bed as a result of his affair.

Remove orgasm as a goal for two weeks during these daily sex exercises. Your new goal is exploration, discovery, and physical pleasure apart from a climax.

Do the following: With both of you nude, you lie down alone on your tummy. He caresses the entire back half of your body, slowly and sensuously, going everywhere from head to toe. Turn over and allow him to do the same thing over the entire front of your body. Switch places. Now you caress him in the same manner, going down the back part of his body first, then the front. Touch everything on each other during these exercises *except* nipples and genital areas such as penis, clitoris, or vagina for the first seven days. In the next seven days you can add genital touching, but not to the point of orgasm. Tease each other by playing with the genitals, going away from them, then returning. Concentrate only on what feels good to you, telling your partner about your sensations. It is important not to worry about how your partner is feeling.

The above exercises will not only allow you to enjoy yourselves without pressure, and rediscover each other's bodies, but they will reintroduce you to teasing—one of the greatest turn-ons in sex.

What If You Can't Stand the Thought of Him Touching You After Discovery of His Affair?

I can sympathize with your feelings, but it is in your own best interests to try to overcome your repulsion. Don't make the mistake of ordering him out of your bedroom and into the guest room or onto the couch. This may magnify any grievances he is harboring against you and make him say, "The hell with it," and leave precipitously. It may also make him go back to her for sex. Better to move way over to your side of the bed until you can stop recoiling. Let him know that your repulsion is a temporary state, so that he can look forward to sex in the near future.

Anger and hurt are the reasons you don't want him to touch you, so you must quickly go to work on these emotions, in the ways outlined in previous sections—by talking them out with him, gaining control of anger by locking yourself in a room by yourself and screaming out all the worst things you can think of about him, by whacking a pillow or mattress with a tennis racket or towel, and of course by working with him to uncover the roots of the affair and what your role in it may be. It is amazing how quickly anger dissipates, once you understand how you have contributed to his affair. Taking charge of the situation also helps dispel anger. You concentrate on doing something about it, rather than blaming him or lusting for revenge. There is an element of revenge in prolonged sexual refusals.

While you work to banish your fury, you can employ a temporary measure to try to bypass negative feelings so that you can feel and act sexual toward him again quickly. It is a technique used in sex therapy for people who have developed aversion to sex with their partners. It is based on the accepted theory that people actually turn themselves off. Of course, when this happens, it is involuntary and unconscious, as in your case, but you can learn to control your reaction consciously.

Here is what to do. When your partner approaches you, monitor whatever thoughts come automatically into your head. You will probably discover negative images connected with him. You may think about his affair, picture him with her, remind yourself how much pain he has caused, or remember what an untrustworthy rat he is. Your thoughts are what are destroying your sexual response to him.

You have to learn to recognize and squelch these negative images as soon as they start to surface. Think ahead of sex time about some quality that you still like in him, or some wonderful memories of the two of you together. Summon up one of these prepared positive thoughts and substitute it for negative ones the minute they start to arise. Flooding your mind with good thoughts rather than bad ones allows sexual feelings to flow again.

Interestingly, for many women, an affair acts the opposite way—it is a turn-on. Very often there is a sexual honeymoon that occurs between a man and a woman after his infidelity is uncovered. Sometimes this is a sign of reconciliation.

However, even if the affair is still not resolved, some women find themselves mysteriously excited by the thought of him with another woman. Occasionally, if you have hidden masochistic tendencies, it is the pain of the thought that ignites you. For more women, however, it is a sense of competition with the lover that revs up their motors. Most often, the hidden factor in hot sex after the revelation of an affair is the tension in the atmosphere. A well-known study examined the erotic responses of people purposely placed in anxiety-provoking situations. The researchers found that anxiety facilitated sexual arousal. Some experts even theorize that some of the sexual turn-on in a secret affair is the anxiety attached to it.

The anxiety you are feeling now concerns questions like these: Will you be able to get him to give her up? Will he go back to her in the future? Will he leave you? Will you forgive him or kick him out? Can anything ever be right between you again? These may rightfully seem like painful issues, but the stress you are under, curiously, may help turn you on as well.

Make the most of it, if this happens. Try to bring back sexual feelings if it doesn't, and remember that either state—hyped-up or "don't touch me"—is probably temporary. For a permanent fix, you have to work in the ways I have outlined to understand each other more and to make your relationship and sex better.

Affairs may be the end of blind faith in your relationship, but they don't have to be the end of the world. More and more couples today who make the right moves are finding infidelity to be the beginning of a much better life together.

"I would never again want to go through what I did after I found out about his affair," explains one wife. "It was agony and hell. But without that experience we would never have had the terrific relationship we do now."

This woman and her husband were willing to let infidelity be a springboard for learning, sharing, improving. "I will never forget it," she says of his affair. Neither will you. You can't forget it, but, like this wife, you can forgive and start on a road that will lead to a richer, happier, sexier life together from now on.

Afterword

MANY COUPLES ARE SUCCESSFUL IN HEALING THEMSELVES OF the wounds caused by infidelity. Sometimes, however, even with the best of intentions, couples find they have trouble working together on their own. They need a third person, an impartial arbiter, to help them along the road to recovery. Although many of the steps I have recommended in this book are based on the therapeutic process, you may find you need the actual presence of a trained professional to act as a referee, to facilitate disclosure, and, in general, to help straighten things out. If emotions are running too high or you run into too many snags, I recommend that you contact the American Association of Marriage and Family Therapists to get the name of a qualified, *licensed* couples therapist in your area. The national headquarters of the AAMFT is located at 1717 K St., N.W., 407, Washington, D.C., 20006.

Appendix 1

THIRTEEN WAYS TO AFFAIR-PROOF YOUR MARRIAGE

1. Create frequent surprises. Surprise notes to each other, unexpected gifts, a new hairdo, a plan for unusual activities—anything that neither of you expects, if done on a regular basis, will keep the relationship from becoming much too predictable and dull. Boredom at home often drives a man to seek out the refreshing excitement of an affair, so keep things lively between you with unexpected acts and gestures.

2. Keep romance alive. Studies have shown that the desire to have a romance again is what starts some men straying. Other studies indicate that a man is more apt to remain monogamous if he feels a continuing sense of romance with you. Therefore, it is in your best interest to go out of your way to have frequent "dates," to hold hands, to whisper love messages in each other's ears, and to dress seductively—just as you did before you became an established couple.

3. Give sex a high priority. Most couples gradually demote sex to last place on their list of things to do. They make love after all the other chores are taken care of, at the end of the day when they are most tired and least inspired, or they forget to make love at all because they are so distracted or sleepy. If you want to prevent extramarital sex from looking like a shining alternative to what is going on at home, put aside prime time each week to make love when you are still fresh and can still summon up some enthusiasm and imagination. Do this even if it means knocking off earlier from work sometimes, or teaching the kids that a closed door means "off limits."

4. Be especially careful of your relationship when you are pregnant. Unfortunately, the time in life when you may feel the happiest is also the time when many men have their first affairs. Keep lines of communication open. Talk to each other about your *inner* thoughts at this time. In particular, search out any troublesome feelings that may be silently bothering him. Common male conflicts that lead to extramarital sex include the following: He may be feeling more trapped because of the extra responsibility he faces, with fatherhood looming. He may, at this time, be thinking of you more and more as a mother and less and less as a lover, which makes him lose sexual interest. He may find your ballooned-out shape a temporary turn-off. He may be under the false illusion that he could harm the baby through intercourse, which makes him avoid sex with you.

On the other hand, you may have stopped acting seductively with him. Or, as you became engrossed in your pregnancy, your libido took a vacation. Your lack of sexual interest may have made him feel unloved or rejected. By getting hidden fears, feelings, and attitudes out in the open, you can empathize with one another, reassure one another, clear up misconceptions, or change your behavior if that is necessary, and thus create a stronger bond between you, instead of growing farther apart, which happens often when hidden fears are not addressed. He will be less tempted to solve his inner conflicts through an affair if you are privy to them.

5. Make sure he gets enough attention after you have children. Another common time when men start affairs is after children are born and the wife starts giving the offspring the lion's share of her attention. Feeling shut out or rejected, some men take out their hidden resentment or try to feel more accepted in the arms of another woman, so don't forget your husband, no matter how busy you are with the kids.

6. Let him know you appreciate him. Many spouses start to take a partner for granted once they have married.

Although they remember to criticize, they forget to compliment. When this happens, a man often begins to feel unappreciated by his wife. He becomes more vulnerable to an affair with another woman who makes him feel admired and cherished again. Frequent statements of affection, caring, and esteem from you can keep him from looking for it elsewhere.

7. *Address problems as they arise.* Affairs often start because the man feels that something is lacking in the marriage. Instead of telling the spouse about it, he goes out and finds another woman. If you can keep communications about the state of your relationship open, you will be able to discuss problems as they occur and try to solve them together. One way to do this is to agree to periodic checkups—discussions every few months devoted entirely to the topics "How are we getting along?" and "Is there anything either of us is doing (or not doing) that should be changed?"

8. *Watch your weight.* Two studies have indicated that infidelity starts for a lot of men when a wife gains too much weight. You don't have to be model-thin. Most men can tolerate a few extra pounds, but when your weight verges on obesity and you really have lost your figure altogether, it becomes dangerous. Maybe he *should* love you for yourself, but that won't stop him from being attracted to someone else's slimmer body. So if you don't want that to happen, keep tabs on your weight.

9. *Be particularly attentive, loving, and seductive as he approaches end-of-decade birthdays.* As ages thirty, forty, fifty, and even sixty approach, men sum up their accomplishments, reasses their marriages, and figure out what they have missed in their lives to that point. Disillusionment with careers, the feeling of shrinking time, and the desire to stay young all loom larger at end-of-decade anniversaries. A common solution to the emotional turmoil that accompanies these birthdays is an affair. By giving him extra doses of tender, loving care, doing more enjoyable things with him, and getting him to talk, if you can, about his feelings, you can do a lot to head off extramarital urges.

10. Make sure you spend enough time together. One study showed that couples spend less than one percent of their leisure time with each other. It is hard to keep a relationship close and healthy without sufficient time alone to get in touch with each other again. When couples grow emotionally apart because they don't spend sufficient time together, the possibility of an affair increases. So turn off the TV set a couple of nights a week, make it a rule to get home early at least once a week, get in the habit of taking evening strolls together, and, on a regular basis, hire a baby-sitter or send the kids off to a relative or a cooperative neighbor, so you can have time to just enjoy each other.

11. Be particularly supportive at times of job-related stress. If a man is having trouble in his career, he may feel his masculinity under attack. To compensate at times like this, some husbands start affairs. Extramarital sex is an attempt to feel more manly. He is far less likely to resort to this kind of solution to his problems if you empathize with him, act like a loyal partner, help out financially if you can, and let him know you believe in him and still think he is the greatest guy you have ever known.

12. Keep in close emotional and physical contact with him at transition times in life. When you move from one geographic locale to another, when you take a job after having been home for a while, when he has started working for a different company after a long time at another one, and when the children leave home are all danger points when chances of extramarital affairs increase. Talking about the anxieties attached to great changes in career or home life will let him air and thus reduce the stress and discomfort he may be feeling. Affairs are often an unconscious attempt to handle the greater-than-average stresses that arise when life changes radically.

13. Keep recharging your sexual batteries. Periodically, try something new—whether it is a different position you have read about, or having hugging, kissing, and touching sessions without actual intercourse. It could be watching a risqué movie on your VCR together, pretending to be two different people, necking in the backseat of your car the way you used to as kids, or going away for weekends to different romantic places for sexy mini-vacations. Take turns dreaming up what the new thing of the month will be. Stay receptive to novelty; don't turn down any reasonable suggestion unless you have tried it with an open mind at least once.

Recharging your sexual batteries also means solving any sexual problems that exist between you, even if it takes a series of visits to a sex therapist together to get things straightened out. Men place great value on good sex, and they are much less likely to get interested in someone else if they have a compatible, enjoyable, interesting, and innovative sex life with you.

Appendix 2

(ALTHOUGH ONE OF THE FOLLOWING QUIZZES IS FOR WOMEN and one is for men, both sexes could learn even more about infidelity by taking both quizzes.)

HOW MUCH DO YOU KNOW ABOUT AFFAIRS?: FOR MEN

		True	False
1.	It is in men's natures to want other sex partners.	___	___
2.	A woman's family background has nothing to do with a man being unfaithful to her.	___	___
3.	Sex is the most important reason for most men's affairs.	___	___
4.	Knowing others who play around makes it more likely that a man will be unfaithful.	___	___
5.	No harm is done to a relationship if a man's partner doesn't find out about his sexual adventures.	___	___
6.	Very few women cooperate in a husband's affairs.	___	___
7.	The closer a man feels to a woman, the less likely it is that he will want to have an affair.	___	___
8.	A man doing poorly at his job is more likely to have an affair.	___	___
9.	Sex is always better with an extramarital partner than with a man's wife.	___	___

275

True　　　False

10. Men who are outgoing are more likely to have affairs than shy men.　　　　　　　　　　　———　　———

11. Married men are more likely to have affairs with strangers than with women they already know.　　　　　　　　　　　———　　———

Answers

1. *True.* The desire for novelty seems to be stronger in males, according to some experiments with monkeys, rats, and humans, while females seem to respond more to familiarity in partners. Men are always battling this side of their natures, which is in conflict with an equally strong need for a home life with a steady partner they can count on.

2. *False.* Studies have shown that a woman who comes from a home where a parent committed adultery is much more likely to choose a man who will be unfaithful to her.

3. *False.* Although sex is often cited by men as the conscious reason for getting involved with another woman, unconscious motivations such as the need to validate his attractiveness as a man, to create more space in his primary relationship, to avoid feeling trapped, and to assert independence from and anger at a partner are more common reasons for cheating.

4. *True.* Experts agree that it increases the odds of infidelity if a man knows other men in either his business or personal life who are fooling around.

5. *False.* Therapists these days feel that some distancing unavoidably occurs in the original relationship when a person has an outside affair. The man is hiding things from his mate, he becomes more closemouthed, he may spend less time at home, he may start to feel resentment because his partner is keeping him from his freedom, and he may be mentally preoccupied with his affair, which makes him more aloof with his mate.

6. *False.* An unconscious collusion between partners is more common than is usually imagined in cases of infidelity. A wife can, in a hidden way, foster her husband's infidelity if it suits her own needs for distance in the relationship, or if she herself does not want to be bothered for intercourse or certain sex acts that the husband has been pressuring for, or if she feels it is worth it to her to trade off his affairs for maintaining the status or security of her marriage.

7. *False.* For some men it works his way, but for a large number, closeness actually creates an opposite effect—too much emotional proximity may make a man feel uncomfortable. He may either consciously or unconsciously worry that he is becoming too dependent on his partner, he may feel suffocated or trapped, he may simply feel a vague anxiety that he can't define, although it comes from getting too close for comfort. Many men solve this discomfort attached to intimacy by having an affair.

8. *True.* Many men feel that their masculine pride is under attack when their careers have a setback. They use a sexual conquest to counter this. An affair can make the man feel more potent and masculine.

9. *False.* Sometimes, but not always. One survey done for *Playboy* found, surprisingly, that most husbands felt sex at home to be more fulfilling overall than the sex in their extramarital encounters: 67 percent of the married men who had affairs rated the sex in their marriages as "very pleasurable," but only 40 percent gave this rating to their affairs.

10. *True.* Researcher H. J. Eynsenck's studies show that extroverts have more sexual partners and start their sexual adventures earlier in life.

11. *False.* Most often the "other woman" is a friend of the family, someone the man works with, the wife of a couple in his social circle, a woman who started out as just a friend. Proximity has proven to be the greatest determinant in who becomes a partner in an affair.

How Much Do You Know About Affairs?: For Women

	True	False
1. A man who has had many pre-marital sexual partners will have sown his wild oats and will be less apt to cheat in marriage.	_____	_____
2. Most women are completely surprised by the discovery of a man's affair.	_____	_____
3. A man's family background has a lot to do with whether he will cheat or not.	_____	_____
4. Heavy drinkers and drug users are more likely to cheat.	_____	_____
5. A womanizer has a higher-than-average sex drive.	_____	_____
6. All men think about sex with other women.	_____	_____
7. All affairs are a threat to a marriage.	_____	_____
8. Children won't know about their father's affair if you don't tell them.	_____	_____
9. The other woman is always a better sex partner or a more attractive woman than you are.	_____	_____
10. Some unfaithful men are sex addicts—they are hooked on sex the way others are on liquor or cocaine.	_____	_____
11. The discovery of a husband's affair always works to the detriment of the marriage in the future.	_____	_____

Answers

1. *False.* Studies indicate that men who have had a lot of premarital sexual experiences are actually *more* likely to cheat as husbands.

2. *False.* The majority of women know instinctively that something is wrong, that somehow he has changed or is different. When the possibility of an affair surfaces in their minds, however, the tendency is to push it away. It is too painful or frightening for many women to face the possibility of a man's infidelity, so they continue to deny what their intuition is telling them. When the affair finally comes out in the open, if they are honest, most women will tell you that they had an inkling beforehand.

3. *True.* The odds for infidelity increase considerably if a man's father had affairs or if he comes from an ethnic background that supports the notion that infidelity is a male privilege.

4. *True.* People with alcohol or drug dependencies have a higher-than-average rate of infidelity. Inhibitions that might be there when they aren't using drink or drugs drop with the use of these substances.

5. *False.* Most chronic philanderers are driven by poor self-images rather than runaway libidos. Feeling insecure as men, they use sexual conquest to validate that they are, indeed, attractive and desirable.

6. *True.* Almost all men have sexual fantasies about other women. However, daydreaming about infidelity is different from actually engaging in it. There are many monogamous men who have these sexual fantasies without acting on them. Jimmy Carter, when he was president, confessed in a magazine interview to lusting after women other than his wife, yet Jimmy Carter is a firm monogamist.

7. *False.* I would say that most infidelity isn't a threat as far as husbands are concerned. Two surveys have indicated that half of the men who have affairs consider their marriages to be happy. Most men want to have their cake and eat it too; they don't want to dissolve their marriages. Some husbands even find that an affair makes it easier for them to be married and allows them to be more giving with their wives. These are men who feel "trapped" in marriage. An outside involvement keeps them from feeling so imprisoned.

8.   *False*. If the affair is causing ongoing turmoil between spouses, the children will always know that something is wrong. It is a disservice to them to tell them everything is all right in these circumstances. Better to let them know that you and their father are having problems, but that you are trying to solve them, and that the problems are adult matters that are not caused by anything the children have done.

9.   *False*. Although it is an almost universal female response to compare yourself unfavorably with the rival, the man generally finds his sexual excitement generated more by the fact that she is a *new* partner than by the fact that she is sexier or better looking. As proof that novelty is a stronger lure than sexual skill or physical attractiveness, remember that the world is full of very beautiful women and world-class sex partners who have been cheated on.

10.   *True*. Experts have come to recognize that some men lead sex lives that are out of their control, and that even if they swear off other women they are unable to stop their philandering. To be a true sex addict, the man generally feels some shame or unhappiness about his sexual patterns. However, he is at a loss as to what to do about it. Some of these men, because they lead a very active other life in secret, feel very isolated by their sexual addiction.

11.   *False*. Many wives and husbands have found that the affair was actually the beginning of a better marital life. Problems that had been previously neglected were addressed and corrected, communication and cooperation increased in the aftermath of discovery. Most marriages survive infidelity, and some do quite well when both partners are willing to work at healing the rift.

Selected Bibliography

Alpert, Hollis. *Burton*. New York: G.P, Putnam & Sons, 1986.

Athanasiou, R., and Sarkin, R. "Premarital Sexual Behaviour and Postmarital Adjustment." *Archives of Sexual Behavior* 3, no. 3 (1974): 207–225.

Athanasiou, R.; Shaver, P.; and Tavris, C. "Sex, a Report to *Psychology Today* Readers." *Psychology Today* 4 (July 1970): 39–52.

Barbara, Dominick A. "Neurotic Motives for Sex." *Medical Aspects of Human Sexuality* (May 1975): 159–160.

Bernard, Jessie. "Infidelity: Some Moral and Social Issues." In *Beyond Monogamy*, edited by J. R. Smith and L. G. Smith. Baltimore: Johns Hopkins Press, 1974

Berger, Amy. "His Cheatin' Heart." *Woman's World*, August 4, 1987.

Blumstein, Philip, and Schwartz, Pepper. *American Couples*. New York: William Morrow and Co., 1983.

Carnes, Patrick, Ph.D. *Out of the Shadows*. Minneapolis: CompCare Publications, 1983.

Clements, Marcelle. "The Dawn of the New Bimbo." *New York Woman*, vol. 1, no. 4 (March/April 1987): 125–128.

Collier, Peter, and Horowitz, David. *The Kennedys: An American Drama*. New York: Warner Books, 1984.

Cuber, John F., and Harroff, Peggy B. *Sex and the Significant Americans*. Baltimore: Penguin Books, 1966.

Davis, John H. *The Kennedys' Dynasty and Disaster 1848–1984*. New York: McGraw Hill, 1984.

Edwards, John N. "Extramarital Involvement: Fact and Theory." *Journal of Sex Research*, vol. 9, no. 3 (August 1973): 210–224.

Edwards, John N., and Booth, Alan. "Sexual Behavior in and out of Marriage: An Assessment of the Correlates." *Journal of Marriage and the Family* 38 (February 1976): 73–81.

Elbaum, P. "The Dynamics, Implications and Treatment of Extramarital Sexual Relations for the Family Therapist." *Journal of Marriage and Family Therapy* 7 (October 1981): 489–495.

Ellis, Albert. "Healthy and Disturbed Reasons for Extramarital Relations." *Journal of Human Relations* 16, no. 4 (1968): 490–501.

Eysenck, H. J. "Hysterical Personality and Sexual Adjustment, Attitudes and Behavior." *Journal of Sex Research*, vol. 7, no. 4 (November 1971): 274–281.

———. *Sex and Personality*. Austin: University of Texas Press, 1977.

———. "Personality and Sexual Behavior." *Journal of Psychosomatic Research* 16 (1972): 141–152.

Feldman, Harold. *Development of the Husband-Wife Relationship*. Ithaca, N.Y.: Cornell University Press, 1967.

Gagnon, John H., and Simon, William, eds. *The Sexual Scene*. Chicago: Aldine Publishing Co., 1970.

———. *Sexual Conduct: The Social Sources of Human Sexuality*. Chicago: Aldine Publishing Co., 1973.

Glass, Shirley P., and Wright, Thomas L. "The Relationship of Extramarital Sex, Length of Marriage, and Sex Differences on Marital Satisfaction and Romanticism: Athanasious's Data Reanalyzed." *Journal of Marriage and the Family* 39, no. 4 (1977): 691–703.

———. "Sex Differences in Type of Extramarital Involvement and Marital Dissatisfaction." *Sex Roles*, vol. 12, nos. 9/10 (1985): 1101–1120.

Greene, Bernard; Lee, Ronald L.; and Lustig, Noel. "Conscious and Unconscious Factors in Marital Infidelity." *Medical Aspects of Human Sexuality*, September 1974: 87–111.

Hansen, Gary L. "Extradyadic Relations During Courtship." *Journal of Sex Research*, Vol. 23, no. 3 (August 1987): 382–390.

Hedaya, Robert, M.D. "The Womanizer." *Medical Aspects of Human Sexuality*, January 1985: 113–114.

Higham, Charles. *Charles Laughton*. Garden City, New York: Doubleday, 1976.

Hite, Shere. *The Hite Report on Male Sexuality*. New York: Alfred A. Knopf, 1981.

Hoon, P.; Wincze, J.; and Hoon, F. "A Test of Reciprocal Inhibitions: Are Anxiety and Sexual Arousal Mutually Inhibitory?" *Journal of Abnormal Psychology* 86 (1977): 65–74.

Hunt, Morton. *Sexual Behavior in the 1970s*. New York: Playboy Press, 1974.

———. *The Affair*. New York: World Publishing Co., 1969.

Husted, John R., and Edwards, Allan E. "Personality Correlates of Male Sexual Arousal and Behavior." *Archives of Sexual Behavior*, vol. 5, no. 2 (1976): 149–156.

Johnson, R. E. "Some Correlates of Extramarital Coitus." *Journal of Marriage and the Family*, vol. 32, no. 2 (August 1970): 449–456.

Kelley, Kathryn, and Musialowski, Donna. "Repeated Exposure to Sexually Explicit Stimuli: Novelty, Sex and Sexual Attitudes." *Archives of Sexual Behavior*, vol. 15, no. 6 (December 1986): 488–489.

Kelley, Kitty. *His Way: The Unauthorized Biography of Frank Sinatra*, New York: Bantam Books, 1986.

———. "The Dark Side of Camelot." *People*, February 29, 1988: 106–114.

Kernberg, Otto. "Mature Love: Prerequisites and Characteristics." *Journal of the American Psychoanalytic Association* 22, no. 4 (1974): 743–768.

Kinsey, Alfred C.; Pomeroy, Wardell B.; and Martin, Clyde. *Sexual Behavior in the Human Male*. Philadelphia: W.B. Saunders Co., 1968.

Klimek, David. *Beneath Mate Selection and Marriage*. New York: Van Nostrand Reinhold Co., 1979.

Lasch, Christopher. *The Culture of Narcissism*. New York: W.W. Norton and Co., 1978.

Maraniss, David. "A History of Failing to Explain." In *The Philadelphia Inquirer*, May 10, 1987: 1-E and 4-E.

Michael, R. P., and Zumpe, D. "Potency in Male Rhesus Monkeys: Effects of Continuously Receptive Females." *Science* 200 (1978): 451–453.

Neubeck, Gerald, and Schletzer, Vera. "A Study of Extramarital Relationships." *Journal of Marriage and the Family* 24:3 (August 1962): 279–281.

Neubeck, Gerald, ed. *Extramarital Relations*. Englewood Cliffs, N.J.: Prentice Hall, 1966.

Newcomb, Michael D. "Sexual Behavior of Cohabitors: A Comparison of Three Independent Samples." *Journal of Sex Research* 4 (November 1986): 492–513.

Offit, Avodah K. *The Sexual Self*. New York: Congdon and Weed, 1983.

Peyser, Joan. *Bernstein*. New York: Beech Tree Books, William Morrow, 1987.

Pietropinto, Anthony, M.D., and Simenauer, Jacqueline. *Beyond the Male Myth*. New York: New American Library, 1977.

Pittman, Frank S., M.D. *Turning Points: Treating Families in Transition and Crisis*. New York: W.W. Norton and Co., 1987.

Richardson, Laurel. *The New Other Woman*. New York: Free Press, 1985.

Roebuck, J., and Spray, S. L. "The Cocktail Lounge: A Study of Heterosexual Relations in a Public Organization." *American Journal of Sociology* 72 (January 1967): 288–295.

Rollins, Boyd C., and Feldman, Harold. "Marital Satisfaction over the Life Cycle." *Journal of Marriage and the Family* 32 (February 1970): 20–28.

Sager, Clifford. "The Role of Sex Therapy in Marital Therapy." *American Journal of Psychiatry* 133, no. 5 (May 1976): 555–558.

Salzman, Leon. *The Obsessive Personality: Origins, Dynamics and Therapy*. New York: Jason Aronson, 1975.

———. "Understanding Adulterous Behavior by Men." *Medical Aspects of Human Sexuality*, vol. 14, no. 8 (August 1980): 117–118.

Schenk, Josef, and Pfrang, Horst. "Extraversion, Neuroticism and Sexual Behavior: Interrelationships in a Sample of Young Men." *Archives of Sexual Behaviour*, vol. 15, no. 6 (December 1986): 449–452.

Schwartz, Mark F., and Brasted, William. "Sexual Addiction." *Medical Aspects of Human Sexuality*, vol. 19, no. 10 (October 1985): 103–107.

Seidenberg, Robert, M.D. *Corporate Wives-Corporate Casualties*. AMACOM, 1973.

Shapiro, David. *Neurotic Styles*. New York: Basic Books, 1965.

Sheehy, Gail. "The Road to Bimini." *Vanity Fair* (September 1987): 131–139, 188–194.

Simenauer, Jaqueline, and Carroll, David. *Singles: The New Americans*. New York: Simon and Schuster, 1982.

Spanier, Graham, and Margolis, Randie. "Marital Separation and Extramarital Behaviour." *Journal of Sex Research*, vol. 19, no. 1 (February 1983): 23–48.

Spiegal, Penina. *McQueen*. Garden City, New York: Doubleday and Co., 1986.

Strean, Herbert. "The Extramarital Affair: A Psychoanalytic View." *Psychoanalytic Review* 63 (Spring): 101–113.

Thompson, Anthony P. "Extramarital Sex: A Review of the Research Literature." *Journal of Sex Research*, vol. 19, no. 7 (February 1983): 1–22.

———. "The Extramarital Sexual Crisis: Common Themes and Therapy Implications." *Journal of Sex and Marital Therapy*, vol. 10, no. 4 (1984): 239–254.

Vaughan, James and Peggy. *Beyond Affairs*. Hilton Head, S.C.: Dialog Press, 1980.

Waxman, Harvey, and Long, Janis, V. F. "Adultery and Marriage: Three Psychological Perspectives." In *Marriage and Divorce: A Contemporary Perspective*, edited by Carol Nadelson and Derek Polansky. New York: The Guilford Press, 1984.

Wayne, Jane Ellen. *Gable's Women*. New York: Prentice-Hall, 1987.

Whitehurst, R. N. "Extramarital Sex: Alienation or Extension of Normal Behavior." In *Extramarital Relations*, edited by G. Neubeck. Englewood Cliffs, New Jersey: Prentice-Hall, 1969.

Willi, Jurg, M.D. *Couples in Collusion*. New York: Jason Aronson, 1982.

Index